PLANET

Religious Feminism
and
the Future of the Planet

A Christian-Buddhist Conversation

RITA M. GROSS AND
ROSEMARY RADFORD RUETHER

Continuum
London New York

2001

The Continuum International Publishing Group Inc
370 Lexington Avenue, New York, NY 10017

The Continuum International Publishing Group Ltd
The Tower Building, 11 York Road, London SE1 7NX

Printed in the United States of America

Library of Congress Cataloging-in-Publication Data

Gross, Rita M.
    Religious feminism and the future of the planet : a Buddhist-Christian conversation / Rita M. Gross and Rosemary Radford Ruether.
        p. cm.
    ISBN 0-8264-1302-1
    1. Women—Religious aspects—Buddhism. 2. Christianity and other religions—Buddhism. 3. Buddhism—Relations—Christianity. 4. Feminism—Religious aspects—Christianity. 5. Women in Religion—Biography. 6. Ecofeminism—Religious aspects. I. Ruether, Rosemary Radford.
    BQ4570.W6 G78 2001
    261.2'43'082—dc21   00-052341

About the Cover
Sarasvati is often thought of as the Hindu goddess of learning and culture, but she is also venerated by Buddhists as a divine female who promotes learning and the arts. This portrait of Sarasvati is typical of much Tibetan Buddhist art.

Wisdom is a female-identified figure found in the Jewish Wisdom writing of Hebrew Scripture and continued as a theological motif in Christian theology, sometimes identified with the Christ or the Holy Spirit in God and sometimes with Mary. Wisdom is a cosmogonic, revelatory, and soteriological figure. She is seen as "working with" God in the creation of the World and the means by which God is revealed and humans reconciled with God.

To John Cobb

and our Colleagues in the
International Buddhist-Christian
Theological Encounter

Contents

PART IV: WHAT IS MOST INSPIRING FOR ME ABOUT THE OTHER TRADITION?

PART V: RELIGIOUS FEMINISM AND THE FUTURE OF THE PLANET

Preface

This book of Buddhist-Christian feminist conversations grows directly out of a weekend workshop we co-presented at Grailville in Loveland, Ohio, in October 1999. Even though we, Rosemary Ruether and Rita Gross, have worked together for a long time, this was the first time we had done such an extensive project together. It was also Rita Gross' first visit to the Grail; Rosemary Ruether already had a close connection with the Grail and had been there many times. There, on the Saturday morning of the workshop, we drew up the plans for this book in Rosemary's room. Previously we had imagined the joint publication of a paper of some sort, but it quickly became apparent that a longer publication was more appropriate. We want to thank residents of Grailville for pushing us in that direction.

We decided to speak to the same topics that had been discussed in our workshop, but we also thought it would be helpful to add an introductory chapter on the topic of dialogue itself. In person, we could convey the essence of dialogue through our interactions, but we felt that might not be so self-evident on the printed page. We also decided to add short responses to each other's chapters to capture the flavor of some of the dialogue between us that occurred during the workshop. Though our talks were taped, we worked fresh from notes for this book, without listening to the tapes. The points made are substantially the same as those made in the workshop, but stated in ways more appropriate to the printed page.

In Rita's experience, the specific route to this particular workshop began in Halifax in 1995 when she had first met Grail member Mary O'Brien at a major Buddhist event in the Buddhist capital of her Buddhist world. In 1998, Rita was invited back to Halifax to give talks at Mt. Vincent University and at the local Shambhala Center. Mary O'Brien

1

helped host Rita and again talked with her about Grailville, renewing earlier discussions of something Rita might do there. Mary asked Rita, "With what Christian feminist would you like to engage in a workshop on Buddhist-Christian-feminist dialogue at Grailville?" The response was very easy for Rita, "Rosemary Ruether." Later, we began to receive e-mails from Mary O'Brien and the workshop took shape. Mary flew from Halifax to Grailville to help present this workshop. It is clear that Mary played a key role in the genesis of this book by her unceasing efforts to make the workshop happen, and she deserves our profound thanks. We also thank all our other hosts and facilitators at Grailville, who made the workshop a memorable experience, especially for Rita, who was experiencing the women's community at Grailville for the first time.

However, our work together goes back many years before the Grailville workshop. Both of us have independent reputations in feminist theology and the feminist study of religions, but our work together has centered around Buddhist-Christian dialogue. In 1985, we worked together, for the first time, in the International Buddhist-Christian Theological Encounter, also known as the Cobb-Abe group. At that point, Rita regarded Rosemary as the senior colleague and was slightly intimidated. But Rosemary's graciousness facilitated an easy relationship, and soon we were doing a few shorter presentations together at Buddhist-Christian dialogue events. We have also worked together on other projects not directly linked with Buddhist-Christian dialogue, but we both feel that our primary and most personal link came through the world of Buddhist-Christian dialogue. On the other hand, both of us are committed to the feminist expression of a major world religion, and that common concern about different religions undoubtedly underpins our collegiality.

I, Rosemary Ruether, want to express my appreciation to Rita Gross, both for our years of work together and the frank and creative sharing in the Grailville workshop that was the basis for this book. Although Rita may regard me as a senior scholar, I regard her very much as a peer and a pioneer in religious feminism, in world religions generally and in Buddhism in particular. I think we have an unusual level of reciprocity that makes the kinds of conversations we have had on Buddhist-Christian feminist commonalities and differences particularly fruitful.

I, Rita, wish to acknowledge my profound gratitude to my co-author, Rosemary Ruether. She is slightly older than myself and began publishing on feminist issues somewhat before I did. And, being a Christian feminist theologian, not a historian of religions and new

Buddhist, she had a more ready audience than I did. I remember being in awe of her very early on, and flattered when I received a copy of one of her early books "compliments of the author." Despite my frustration at being labeled merely an imitator of Rosemary Ruether in one critique of my book *Buddhism after Patriarchy*, I count it as keeping good company that the kinship between our work is recognized. Unlike the usual stereotype and reality of the competitive academic world, Rosemary could not have been a kinder and more supportive senior colleague. And I deeply appreciate all the support and understanding I have received from her through the years.

We both also thank our colleagues in the world of Buddhist-Christian dialogue, who provided the context for our continuing relationship as feminist colleagues. I, Rosemary, wish to thank the community of Buddhist-Christian Dialogue for having creating much of the setting that began my dialogue on religious feminism with Rita Gross. I, Rita, have said in other contexts, and would like to state here as well, that my colleagues in Buddhist-Christian dialogue, both male and female, have become one of my closest collegial communities, a community in which I can express myself fully and be received as a friend and a colleague for doing so. Finally, we also wish to thank our editor, Frank Oveis of Continuum, for his enthusiasm for this project and for his help in seeing it through to completion.

Rita M. Gross
Rosemary Radford Ruether

Introduction:
A Dialogue about Dialogue

The first question: "What is interreligious dialogue?"

Rosemary

Interreligious dialogue is a new development in the relationships of the world's religions. It is particularly threatening to many adherents of the Semitic monotheistic religions that have connected the oneness of the (male patriarchal) God with an exclusivist view of religious truth. Judaism, Christianity, and Islam each see itself as comprising the one true people of God with the one true religion. Although they may accept some truth in the other two monotheistic faiths, they position themselves as a people whose special relation to God gives them the fullness of truth and revealed knowledge of the true God.

Christianity sees Judaism as having been superseded by itself, and in deep error for having failed to recognize Jesus as the Christ, while Islam has traditionally been vilified as an infidel deviation from the fullness of revelation in Christ. Judaism sees the other two monotheistic faiths as deviations or corruptions, although at times conceding that they are secondary expressions of true knowledge of God for the gentiles. Islam has a supercessionary view of both of the other two religions, seeing itself as the fullness of revelation, and Jews and Christians as "peoples of the Book" who have a partial, incomplete and corrupted knowledge of God.

All three monotheistic faiths have looked on the Asian religions and indigenous faiths with a plurality of deities as "paganisms" to be regarded either as worshippers of demonic powers, and not the true God, or having only a dim understanding of the true God based on nature but not on revelation. Traditionally their stance toward polytheistic religions has been that they should be destroyed and their people assimilated into the one true faith.

The other world religions have been less exclusivist, although sometimes seeing themselves as the true faith for their particular people. Judaism shares this more ethnic perspective. In some Asian contexts where Buddhism, Confucianism, and Taoism coexist, it is common for people to regard themselves as participating in all three of these religions, in different contexts. Each religion is seen as addressing particular aspects of life, and so one participates in one or the other tradition according to particular needs at different occasions in life.

Some Asian Christians are adopting this view of plural identities, seeing themselves as simultaneously Confucian, Taoist, and Christian (among Chinese), or Buddhist, Christian, Shamanist, and Confucian (Koreans). But such pluralist views of one's identity are still seen as radically unacceptable among many Asian churches, especially evangelicals. One Korean minister who was the President of the Methodist seminary in Seoul was even excommunicated by his church for participating in Buddhist-Christian dialogue. The church insisted that becoming a Christian meant a decisive repudiation of Buddhism as false.

Rita

Interreligious dialogue is one tool for decreasing interreligious tensions and increasing interreligious understanding in a religiously diverse world. The world has always been religiously diverse, and there has always been a certain amount of mutual suspicion and hostility among the world's religions. One of the more common conventional psychological patterns is to fear and scorn those who are different. Such a situation is less dangerous and more understandable when the various religions are geographically separated and do not have many avenues for becoming acquainted with each other, as was more or less the case for much of human history. Until relatively recently, various forms of Christianity had some interactions with each other, especially after the Reformation, and the three monotheistic religions sometimes encountered each other. However, except for Muslims in India, the great Asian traditions were largely unknown to monotheists. But in contemporary times, many parts of the world, especially North America and Europe, are rapidly growing much more religiously diverse, both through immigration and through conversions. Nor is this trend likely to diminish in the near future. In such circumstances, hostility between religions is no longer merely unfortunate; it becomes dangerous. Theological condemnation of religions that are different fuels poisoned patterns of interaction between people who share the same territory and culture. In such conditions, any tools that can promote a more ethical and compassionate stance toward those who are religiously different is imperative.

Actually, I would suggest that interreligious dialogue is a relatively advanced and sophisticated tool for fostering greater interreligious understanding and appreciation. In interreligious dialogue, committed and knowledgeable practitioners of the various religions meet face to face to explore together the meaning of religion in their lives and the reality of divergent points of view on complex and important issues. This conversation requires certain attitudes of mutual acceptance and willingness to tolerate religious diversity; it is hard to imagine a successful interreligious interchange unless all participants accept the premise that religious diversity is a fact and a resource, not a theological mistake. If those ground rules are not agreed upon by all parties to an interreligious interchange, face to face meetings may do more harm than good. Participation in interreligious interchange also requires that one be reasonably well-educated in the religion one is representing in the interchange. People who are ill-informed about the teachings of their own religion simply are not in the best position to speak for it in an interreligious interchange.

Because I regard finding a viable way of accepting and appreciating religious diversity as one of the great moral issues of our time, and because I do not believe that interreligious interchange is an easy exercise, I would advocate use of a great many other tools for decreasing interreligious tensions and increasing interreligious understandings as well. In fact, I would not trust the process of negotiating our way into a viable theology of religious diversity to interreligious exchange alone. I have spent my life and career in the comparative study of religions, and I am completely convinced of the importance of comparative studies for understanding both oneself and for understanding others. I would, in fact, place more trust in comparative studies, required at all levels of education, than in interreligious interchange. I would especially advocate comparative studies of the various religions, taught in ways that are not condescending or triumphalist, as an essential component of all pastoral and ministerial training. In Europe and North America, Christians are still in the majority, and they have a poor track record in appreciating religious diversity. Therefore, the required changes in attitudes toward religious diversity must be built into the training that religious leaders receive. They are the ones who are primarily responsible for educating their parishioners about religious diversity; unless they are properly trained themselves, they will only perpetuate the vicious cycles of suspicion and intolerance that we have seen for so long. This tactic would affect many more people much more quickly than interreligious interchanges among those experts trained to engage in effective dialogues, important and useful as such interchanges may be.

The second question: "What is the purpose in interreligious interchange?"

Rita

I would emphasize that the main purpose of interreligious interchange is to become better informed about important religious issues and, thus, to have more material at one's command with which to think about religion. In other words, the chief purpose of interreligious interchange is one's own growth, the challenge it can provide to one's own assumptions and conclusions. Interreligious interchange is not primarily about affecting one's dialogue partners; it is about one's own spiritual and theological development.

These comments on the purpose of interreligious exchange again come straight from the heart of my concern for a wider perspective, for comparative dimensions to one's understanding of religion. So often, when one "goes abroad" in any sense of that term, from physical travel to academic study of other cultures, the reaction is "I learned so much about myself, about my own culture." It is very hard to have much perspective on one's own angle, one's own version of how things are, if one has never had a glimpse of how they might look from another vantage point. Comparative study can provide such perspective, but for many that perspective is more immediate in interchange with one's peers from other religious traditions. I have been in such interreligious interchanges and have listened as colleagues discussed attitudes that they would never have encountered in their own cultural/religious situations and the impact such information has had on their thinking.

Such purposeful exposure to other points of view is especially important for those who belong to a numerically dominant group. It is very easy for members of such groups to lose all perspective on their own specificity and peculiarity. They are prone to thinking that because there are so many of them, they must be in the right, and have little to learn from minority groups. As a result, members of dominant groups often become quite myopic, whereas members of minority groups usually know a great deal about those in whose midst they live.

Dialogue is based on the presupposition of radical openness to change. There is no point to interreligious interchange if one already has a completely fixed mind and is self-righteous about what should happen in encounters with the other. Many thinkers have commented throughout history that genuine encounter with another always changes one and that it is impossible to predict ahead of time in what direction those changes might take one.

Rosemary

Interreligious dialogue seeks to transcend conflict between religions. Its starting point is an acceptance that there is truth in the other religion with which one engages. This is easier among the three monotheistic faiths which share scriptural roots and many common patterns of theology. Often the problem in Jewish-Christian-Muslim dialogue is more the unacknowledged political issues that divide the peoples of these three communities. It is a greater leap for Christians to move into dialogue with an Asian religion, such as Buddhism, which lacks not only a monotheistic God but any God at all.

Often the last to be taken seriously by Christians are the indigenous religions, which are local rather than universal. These traditions have most particularly been seen as the epitome of "paganism," to be exterminated along with their people, unless these people can be assimilated into Christianity by erasing not only their religion but their entire culture (since there is no distinction between religion and culture in such communities).

It is a much bigger leap for Christians to concede religious truths in every religious tradition, not simply some favored ones. Yet even when such a stance is taken theoretically (which would be my own view), it is still not at all clear what this means in the actual process of dialogue. What is the goal of dialogue? The ground rules of dialogue demand that not simply some truth, but equal truth must be accepted in the other faith. One must reject not only an exclusivist view in which the other religions are false, but also a supercessionist view in which the other religions are conceded some truth, but in a partial way and in need of perfection by Christianity.

The third question: "What is not the point of dialogue?"

Rita

To those unpracticed in dialogue, it is important to understand what genuine dialogue is not. It is not a covert missionary activity in which each side tries to prove the superiority of their religion. It is not a debate, with all the adversarial connotations of the term. Nor is it an attempt to find some commonality between religions, an attempt to discover that, at the bottom line in an esoteric way, all religions really are the same.

Many people have the misconception that, in conversations or dialogue with people of other religious persuasions, one could not help but try to demonstrate the superiority of one's own position to one's partner. "After all," they say, "you are committed to this religious perspective; you have devoted years to studying and practicing it. Clearly you must think that it is the best position." The question in response is "Best for whom?" A pluralistic theology of religions easily accommodates love of and enthusiasm for one's own religious position with deep appreciation of other positions. One does not have to be very psychologically sophisticated to realize that religion cannot be a "one size fits all" phenomenon. There is no reason to expect that the religious symbols and practices to which I can deeply relate have the same resonance for everyone. Being defensive about one's own perspective is the stance least likely to produce successful dialogue.

Debate is also less than ideal as a format for dialogue, and, in fact, it is never used as a format for dialogue, to my knowledge, even though some might think dialogue would be debate. Debate is an exercise in which the most skilled debaters "win," which does not prove the truth of their position: the agenda of debate is to score points for oneself, not to understand the other.

Probably the most widespread misconception about interreligious dialogue is that its purpose is to find common ground, areas of agreement between the religions, so that mutual suspicions and hostilities can end. After all, if all religions really teach the same things in the long run, what's there to fight about? This understanding of dialogue carries a covert theology of religions with it. Genuine religious diversity is still seen as a problem if this is one's concept of the purpose of dialogue. It is felt that there must be some common meeting point for all the religions, if we could only find it, and that finding it would promote better relations between the religions. But why do we need a common meeting point? Can't we just appreciate the diversity of religions? Most people who have specialized to some extent in interreligious dialogue do not hold the view there is a common ground upon which all the religions can agree, nor do they think that it would be preferable for there to be a common ground for all religions.

Rosemary

Like Rita, I claim that the goal of the dialogue is not conversion of the other dialogue partners, or even convincing them that one's own faith has better ideas that could improve on the other tradition. Rather the goal of dialogue is simply in the process itself of mutual understanding. This may lead persons from each of the traditions to be enriched by the other faith, in the sense of finding insights that illuminate areas of religious experience that are either lacking or latent in one's own tradition. Some dialogue partners may even find ideas in the other tradition so much more helpful than one's own that they may come to identify with it, but this is a voluntary side effect, not the goal of dialogue.

Primarily, I see the goal of dialogue as something like learning another language and culture. One becomes somewhat bilingual and bicultural, but not in a way that eliminates one's own religious tradition as one's "mother tongue," one's primary language. Rather one enriches one's own experiences and understanding with insights from the other tradition. This doesn't mean making a new synthesis of the two traditions. The tendency among Christians is to want to reach for a new confessional unity that combines the two traditions. But this inevitably uses one's own tradition as the norm and forces the other tradition into a schema defined by one's own language.

I have found it more helpful in Buddhist-Christian dialogue to see the outcome as an intercultural journey which does not lend itself to a new synthesis, but rather a development of an ability to partially experience another religious way that can't be synthesized in a new union. I see Buddhism and Christianity as both being complete ways which stand parallel to one another, each having a full truth, but not one that can be reduced to one system. My analogy to this is quantum physics, in which the wave theory and the particle theory of light are both true, but can't be reduced to one system. They are true in different contexts. I don't know whether this analogy will hold up as I enter into further engagement with Buddhism, but it is my working analogy at the moment that allows me to participate in both without trying to create a new system that integrates the two.

The final and most difficult question: "What about cultural relativity, especially regarding sexism and the oppression of women?"

Rosemary

A question I want to ask in this introduction to a feminist Buddhist-Christian dialogue between Rita and myself is whether there is any basis for critique of a religion given a stance of mutual tolerance? Can anything be questioned or falsified in the other tradition without assuming that one has a superior truth by which the other is judged? Clearly, as feminists, both Rita and I are assuming some critical principles by which we reject aspects of our own traditions at the point where they justify oppression of women. Thus some principle of equal well-being of women and men stands as a kind of trans-religious principle for us by which we falsify aspects of our own tradition.

Generally we should leave a similar questioning of patriarchal elements in the other tradition to the integrity of its own practitioners. What may look discriminatory to Western eyes may be experienced differently from within a tradition, and it is the women of the tradition that are the best judges of that. But it is another matter to justify male domination in another tradition simply on the grounds that each tradition is "different." I would allow that each culture has somewhat different ways of expressing equality or equivalence of men and women, but there are limits for me to the acceptance of cultural pluralism when it comes to gender. If a tradition says that women, because of the very nature of women, can't assume the full and equal leadership in society or in the religious institutions, such as being monastic teachers in Buddhism or ordained ministers in Christianity, this has to be questioned as discriminatory.

What is the cultural source of this critique of patriarchy that we apply to each of our religions? Is this simply a Western human rights tradition (itself rooted in Western political thought with some Jewish and Christian roots), or do we find the basis of this critique in each of our religious traditions? In other words, is the critique of patriarchy one area where we find a common norm for critique or affirmation of each of our traditions that is partly rooted in different ways in each, but partly transcends them both, and therefore stands above each of them on an intercultural plane of truth?

This question connects to the more general question of whether there is room for criticism of falsehood or evil in any religion, once one has accepted the principle that there is truth in all religions. Or does the very stance of mutual respect assume that every religion's truth claims are unquestioned with the goodness of their particular customs immune to criticism? Does the principle of tolerance and mutual respect reduce us to normless gullibility or polite silence in the face of patterns of religious thought and practice that strike us as unjust, cruel, obsessive, or self-promoting?

This question became compelling to me during my recent participation in the Parliament of the World's Religions in Cape Town, South Africa (December 1–9, 1999). The organizers of the Parliament are not actually advocating ethical neutrality. On the contrary, the 1994 Parliament meeting in Chicago produced a statement of principles of a global ethic to which all the representatives of different religious traditions agreed. The Global Ethic found that all religions concur on certain basic principles: do not kill, lie, steal, or sexually exploit others. To put it positively, all religions agree on the promotion of the values of life, truth, justice, and love.

The Global Ethic was criticized by some at the 1994 Parliament meeting as a Western "universalism" that is incompatible with the acceptance of diversity of religions. The Parliament's adoption of this ethic is based on a split between theology or religious symbolism and ethics. The argument has been that the World's Religions are diverse in theological symbolism, and that these cannot and should not be reduced to one system, but in ethics they have principles that are so similar that they can be formulated in a single system to which all concur.

But this universalism of ethics shared by the world's religions is something of a chimera. The reality is that most of the people who attend the Parliament belong to the "progressive" wing of their traditions that accept certain human rights principles and hence can agree on these principles. But their conservative co-religionists do not see such ideas as gender equality as rooted in their traditions. Thus the question remains: Is there a transcultural norm of the good and what is its basis, if we accept the irreducibility of difference in cultures?

The 1999 Parliament built on this global ethic and sought to apply it to practical "calls" to the dominant social institutions; government, the media, corporations, education, international organizations, non-governmental organizations, and religious institutions. The call to every institution to self-examination and reform in the light of the global ethic assumes a critique, not only by religion of other institutions, but a critique of religions themselves. How do religious institutions measure up to the global ethic? Do we assume that because religions are presented as the primary bearers of these values for society, that religious institutions themselves are better in this regard that other institutions?

The ethical superiority of religious institutions to secular ones would, I am afraid, hardly be borne up by the historical record. Religious leaders have sometimes used their office to promote sexual exploitation. War and violence have been promoted as crusades against infidels or punishment of heretics. The use of religion to accumulate wealth in the hands of religious leaders is hardly unknown. Often these failings are seen as having been in conflict with the principles of the religion itself. Thus one might say that religions teach good principles but individuals fail to live up to them. But this question becomes more difficult when the behavior we see as "bad" has been justified by religious tradition itself. Most of the world's religions have justified gender hierarchy as part of their theology and ethic.

While religion may elevate the best in human capacities, it also seems to exaggerate the worst. These distortions of religion seem to take the human vices of lying, stealing, killing, and sexual exploitation into another dimension, precisely by sacralizing them, by using religion to justify them or cover them up. This, I think, is why many people have felt particularly angry at religion, when they discover their claims to be betrayed, and in the name of religion itself.

This question of the betrayal of ethical principles by religion came up in a session of the Parliament in which I participated. This was a panel discussion of the International Buddhist-Christian Theological Encounter. This group has met for some fifteen years, and has sought to explore in depth the similarities and differences between Christianity and Buddhism. It has established an admirable community of friends that has entered into mutual understanding at a deep level. In our panel at the Parliament we tried to convey something of the success of this effort at dialogue.

Our discussion was challenged by an Indian man in the audience, himself a member of the Jain community and a teacher in Great Britain. He pointed out to one of our Buddhist presenters an experience he had had in a great Buddhist temple in an Asian country. In this temple the Buddha was honored by a statue wearing a crown covered with precious jewels. "How," he asked, "can a religion founded by a prince that renounced the life of royal privilege for that of a wandering ascetic honor him with a crown of jewels?" The Buddhist presenter quickly acknowledged that this was a distortion of the fundamental principles of Buddhism that call for the renunciation of avarice and the desire for wealth.

The Christians on the panel acknowledged a similar history of distortion in Christianity. How does the cross on which Christ suffered as the despised and rejected one, against the powers of injustice in the state and society, get turned into a gold and jeweled artifact to be hung above altars in ornate churches? What fundamental distortion of the message of Christianity is involved in such a transformation of the cross into a piece of precious jewelry? Jeweled crowns on the head of the Buddha and jeweled crosses on which Christ is hung both represent the distortion of the founder's message of critique of the exploitative power and wealth of society into a sacralization of this very power and wealth.

The sessions of the world parliament did not pay much explicit attention to the principles for the critique of religion, although it is implied in the global ethic and the inclusion of religions among those "guiding institutions" which the 1999 Parliament sought to call to account. But as the process continues of calling World Parliaments of Religion on a five year cycle (the next one is due to assemble in 2004), it would not be amiss to reflect on this question explicitly. Are the failings of religion simply ordinary humans failing writ large? Are these failings simply that of individuals, or do religions sometimes officially use their authority to sanction, violence, avarice, untruth, and exploitation? Are there some kinds of failings that are particular to religion?

My answer is yes to all three of these questions. There are certainly the failures of individual religious leaders to live up to their teachings, but religion can also use its official authority to sanction evil. Religions also suffer from a special temptation. From the Jewish and Christian prophetic tradition I would name this particular danger as idolatry. Idolatry is the tendency for religious leaders to translate their efforts to speak in the name of the sacred into a total identification of their person with the sacred. When the leader claims to be completely divine, to have an absolutely privileged claim to speak as the font of divine truth and goodness, then the needed element of humility and repentant self-questioning disappears.

The magnification of evil through false sacralization happens when leaders claim divine privilege to accumulate wealth, exercise authoritarian control, repress dissent, and call for violence toward others. This suggests that one of the criteria of "good" religion versus religious tendencies to evil is the extent to which they keep a healthy principle of repentant self-questioning built in to their quest for relation to the divine. While all religions seek to bring us into relation or communion with the divine, a fusion of the self (particularly of a religious leader) with the divine that eliminates the possibility of self-critique opens up the particular dangers of idolatrous abuse of power.

We readily recognize this abuse when we see it in other religions, but are less alert to our own idolatrous abuses of power. What this suggests is that the most valid critique of religion is self-critique, the cultivation of a mature balance between worship and communion with the divine and a recognition of our difference from the divine. We do this poorly when we use this principle to attack or discredit other religions in whose well-being we have no stake. We do it best when we exercise this principle as self-critique for the sake of our own community's spiritual health and good influence.

But this critique of greed and domination in religion assumes a Judaeo-Christian norm, although one often violated by those religions. Is this a transcultural norm? Since Buddhists found a similar norm in their own tradition of the Buddha, we could easily reach a consensus that each of us had taught a similar truth of renunciation of excess power and wealth, but failed to live up to it. But what do we do when faced with a religion that asserts the divinity and infallibility of its leader as a central revealed principle? That claims that gaining great wealth is an expected fruit of religious piety? How do we dialogue with a religion that insists that gender inequality is divinely revealed in its Scriptures, and hence is unchangeable?

I believe the Global Ethic pushes interreligious dialogue into some acceptance of a transcultural ethic that may be partly rooted in many faiths, but also partly transcends their historical traditions and practice. It is asking not just for mutual acceptance, but also some transformation of each religion to confirm to what is implicitly seen as common "human" principles of justice and well-being. Gender equality is typically the area of this "universalism" that is most unacceptable to the particular traditions. I myself am not willing to accept religiously sanctioned patriarchy as a legitimate diversity between religions that cannot be questioned. In that sense I assume some kind of common humanity that can be discerned across cultures that allows us to ask that women be treated equally with men, and that each religion should reform its traditions to accommodate this principle.

This suggests a need to distinguish between diversity of culture that opens us up to the rich plurality of possibilities of humanness while doing no harm, and differences that do harm, such as slavery, violence, gender hierarchy, racism, and wealth of the few at the expense of a majority of the poor. We need to grope toward some way of affirming diversities that do no harm, and also commonalities that can unite us as humans, as members of one earth community across cultures. The World Parliament functions implicitly with both of these principles, but we do not yet have a clear way of formulating this relationship of religious diversities and ethical commonalities. Perhaps one of the emerging dimensions of inter-religious dialogue is finding a basis for both mutual celebration of our differences and transformations toward shared well-being.

Rita

This question is extremely important in a time when post-modernism claims that no universals can be found—for feminism is, in some ways, the first post-modern position—but feminism cannot survive without adherence to some universal standards of humane and just relations between people. Feminism was one of the first movements to claim that the assumptions of modern culture were limited because they really represented the viewpoint and values of a small, though dominant, segment of the population: educated, economically well off, heterosexual, white, largely Protestant men. Thus, feminism demonstrated that androcentric ways of thinking were a false universal which needed to make room for those experiences that it had excluded, and recognize its own contingency. However, that logic, if allowed to swing to the opposite extreme, makes feminism itself nothing more than another contingency rather than a standard for humane and just relationships between women and men that prevails universally. Indeed, many detractors of feminism are eager to make that claim.

Additionally, when the pluralist appreciation of religious diversity that both Rosemary and I advocate is voiced, some people, usually religious conservatives, state that by giving up claims for the exclusive truth and relevance of one religion among the many religions, we are advocating total relativism, that we have no basis for making any judgements about anything that religions do or advocate. However, while neither Rosemary nor I will accept as universal truths some of the things that we were trained to believe in as universal truths, that does not mean we accept anything done in the name of religion as valid and acceptable. Because we can see truth in every religious perspective and do not regard our own religions as superior to other religions does not mean that religious phenomena cannot be evaluated.

Instead, what we are saying that no religion has a monopoly on either truth or falsity, relevant or harmful teachings and practices. Furthermore, every religion has some of each. In evaluating religious phenomena, I would claim that ethical behavior is far more important than theological doctrines. It is easy to demonstrate, if one studies world religions, that there are many cogent theologies; there is no particular need to rank or evaluate them against one another. If they can be evaluated or ranked at all, the only possible basis for such ranking would be the ethical consequences of theological ideas. When a theological doctrine, by itself, harms people who try to believe in it or when a theological doctrine translates directly into oppressive social practices, then it could be negatively evaluated. Many Jewish and Christian feminists have claimed that the exclusively male language and imagery of deity common in the monotheistic religions is one such example. More generally, I would claim that if people who hold to a set of doctrines are transformed in ethically positive ways by their adherence of those doctrines, they can be evaluated positively, though that does not mean those doctrines are therefore of universal value. If, on the other hand, people are rigid, inflexible, hateful toward those who are different, wasteful of natural resources, or cruel to animals, then the religious doctrines they hold are not working, are not doing their proper job of transforming humans into gentler, kinder, more compassionate beings. According to this standard, all religions have both succeeded and failed, another reason to hold the pluralist position.

As feminists, both Rosemary and I do evaluate how women fare, both in our own religions and in other religions. This, however, is one of the trickiest tasks we face, as we encounter religious teachings and behaviors that are not only patriarchal in familiar ways but also seemingly immoral and unredeemably oppressive. Western feminists, religious and secular, have sometimes been eager to criticize and condemn practices that strike them as completely cruel and unbearable for women. Unquestionably, when a feminist studies some unfamiliar religious contexts, she is likely to heave a sigh of relief that she does not live in that culture. Some practices, such as African genital operations on women, cannot be evaluated as anything but completely horrific by feminist standards. Nevertheless, we must ask if vocal outrage is the most effective way of responding to such practices.

Quick condemnation of unfamiliar religious or cultural beliefs and practices is one of the great pitfalls of cross-cultural studies in general. The purpose and the promise of such study is not to feel smug and superior. Long experience in teaching unfamiliar religions has given me certain insights about how best to proceed. First, the ground rules for looking into and learning from the comparative mirror require suspension of judgment at first, until one is thoroughly familiar with the situation being studied. One must first try to understand why such practices exist and what purposes they serve, according to the viewpoint of the religion being studied. Empathy is the most critical tool for looking into the comparative mirror in ways that do not create further mutual entrenchment and scorn. It must be applied in all cases, even the most unsavory, before appropriate judgments can be made.

If one does not jump to conclusions about how certain religious or cultural phenomena are experienced by projecting from one's experience, but takes more time to reflect on the practice, there may be some surprising conclusions. Some practices that seem undesirable turn out not to be as disadvantageous to women as they might seem at first. For example, arranged marriages can protect women from the need for self-display, the indignities of the singles bar, and the danger of date rape. Polygyny can provide female companionship and help with childcare. Furthermore, every woman who wants to marry can be married in a polygynous culture. Dress codes that require modesty can free women who are trying to find a partner from the need to display themselves as sex objects competing to attract the male gaze.

In other cases, seemingly undesirable conditions are not really very different from what Western women experienced until very recently, or even today. In particular, statements about the inferiority of women and the requirement that women should be subservient to male authority stemming from other religious contexts should not sound too different from the home-grown variety.

Finally, outsiders' judgments about women's situations are often made on the basis of public observation, of what goes on in public spaces. Women do not usually have authority in public spaces, including religious public spaces; indeed they may not even be present. However, if one knows the situation more intimately, one will discover that women often have a great deal of power behind the scenes, and everyone knows that and takes it for granted. As we have become familiar with the cultural and religious systems of India and China, this point has been demonstrated time and again.

However, some religious ideas and practices remain deplorable to a feminist even after much consideration. Then what? Cross-cultural public denunciations from first world countries and former colonists probably only entrench the situation further. Then resisting changes in women's situations becomes part of national pride and resistance to Westernization. It does little good to talk about African genital mutilation rather than African genital operations, or to decry Muslim practices surrounding gender, to name two of the most inflammatory feminist causes. It would probably be far better quietly to work with women from those situations and to support them financially and emotionally.

PART I

Lifestories

1. *Autobiographical Routes to Dialogue*

RITA M. GROSS

For more than twenty years, since 1980, Buddhist-Christian dialogue has been central to my life and my work. In retrospect, it seems as if all the currents that had defined my life previously were funneled into a few events that occurred that year, and as if the directions that have defined my life since then emerged from those concentrated points. Early in that year, the first edition of the book I co-edited with Nancy Falk, *Unspoken Worlds: Women's Religious Lives*, appeared. That book was the culmination and the most significant of my writings as a conventional historian of religions. It was also one of the last such writings. I had already begun to cross the discipline boundaries between religious studies and theology, and after that point, such boundary transgressions became ever more characteristic of my work.

For eighty days between February and April, I had participated, as a student, in the Vajradhatu Seminary, held that year at Chateau Lake Louise in the Canadian Rockies. This intensive, demanding period of sitting meditation and study is the major training program in the curriculum of the Buddhist group which I had joined a few years earlier. It is the gateway for beginning to do Vajrayana Buddhist practices and studies, the first of which is 100,000 full prostrations. One must prove that one is serious if one wants to participate in this world: the difficulty and effort involved an apprenticeship that includes 100,000 full prostrations indicates the unreliability of the popular literature that promises easy access to "Tantric secrets."

The point of deepest concentration, however, was the First International Buddhist-Christian Dialogue Conference, held for two weeks in June at the University of Hawaii. I had never been involved in Buddhist-Christian dialogue, or any interreligious interchange, for that matter, but I eagerly submitted a proposal to present a paper when I received a single sheet flyer announcing the conference. I was invited to present a plenary address on "Buddhism and Feminism." That talk stands as a central reference point when I reflect on my life. It was a "coming out" event in many ways. Though I had done unconventional work before, this felt like the most daring and dangerous thing I had done to date, and, indeed, it was. In the high energy of my immediate post-seminary experience, I had composed an eighty page paper that said everything I wanted to say about Buddhism and feminism at that time. But when it came time to do the actual plenary, I put the paper away and relied on a few notes. It was the first presentation I ever gave on Buddhism and feminism, and the first time I had spoken openly as a Buddhist practitioner to an academic audience. The audience was fairly large and I was on stage in a darkened theater-style auditorium. Every now and then I would notice some of the more academic attendees of the conference coming into the back of the auditorium, looking puzzled, and leaving after a few minutes. But in the middle of the auditorium sat Robert Aitken, Roshi, head of the Diamond Sangha of Honolulu. The longer I spoke, the more broadly he smiled; I knew I was doing something right. The response when I finished was overwhelming, and all that summer as I went about the conference trail, people were still discussing that talk. It was one of several times when I have given an utterly daring presentation that took every ounce of my energy and courage, when I have said or done things in a plenary that people just don't do. It's always worked, as it did that time in Honolulu.

In a way, everything to which I've devoted my scholarly attention was concentrated into that one talk: feminism, non-Christian religions, accurate information about world religions, Buddhism, Buddhism and feminism, interreligious interchange, even theology of religions. The response energized me to continue with what I knew was going to be an arduous task—writing the first feminist account of Buddhism—and to continue with my peculiar methodology that straddled religious studies and theology. What I was up against, as a Buddhist feminist theologian, was also revealed at the conference. Though the Japanese (male) delegates didn't talk with me, they talked with my Western male colleagues who reported to me. "That crazy American woman," they said. "What is her problem? We can understand that Christian women might feel a need for feminism—after all there's the male priesthood, the male deity, and so on. But we Buddhists have solved all those problems. According to Buddhism, deserving women are reborn as men!"

The second such conference was in 1984. At the conference, the prestigious Cobb-Abe International Buddhist-Christian Theological Encounter made its all-male debut. The conference attendees exploded about the lack of women and one of the organizers defended the group, saying "We invited Rosemary Ruether, but she turned us down." My name was put forward by people attending the conference and I was quickly invited to join the group. I was terrified. I had not prepared in any way for this turn of events and suddenly I was the only woman on stage with some of the most prestigious male theologians in the world. But I just did it, I just made myself sit there, though I didn't say anything at that dialogue. When we debriefed, I told John Cobb that I would not stay with the group unless at least two Buddhist and two Christian women were invited to join the group. Needless to say, they agreed, but asked me to do a major paper for the next meeting. I still felt intimidated, but went ahead anyway. As I gained my voice more and more, my intimidation dropped away; this is now one of my favorite groups of people in the world. I must also say that every man in this group has always been kind and gracious, and never condescending to me.

After the 1987 conference, the Society for Buddhist-Christian Studies was organized and I became its first vice-president and second president, succeeding John Cobb. When the Society's by-laws were written, care was taken to ensure equal representation on the board and in the leadership of the Society, not only between Christians and Buddhists, but also between women and men. I know that was in part due to my active participation in the Society. But I would argue that, if feminists get out into the bigger world, such results are not improbable or impossible. I have become quite tired of the self-isolation of many in the feminist theological movement today and find their worldview, which usually doesn't include much concern with religious diversity or non-Christian religions, to be quite stifling. I have continued with active participation in the Society and in the Cobb-Abe theological dialogue and also am co-editor of the Society's journal at this point.

But why would I have devoted so much energy to Buddhist-Christian dialogue? After all, I'm a historian of religions by training and a Buddhist by confession. Furthermore, becoming publicly identified with such a theological venture is professionally dangerous for someone whose major academic hat is being a scholar of an Asian religious tradition. I remember that when I saw the flyer for the 1980 conference, something very deep in me, beyond considered choice, responded—"Yes!

I want to do this," though I don't think the idea of participating in inter-religious exchange had occurred to me before. I did not rationally make the choice "I should do this because…" I believe the activity so compelled me because of my own traumatic history with Christianity. I longed, and long, for contact with a Christianity that is sensible and compassionate, and I have found it in the world of Buddhist-Christian dialogue.

It is early 1965. I am a senior in college, a philosophy major, rapidly becoming somewhat proficient in the Hebrew language, nearly perfect GPA, about to head off to graduate school in the history of religions at the University of Chicago. My mother has been dead for two months and I have come home to attend another funeral. The pastor of the Lutheran church in which I had been confirmed suddenly appears at the door. He is looking for my father; he did not know that I was home. But this is his chance for the confrontation he obviously feels is appropriate. At my mother's funeral, he had as captive audience, myself, my cousin who had become Catholic when she married, and my wayward uncle who had lived with several women over the years. The funeral sermon was mainly directed at me, though he reprimanded everyone else as well, and it was quite aggressive. Mainly the sermon was anti-Jewish because I had been studying Judaism for a number of years, but it was also intensively anti-learning as well. I do not remember much of the actual content but I do remember the feeling, sitting in the front pew—"If this wasn't my mother's funeral, I'd just get up and leave."

He began asking me very specific questions concerning my religious views about various matters, but when I tried to explain anything, he interrupted me immediately with "the truth." I got it relatively quickly and refused to stop speaking when he began, but he paid no heed and just kept up his monologue, no matter how long I continued. Finally he yelled, "I don't care what you think about anything. Just give me a 'yes' or a 'no' answer. Do you still hold completely to the doctrines to which you swore your lifelong allegiance when you were confirmed?" (at the age of fourteen). "That's exactly what the Catholic church demanded of Luther at the Diet of Worms," I replied. He turned away and slammed the door of my house so hard he almost broke the glass. A few days later, I got the letter telling me that I had been excommunicated and was going to spend eternity in a very hot place unless I apologized to him and repented of my sins. "You have sold your soul for a mess of academic pot-tage," I was told. My numerous sins? An earlier reprimand session, in which I was being castigated for singing in the choir at the wrong kind of Lutheran church sums it up: "I always knew I'd have problems with you someday. You asked too many questions." Most of all, I simply could not accept that all non-Christians and most non-Lutherans would end up in hell because they had the wrong religious ideas and didn't believe in Jesus. "There will be some Catholics in heaven," we were told. "But we don't know how they're going to get there given what they believe." Twenty-one seems a little young to be a confirmed heretic, but there I was—excommunicated for heresy.

My childhood was not of this century. I have a picture of myself in the second or third grade. I have traditional braids, as my hair had never been cut. I am wearing an old-fashioned looking dress and the horrible long brown cotton stockings and ankle-high scuffed brown shoes that I was made to wear at that age. I am standing on an unpainted stoop against the background of an exterior wall with flaking paint. I look like something out of Laura Ingalls Wilder; most people would assume it was a photograph from the nineteenth century. That was how we lived. I grew up in a log cabin that my parents had built. My mother skidded the spruce logs out of the woods with a horse and my dad notched them and put them together, like children might do with toy building components today. The house stood in the middle of forty acres of land; neither the highway nor any neighbors were visible. Heat and energy for cooking came from two wood burning stoves, one in the living room and one in the kitchen. The enormous quantities of wood required for heating and cooking had to be prepared each year: felling the logs, buzzing them up, splitting them if necessary, stacking them, and hauling a fresh supply of wood into the house every day. Water for all purposes—cooking, washing, bathing, and doing laundry—was carried from a spring some distance from the house. There was no indoor plumbing; outhouses worked quite well. We did have electricity. I vaguely remember the electricians putting in the wiring when the Rural Electrification Project brought electricity to areas such as ours after World War II. We never had a TV, or, much worse for me when I was a teenager, a telephone.

My parents survived the depression somehow, living from hand to mouth, and as a result my mother was a consummate packrat. We saved everything "in case of bad times." By the time I was around, my dad had gotten a job doing shift work in a local factory that made pallets. We also had a cow or two and my mother raised chickens for both eggs and meat for a number of years. She also churned butter and my parents had a route in town to deliver butter, eggs, and chickens, as customers ordered.

My mother hated raising chickens and was more than happy to get a few more cows, start selling the milk, and quit the butter, eggs, and chicken route. We had a large garden and my mother canned virtually everything you could think of, including peaches and other fruits that were bought in the store. There was a root cellar under the cabin, with shelves lined with home canned products, including meat, and a large potato bin. Every day someone got the potatoes for our daily home-canned meat and potatoes supper—usually me, as soon as I could.

We got our first tractor in 1949. What a day! My dad had to drive it home from town, seven miles, which took quite a while with a 1940s tractor. With cows around we had to make hay every summer, which became one of the dominant realities of my life until the summer after I graduated from college. When I was almost seven, we got our first horse, the fulfillment of my mother's dreams of many years, and mine too. She must have taught me that I wanted a horse, but I still love horses. Those were happy years. My parents still got along well and seemed to enjoy each other's company, and the work load, while heavy, was not over-whelming. Things changed a lot after we acquired "the farm." My moth-er had grown up on it and it had been farmed by her younger brother, who had died suddenly of a cerebral aneurysm. None of the other broth-ers wanted to farm but my mother couldn't bear to see the property leave the family. Besides, my father's factory was going to close any day; every-one knew it and he was too old to get another factory position (of which there were very few to be had anyway). So we acquired the farm—160 acres kitty-corner with our own forty—when I was eleven.

If I were to be more analytical, using an out of favor analytical model, I could say that my childhood and teenage years were dominated by the natural world and a cultural order. They were quite contrasting in the extent to which they nurtured me. The memories I narrated above are early. My more dominant memories involve the years of working the farm and all that entailed. Even in the 50s, it was a marginal farm, too far north and too small to provide livelihood above the poverty level. I worked on the farm from late grade school through college.

My favorite memory of the farm, based on experiences which pre-vailed all through high school and college, occurs in the summer. I get up at about 4:00 A.M.; my parents have already been up a while. I go out to the little barn near our house and saddle the horse I am riding. My dog, a collie whom I had named "Lassie" when I was younger, has been unchained and is excited to be out for a ride and a run. The big barn, where the dairy herd is kept, is a ways away from our home site and my mother and I both ride horses back and forth. We three, dog, horse, and I, take off across a home built wooden bridge and through the woods. We come out of the woods at the base of a large hill; all the fields are at the top of that hill. The sun is very new in the sky; the light is soft—a golden, soft, open light that I still find impossible to describe. As we move through the grass, we leave trails in the heavy dew. We reach the barn; I lean down beside the horse's neck so that I don't have to dismount till we get to her stall. Her hooves clop on the cement floor and all the calves begin bawling; they know they'll soon be fed. I grab a milkstool and milkpail and get a cow into the proper position to be milked, lean my forehead into her flank to remind her to stand still and start in. To be milked properly, a cow has to be milked very fast and it's quite hard work. Twelve to fifteen minutes and there is a full pail of milk. Some is measured out for that cow's calf and it is fed. Repeat ten or twelve times. If I never milk another cow, it will be too soon, though I didn't mind it at the time. (We had milking machines and all the equipment needed to use them. My mother refused to do so.)

Later, after the dew dries off, it's time to make hay, one of the most important and labor-intensive aspects of the kind of farming we did. I either drove a tractor or worked loading and unloading hay bales all day. I actually did more of the work with hay bales because my mother could not do that kind of work due to a childhood injury. She did more tractor-driving, which is a sit-down job. That meant that I spent most of my time, as a pre-teen and teenage girl, working with a small crew of men, and I took pride in the fact that I could throw a bale of hay almost as well as they could, though, realistically, I had to stay with the lighter jobs of top-loading the wagon and then throwing bales into the haymow where the men worked to stack them. At the end of that kind of workday, the cows had to be milked again. Twice a day, 365 days a year, cows had to be milked; there was no such thing as a break.

Dominant winter memories are somewhat different. Fortunately, my mother did not make me do barn chores on school days. Instead, I walked home from where the school bus dropped me off, let myself into the house, and rekindled the fires in the cook-stove and the main heater. (Thus, I was a "latch-key" child, and I don't see any problem with that practice.) A pot of water was boiled and I did the dishes from the preceding day. Then I did whatever housework needed to be done—ironing, patching. By then I made most of my mother's clothes and all of my own.

I cooked dinner (we called it "supper") on the wood-burning cookstove. My parents came home from the barn and we ate. They went to bed almost immediately after supper and I did homework, or—luxury of luxuries—simply read for pleasure. The only place warm enough to do so was sitting right next to the cookstove, sometimes with my feet in the oven. I have vivid memories of sitting there wondering whether I dared put one more piece of wood in the stove and read just a little longer. I could regulate the temperature of that stove so precisely that I could bake a cake in the oven, and I knew just how long I could get out of one more piece of wood.

Weekends found me in the barn again. The cows got very dirty, lying in their own manure part of the time. (There were gutters for their manure, but they often missed.) Milking them by hand, they had to be somewhat clean or the milk would be too dirty to use. So I kept them curried in the winter. Actually, I loved the barn in winter. I have an especially vivid memory of sitting there one evening. The chores were all done; the cows had been fed new hay and were happily munching away. The sound of thirty or so cows chewing their hay is indescribable. I was sitting on a bale of straw, my dog happily cuddled beside me. It was an experience of pure contentment. "What's so bad about being born in a barn?" I asked myself. (It must have been near Christmas.) As my dog and I cuddled and hugged each other, I asked, "What's so evil about touching?" (We were forbidden to dance because it was too dangerous to touch that way.)

After my dad quit farming, I bought his half of the farm from him and kept the land and the barn for many years. I just couldn't let go of it. My cousin farmed it, paying me the cost of the property taxes. After the barn finally burned down a few years ago with forty-five head of cattle in it, I called my cousin. We tried to talk, but all we could do was hold the phone and weep. Even now, just writing this makes me weep all over again. There was something so unfathomably profound about the land and the animals, so many vignettes of unsurpassed beauty, so many little corners of the land here and there that stop the mind and break the heart. Even saying the word *beauty* to describe their quality is far too trivial.

And then there was culture. I grew up in northern Wisconsin, which was quite provincial then. For example, I never saw a black person until I went to college, though I angrily listened to my Milwaukee relatives complaining about the " n_____s." Speaking up to them was not appreciated. Neither of my parents went to high school. Education was not particularly valued, either by my family or the culture. Intellectual inquiry was even less understood or tolerated.

My struggle to find enough books to read is indicative of what the culture was like. I spent the first four years of grade school in an old-fashioned one-room school house with one teacher for all eight grades. The library consisted of two small bookshelves, one for grades one through four on one side of the room and the other, for grades five through eight, on the other side. By the time I was in the third or fourth grade, I was reading at the seventh or eighth grade level and I had more than exhausted all the books in the book shelf for the lower grades, many of which were intended for children just beginning to learn to read. But I was forbidden to cross the invisible line that separated the other bookshelf from the one to which I had access. "You'll just have to wait until you're older," I was told. It was suggested that I should take books out of the lending library in Rhinelander, a town seven miles away in which we shopped regularly anyway. That worked for a few weeks until the librarians realized that my parents' cabin was a few hundred yards on the wrong side of the county line. "Your parents don't pay taxes in our county, so you can't read our books." Instead, they were told to take me to Merrill, thirty-five miles away, to borrow books there. That was not going to happen, given the time and money it would have taken.

A few years later, when we had acquired the farm, I went back to the librarians. "My parents now own land in Oneida County, so we pay taxes here." The reply, "That's not enough. You actually have to live in Oneida County to read our books." From fifth through eighth grade, I attended the Lutheran parochial school in Rhinelander, two blocks from the library. Though I was still forbidden to cross the street by my over-protective mother, I went to the library anyway with my friends. I picked out books, which they checked out on their library cards. The librarians figured out what was going on. "If you let her read books on your library cards, we'll take your library cards away from you. She's not permitted to read our books." Finally, I was in high school in Rhinelander and by law was permitted to have a library card. The librarians still tried to keep me out of the adult library as long as they could and were always complaining about the number of books that I checked out.

One of my attempts to find something to read resulted in an eerie experience for which I have no real explanation. I was probably in the third grade. My parents had gone to visit some friends, taking me along, as always. (My mother prided herself on the fact that she took me every-

where and never left me with an older relative or friend.) These friends
had somehow acquired some cast-off school books. Among them was a
coverless geography book with half its pages missing, but I hadn't seen it
before, so I settled down to read it instead of playing with my parents'
friends' kid. Amazingly, for a book that was already old in 1952, it
included a chapter on Tibet, which I started reading. All sorts of information was presented, including the claim that Tibetans were a very dirty
people who hardly ever bathed. It was explained that their climate was
too cold and dry to permit much bathing, but I said to myself indig-
nantly, "That's not true! We are not dirty!"

Not much needs be said about the schools. The restrictions on library
use at the one-room school house say enough. At the Lutheran parochial
school, the main emphasis was making sure we didn't hear about anything that was not correct according to church dogma. That made it very
difficult to teach science, and I had virtually no education in science until
high school biology. (The library at the Lutheran school isn't even worth
mentioning; everything was censored by quite a number of criteria.)
High school, however, was another matter. Whatever its limitations,
including few classes intended for the more academically oriented students, it was a gateway to another world, the world beyond Rhinelander,
Wisconsin, and the seventy mile radius around Rhinelander that consti-
tuted the world I had physically experienced. In those days, some things
about the education system in general were better than they are today.
For example, I was able to take two years of Latin in this remote and
provincial part of the country. Studying Latin was a whole new window
on the world and I was rapidly following my gaze out that window.

The social milieu was very difficult, however. There are two parts to
these difficulties, one due to the culture in general and one more specific to my socialization. Girls were less valued, and I knew that from a very
young age, not from anything overt on the part of my parents but from
general and widespread cultural signals. A reproduction of a well-known
religious painting hung on one of the cabin walls. It showed two children
crossing a flimsy bridge over a deep ravine, with an angel behind them,
obviously guarding them and watching over them. I was still very young,
perhaps even pre-school, when I began to take comfort from that picture.
"Jesus was a man," I mused, "and so is God. Where does that leave me?"
Then I would look at the picture. "Ah, but the angels are women!" Later,
the message was delivered in confirmation class. The role of a Christian
woman was to be married and have children if at all possible. But those

unfortunate women for whom that did not happen could still help in the work of God's kingdom. Women were to obey their husbands and be subservient. How do we know this? From the fact that both Jesus and God are male. I put up my hand. "But the angels are women," I protested. "No—that's not the case. The artists make it look that way, but they're really painting the angels incorrectly. They are also men." This was the same pastor who later excommunicated me.

I spent many of my pre-teen and teen years desperately wishing, "If only I hadn't been a girl. Why did I have to be a girl! Girls can't do anything that I want to do. I don't want to have kids, I want to explore the world and to think!" Finally one day, it occurred to me, "It's not me—there's nothing wrong with me. It's the system." My anger switched from being focused on my female body to being focused on the system, but this was well before the emergence of the feminist movement and I tried hard to conceal my anger because it was so unacceptable.

Socially things were also very difficult, due to the way I had been raised. My mother was a very difficult person—extremely over-protective and domineering. When I was younger, I was never allowed to do anything the kids in my rural neighborhood did, especially ride their bikes exploring the countryside, because "you might get hurt. I don't know about these other parents, they let their kids run all over, but I love you, so I'm going to keep you right beside me all the time." Needless to say, I didn't develop very good social skills, which, combined with being female and being bright in an era and area that did not value brightness in children, made for a miserable social life, all through high school. I also remember saying to myself, "I wish I weren't so smart so that the other kids would like me." They liked me well enough when they needed to borrow and copy my homework, but that's as far as it went. By high school, I was simply hanging on, waiting to get away to college where there might be other people genuinely interesting in learning, who were not just putting up with school.

My mother cared little for my grades; it just didn't matter to her one way or the other. Her sole ambition for me was that I would marry a farmer and build a house right next to hers so that we could be together forever. She tried to control, not only that big decision of my life, but every detail. For example, when I was in college, I needed new glasses and she insisted on picking out the frames, even though I was twenty years old, largely self-supporting, and worked like a dog, without pay, for my parents on the farm every summer. I had picked a stylish pair of glass frames that I thought made me look rather good, but she picked a dowdy, bland pair of frames that she said were "more sensible." By then I had learned not to fight back but to wait it out. I refused to settle for her chosen frames. It took all day, with the optometrist finally intervening to say that the frames I had chosen were perfectly okay, but I got the frames I wanted.

By then she and my father were not getting along very well. She constantly criticized him. He couldn't do anything right; he couldn't milk a cow right, he couldn't spread the bedding straw right, he couldn't even carry in an armload of wood into the house without spilling too many chips and pieces of bark, and he was too slow at everything he did. They didn't spend much time working together but I constantly heard from my mother about how dissatisfied she was. That dissatisfaction intensified her compulsion to keep me near at hand. But it was inevitable. As much as I loved the farm, my gaze was going out that window opened by the study of Latin and it was becoming clear to me that what I wanted to do in life could not be done in Rhinelander, Wisconsin. The first time "The Subject" came up, she exploded with rage. "How dare you think of planning your life so that you leave here. Don't you see what you'd be leaving me with?" I took off on my horse for a long ride in the woods, my usual way of dealing with such confrontations. After that, there was always a lot of tension, though as long as "The Subject" didn't come up, we got along easily and worked well together. Unlike my father, I could milk the cows and spread the bedding straw according to her specifications. But "The Subject" was always just beneath the surface and often came stingingly out in the open. One example is enough. After the morning milking had been finished and before the day's hay-making began, we were riding our horses home after taking the cows out to their pasture. Suddenly it somehow came up. "I don't know what I ever did to deserve a kid like you. Everybody else is content to graduate from high school and settle down around here. What makes you think you're so special?"

Other things from her have stayed with me. Our little house was always full of plants. My much bigger house is also full of plants, a few of which come from plants that she had over fifty years ago. She also kept magnificent flower gardens, especially before the farm became overwhelming. I, too, have extensive flower gardens in my city yard. Some joggers and walkers modify their route to take in my flowers. Some of them also were dug out of the yard in Rhinelander and replanted in Eau Claire. Sometimes I cannot help wondering what would have happened if she had lived longer. Would she ever have been able to let go of her version of me and make a relationship with her Buddhist feminist daughter who did not want to milk cows for the rest of her life? I have my doubts.

My dad and I got to know each other after she died. I found that he was a very gentle, genial man, easy-going and easy to get along with. We would spend hours talking about how difficult she had been to live with, which was very healing. My dad told me that he had tried to intervene on my behalf, but that he just couldn't stand up to her determination that she would protect me from everything so that I wouldn't "get hurt or make any mistakes." Two stories about my father that I treasure came to me by way of my step-mother. After my dad retired from farming, he worked part time as a janitor's aid at the local school. Every afternoon, he went to work a little early so that he could have a cup of coffee with the principal and chat. One day he told him, "I might only be a janitor, but my daughter is a college professor." My step-mother also told me that he prayed every night that some day I would come back to "the church." But I never heard a single word about it from him.

The process of selecting a college to attend was complicated by poverty and by a lack of experience in the whole world of higher education on the part of my family and the people with whom we socialized. Eventually, I wound up realizing that the University of Wisconsin at Milwaukee was both my best and my only choice. It was the best choice because it had a philosophy department—something most UW campuses, only recently converted from being state teachers' colleges, lacked. It was the only choice because it was a commuter school and did not have dormitories. Therefore, UW-M could not require undergraduates to live in dorms, which was the norm when I went to college. Tuition, which was then very low, could be scraped together somehow, but dorm and cafeteria fees were out of the question. It was much cheaper to rent a room in someone's attic and cook on a hot plate.

The transition from the farm to college life in a city was one of the two most thorough changes in consciousness I have ever experienced. (The other was when the scales of androcentrism dropped away from my eyes and I began to realize just what had been done to me by social convention, both intellectually and spiritually.) For most of the first semester, I felt numb and disoriented, but that didn't prevent me from studying well and making good grades. By the end of my first year, I felt much more adjusted and began to enjoy my new lifestyle. My high school dreams of finally having intellectual companionship had to be given up, however. My nick-name in college was "curve-wrecker," but by then I didn't much care about downsizing myself to be acceptable to my peers. UW-M was more like a community college than a university in terms of why most students were there and what they wanted. Furthermore, there was little campus life because almost everyone took a city bus home by late afternoon. For the most part, the course work was adequate, though not outstanding, but UW-M was much what high school had been—a gateway to other things.

But the neighborhood, not the university itself, was the gateway to my involvement in and eventual conversion to Judaism. Though I could not officially study religion at UW-M, my interest in religion only increased through my college years. I was in a position to explore other forms of religion, including the choir at the "wrong" kind of Lutheran church, and I did. Across the street from the campus was a Reform Jewish synagogue with a charismatic, liberal Rabbi who was very involved in the civil rights movement. A non-Jewish friend of mine had attended services there and spoke positively of the experience. So one Friday night I put on my Sunday clothes, timidly entered the synagogue by myself, and took a seat somewhere near the back. I don't think anyone noticed me. I was shocked by the familiarity of parts of the service. I've always found good liturgy very appealing and it didn't take me long to figure out the traces from the Jewish service through the Catholic mass and into the Lutheran service. I found myself continuing to come back and eventually people noticed me and befriended me. I met the Rabbi, who became an important mentor to me, and became quite familiar with the liturgy, and increasingly, with a Jewish understanding of the world. In my senior year of college, I began the study of Hebrew language and Hebrew civilization at the university. I was slowly becoming convinced that this was where I wanted to be religiously, but I took my time. For well over a year, I did choir practice on Thursday evening, Jewish services on Friday evening and Saturday morning, and then church on Sunday (at the wrong kind of Lutheran church). I also wanted to leave Milwaukee before I converted, to make sure I was converting to Judaism and not to this particular congregation.

When I left for graduate school at the University of Chicago Divinity School, I eagerly went to the Hillel Foundation. I was delighted that I was able to "pass;" my Jewish knowledge was such that no one suspected I wasn't Jewish by birth even when they found out somehow that I was from northern Wisconsin. The Hillel community and environment were extremely appealing and satisfying to me. I formally converted about six months after I entered graduate school. During my years at the University of Chicago, I was deeply involved in the Hillel community. During my first year there, a new worship group, the "upstairs minyan," was formed. It was to be both traditional and innovative at the same time. I was a member from the very beginning. Early in its history, the minyan began to raise the issue of women's participation, or lack thereof, in traditional Jewish synagogue liturgy. I was one of the leaders in that development and we slowly broke all the traditional barriers to women. By the time I left, women were serving as cantors for our High Holiday services, which were attended by a large public audience. (I never filled that role; I couldn't sing well enough, despite all my years singing in Lutheran choirs.)

Eventually, my Jewish practice did not survive my transition out of the Hillel environment and into the environment of a congregation, especially after I moved to Eau Claire, where a fairly Jewish-illiterate congregation held services once a month. There were very few people like me—young, female, single, professionals—in that congregation. In addition, I had begun meditating, and, as Judaism eventually proved more attractive than any version of Christianity I encountered, so Buddhism eventually proved to be more appropriate for me than an active Jewish life. But I did remain significantly involved long enough to write several essays in Jewish feminist theology, including the first discussion of female god-language in a Jewish context, which was eventually published in the landmark anthology *Womanspirit Rising.*

People sometimes ask me in a truly mystified manner—"Why Judaism?" I reply that, even now, I do not consider myself to be an ex-Jew, though I do not choose an active Jewish practice. Judaism offered two things that were literally life-saving to me. I became part of a community in which I was accepted and in which I could participate whole-heartedly. And in Judaism, it is okay to have a brain. At a time when I had had few nurturing social reference points, I was accepted, liked, and valued for who I was and what I could contribute. That has been a rare experience in my life.

UW-Milwaukee was also that the gateway to graduate studies at the Divinity School of the University of Chicago, though I was quite naive and had no idea what I was getting into when I chose that direction. First, it was rare for women to pursue graduate studies in those days, so rare that I was assured by one of my more concerned college mentors that, despite my impeccable academic record, I would not receive a prestigious Woodrow Wilson Fellowship to attend graduate school. With some impatience, he said to me, "You can't expect them to give that kind of fellowship to you. You're an attractive woman; you'll get married and it will go to waste."

My studies of philosophy convinced me that I did not want to continue with that field, that I was much more interested in religion, because it seemed to me that religion is much more at the core of life and deals with the whole person, not just the intellect. Again I faced discouragement. The college mentor who helped me the most, a female professor of English, begged me not to go into that field. "A woman can't make in religion," she told me. Once I had decided to pursue graduate studies in religion so that I could study how people dealt with ultimate questions of life and meaning, it immediately seemed obvious to me that it is pointless to pursue such study only within the context of the culture of one's birth. I have never understood why people who are interested in religion wouldn't want to study it in a cross-cultural perspective.

My winding up at the University of Chicago to study the history of religions during the heyday of that school's impact on the field of religious studies was serendipity or good karma. I really didn't know anything about the merits and demerits of the various programs in religious studies, and no one at UW-M had a clue either. So I received no advice and knew precious little about the process of getting a Ph.D., though I knew that was my goal. I was so intent on what I wanted to do that I only vaguely noticed that now I was the only woman present in many contexts. There was a huge influx of female students into the Divinity school in 1965, the year I entered—six. That brought the female population of the Divinity School to twelve women among four hundred students. The professors were wondering what the field could possibly do with all these women now wanting to study religion, and some of my professors censored some of their usual course readings because they felt they couldn't talk about anything explicitly sexual with women present.

I found that my Lutheran training, minus its rigidity, had provided me with me a good basis for quickly passing my exams in Bible and Christian Theology. No matter the field in which one was intending to specialize, all students were required to pass exams in all the fields offered by the Divinity School. For those of us going into the history of religions and intending to specialize in a Asian religion, that meant we still had to pass exams in the six Western-oriented fields of the Divinity School. I passed those quickly, and also passed the required German and

French competency exams. Then I settled into the foundation of a history of religions specialty, an Asian language—Sanskrit in my case. My life became one endless Sanskrit dictionary; it seemed there was no time for anything else.

In my second year, spring 1967, I was taking the required courses from Mircea Eliade in "primitive religions," as they were then disparagingly called. I was also getting more and more frustrated with the role of women in Western religions in general and decided to write my two-course paper, "The Role of Women in Australian and Melanesian Religions," "to find out if things are as bad for women everywhere else as they are here." That paper turned out to be a life-shaping, life-changing event. Almost immediately I found some extremely interesting materials. Quickly I saw that the issue was not so much what kind of role women played in Australian Aboriginal religion, but how that data had been understood by Western scholars. They said that women have no religious life, that religion is something for the sacred men and that the profane women have no role in religion. But the field reports I was reading documented all sort of things that women did religiously, though they were not what that the men did. Part of that paper was simply a report on all the data I had found, but something else seemed clear to me. It seemed clear to me that one would not get an accurate portrait of a religious community if one studied only the men and that it was a methodological flaw to do so.

I thought my mentors in that the history of religions would be very interested in these findings. Indeed, Mircea Eliade was, more, I think, for the data I was noticing than for the methodological implications involved in noticing or not noticing those data. When he gave the paper back to me, he told me that I was seeing things in the materials that he had seen. "You're going to do your dissertation on this material, aren't you?" he asked. I replied, "No, I want to do my dissertation on something important." But he really encouraged me to proceed with these investigations and eventually I began to consider doing so.

Again, I was naive and didn't know the ropes professionally, and no one gave me good advice. I was well into my Sanskrit studies and South Asian focus, which I didn't really want or intend to give up. But, given the feedback I had gotten on my paper, my dissertation proposal mushroomed into a comparative study on the role of women in religions, with South Asian religion as one of the components. I prepared for my written preliminaries and my oral defense of the dissertation proposal (which is what one defends at Chicago for some strange reason). The oral defense would be on the first set of materials, those on Aboriginal Australia. By 1968, I already had the beginnings of a genuinely feminist methodology well in hand. The first sentence of my statement read, "History of Religions is very concerned with *homo religiousus* but it ignores *femina religiousa*." My materials demonstrated that studying women makes a difference to one's understanding of any specific religion. By July, my statement was ready for an October defense. The only feedback I received was that I should publish as soon as my defense was completed.

Finally the day arrived. I knew something was wrong when I walked into the room, in which sat not only my committee but some visiting professors who had been invited to sit in. When it was over, one of my major advisors said, "You're an intelligent person. Don't you understand that the generic masculine covers and includes the feminine, thereby making it unnecessary to look specifically at women?" From that day on, the Divinity School faculty fought over whether someone who wanted to write a dissertation on something as unimportant as women and religion should be allowed to continue. I learned later that one of visiting professors, who had a major grudge against Eliade, had insisted that it was scandalous for the University of Chicago to be taking such an unscholarly topic seriously. Except for Eliade, the male professors who had previously encouraged my project now bowed to their male colleagues' pressure. My status was in limbo, and for months I heard rumors and saw the edges of the fight in the faculty. Finally the visiting professor left and I was set free from limbo and told to proceed with my dissertation as if nothing untoward had happened, with the understanding that it should be scaled back to cover only the materials on Aboriginal Australia. I proceeded, and left Chicago in 1971 for my first teaching position with about a third of dissertation finished and approved.

But it wasn't over! My committee started fighting among itself. The University of Chicago itself was not big enough for two of them. One of them had to become my primary advisor under these circumstances and the one who had actually worked with me quite a bit made the most sense. He soon left the University of Chicago but was given permission to finish up with his doctoral students. He forbade me to have any contact with the other professor. It was all very traumatic and confusing. I found myself completely consumed by the demands of teaching in my first few years as a professor, especially since I have always been expected to cover all of Asia in my course work. But I also knew I had to finish the dissertation, which I did in a grand push in the summer of 1974. By then I had already published several articles on the importance of studying women and religion and some of the methodology involved. My major professor, I found out later, thought that it was fine to study women, but couldn't believe that the methodology of history of religions itself was flawed or that androcentrism was a methodological problem. I submitted in my dissertation in late August. Months went by and it hadn't been read. Even before it had been read, the content of my dissertation was well-known and thought to be important by some, but the Divinity School faculty was also still fighting about the appropriateness of studying women and religion. After tumultuous interchanges between my major professor and a number of Divinity School graduates at the seventy-four AAR's, it was unclear to me whether my major professor would ever read my dissertation, and I did not know what to do next. Finally, one evening in December he called me. I'll never forget that moment. "Congratulations, Dr. Gross," he said. "You should publish this stuff in some journals." He wanted a few minor revisions and that was it, except that the other professor still tried to sabotage my work. Sections of the dissertation he had previously approved as more than adequate he now wanted completely redone. But he had no power at that point.

By December, 1974, all the paperwork was completed. All that remained was to have the dissertation retyped and actually to have the degree conferred. I chose to miss the March commencement because it didn't fit my schedule. After all I been through, I was going to march to receive my degree, damn it, and march I did, in the June commencement—under the huge bell tower and carillon of Rockefeller Chapel and down the long aisle, the carillon, organ, and brass choir all sounding as triumphant and joyful as I felt! By a short margin, it was the first Ph.D. conferred for study of women and religion and I was the only woman in doctoral robes at my commencement. As I walked around campus and met people, I found out that my dissertation and I were still controversial among the faculty: women and religion was not a valid topic and someone who wanted to study that topic could not be up to University of Chicago standards, it was claimed.

That same spring, the Divinity School of the University of Chicago sponsored a conference on women and religion. I was not invited! Later I got blow by blow accounts from several women friends about how the conference organizers had been made to feel the heat for not inviting me. But that didn't change the fact that, though I had done the tough pioneering work, my work was not acknowledged or recognized by my graduate school.

People often tell the story of the child who is the only one brave, naive, and honest enough to point out that the emperor is not wearing clothes, though he declaims about his wonderful suit. The implication of that story, as usually told, is that everyone awakens to the child's wisdom and insight. But I think the story goes differently. Instead, the kid is smacked on the mouth and told never to talk that way again. If you say, "But look, the emperor *really* isn't wearing clothes," you are then sent to stand in the corner. It is amazing to me that the learned professors at the University of Chicago didn't realize I was on to something in 1968, and celebrate and foster what one of their own was doing. That it could ever have been controversial simply to study women and religion remains unfathomable to me. The need to study women's religious lives is not a very monumental insight, in and of itself. After all, I was barely off the farm and had never been through a top-notch educational process when I realized, with blinding clarity, that the study of religion was flawed by its failure to study women's religious lives and roles. But, instead of being recognized, I have been made to stand in the corner for a long time.

The corner to which I was sent was a regional state university. Regional state universities are the factories of academia. Like the schools I had attended most of my life, I was now teaching in a school where learning was not a high priority for most of the students and I had few intellectual comrades among the faculty. Furthermore, in such a school, religious studies is a "service program," which means that our main reason for existing is to offer humanities general studies classes for students majoring in other fields. They are not reticent to tell professors that their course in religious studies is not a high priority and that course requirements should reflect that fact. My major teaching responsibility was a freshman course in world religions, and every course I taught was relatively introductory. For many many years, I was the only woman in the department, the only single person, and the only person who cared about Asia (in the whole university at first). There were also precious few feminists when I arrived in 1973. The collegiality offered to me consisted of urging me to join the football pool. There were almost no men with whom a sustained relationship was possible and there was never a community of like-minded people. The three things that are so essential to a nurtured life—collegiality, community, and the companionship of a life partner—have been largely denied me here in this corner.

I was also the only department member with a significant scholarly life and a national or international reputation. Early on at UW-EC, I was told not to expect my scholarly activities to make much difference in terms of salary or promotions, because "that's not what this school is about," and, despite my scholarly record, my salary was always well below the median for my rank. I found that if I did mention a publication or a speaking engagement, the reaction was that "Rita is bragging again." Therefore, for that the most part, I kept quiet about my scholarly successes.

As the years passed, this situation became more and more intolerable. When I traveled, I would discover that my writings were being widely taught—by other professors at good schools, while I was ignored at UW-EC. Graduate students from other institutions wrote to me and called me, sent me their papers, and were eager to meet me at conferences or other speaking engagements, and even asked if there was some way they could study with me. Meanwhile, students at UW-EC shopped for the easiest courses and complained that I was too demanding, even though the few students who were genuinely interested in thinking and in studying religions repeatedly enrolled in my courses. In academia, the penalties for doing innovative work, for blending disciplines, and for focussing on women and religion are very high. But at least I have the satisfaction of knowing that I have done something worthwhile and helpful to others with my life and my work, that I have done more than work on articles that are seldom read or used by anyone. Despite all the hardship, I would make the same choices again.

In September, 1973, when I had just moved to Eau Claire, I was walking across the parking lot to teach my Buddhism class. I had just returned from visiting my lover, who was dying of an inoperable brain tumor, for what I knew would be the last time. I knew no one in town and already realized that Eau Claire was not going to be a supportive and nurturing place for me. I was lonely and miserable. I was also trying to think about the Four Noble Truths, which I didn't think I understood very well, and which I needed to teach in the upcoming class. In an instantaneous flash, I saw how much my misery was caused by the fact that I desperately wanted things to be different, that I wanted what I couldn't have. I wanted those things so badly that I couldn't really experience the beautiful fall day in northern Wisconsin. I stopped and said to myself, "The Four Noble Truths are true!"

When that insight hit, unlike many academics, I did not confine myself to the first three noble truths, which can be rather philosophical and remote without Buddhist practice. I looked into the Fourth Noble Truth, with its insistence on the necessity of meditation, as well. It didn't make much sense for the other three truths to be true and for this one to be irrelevant. I decided then and there that I must learn to meditate, though I also justified it to myself by saying that I really needed to know what this part of Buddhism was about if I were to teach Buddhism successfully. Acting on that decision took some will power and persistence in northern Wisconsin in the early seventies, but eventually, it did happen. In early 1975 I attended a workshop on Zen Buddhist meditation in Madison and meditated sporadically. That summer, when Nancy Falk and I began our work on *Unspoken Worlds*, I attended some sessions lead by a visiting Hindu guru, but I didn't think that was that the path I wished to follow. Finally, in early 1976, a dear old Chicago friend who had already become involved with Vajradhatu came through Eau Claire recruiting for Naropa Institute. We had arranged his visit so that I could receive meditation instruction, for I knew from the beginnings of my personal interest in Buddhism that Vajrayana Buddhism was the path that I would follow. That summer I went to India for the first time and when I came back, I had largely stopped meditating. One talk with my old friend got me back on track. Since then, even if for some reason I miss meditation for a period of time, I have defined myself as a meditator. It became part of my life and I knew I would never quit.

The following summer, I went to Boulder for the first time to teach at Naropa Institute. I was cautious and suspicious about what I might find there. I had decided that meditation was a good thing and that I would continue with it, but I had also decided not to become involved with Buddhism as a religion. After all, I said to myself, "I've already been through two religions, and that's enough." Besides, I knew that Buddhism had its own share of problems with patriarchy and by then I was firmly identified as a feminist and had already made a reputation for my work on feminism and religion.

But I fell hard that summer for the actual experience of the Buddhist community, the presence and magnetism of Buddhist teachers, and the whole general milieu we called "the scene." I could not believe myself when I found myself asking to "take refuge," to become a Buddhist in my first formal meditation interview, but that's what happened. Even more surprising, the teacher listened to me and said, "You've waited too long already." (Usually people are asked to wait for some time before taking refuge.) After that, I moved quickly through the curriculum of study and practice leading up to Vajradhatu Seminary (at which point this narrative began) and beyond. I also began teaching Buddhadharma in the context of Shambhala meditation centers and other Buddhist institutions relatively quickly. This Buddhist journey has definitely not been without its own frustrations. My own Buddhist community is relatively apolitical and deliberately ignores gender issues, even though women do quite well up to the point of a glass ceiling that is relatively high. I also faced the dilemma of needing to stay in Eau Claire, where there is no Buddhist community, so that I could have an academic position that would allow me to write about Buddhism and gender and about Buddhist-Christian dialogue. But I did gain a national community of dharma friends to complement my national and international community of academic friends.

As for Buddhist patriarchy, I always knew that if I became a Buddhist, I would end up doing a feminist critique of Buddhism. I guess I just decided that it was better to roll up my sleeves and work through the issues of patriarchy and religion one more time in another context than to turn my back on something that was so compelling and so comforting. I have never regretted that choice. In fact, I doubt I could have survived all the difficulties I have faced, had it not been for meditation and the dharma.

2. Autobiographical Roots of Dialogue

ROSEMARY RADFORD RUETHER

OPENNESS TO INTERRELIGIOUS dialogue has particular biographical roots for each person. For both Rita and me, very different family patterns disposed each of us to be open to dialogue and to come to repudiate a Christian exclusivism that assumed that there is only one true religion and that all other religions are inferior or even false. My own family, the Radfords on my father's side and the Ords on my mother's side, were religiously plural and had an international and inter-cultural perspective that disposed me to be open to such experiences of other religions.

Both the Ords and the Radfords were very conscious of having old established American roots, going back before the Revolutionary War. They had a tradition of government service. My great-grandfathers, Edward Otho Cresap Ord and William Radford, were respectively a general and an admiral in the Civil War. Admiral Radford built a house in Washington, D.C., after the Civil War that still stands. His younger daughter, Sophie Radford, made her debut in Washington society in 1873 and married Vladimir Alexandrovitch D'Meissner, a diplomat of French and Russian ancestry in the service of the Czar. They lived in several parts of Europe during their marriage, including St. Petersburg.

My great aunt wrote novels based on Russian folk tales, as well as the biography of her father, an Admiral (*Old Naval Days*, 1920). When her husband and then her son died she wrote a book about her spiritualist experiences titled *There Are No Dead* (1912). I remember her as an elegant old woman in her nineties living in Washington, D.C., who encouraged my sisters and me to learn French. We continue to be in touch with our French cousins, descendants of the French side of the D'Meissner family. Another cousin, Horace Torbert, son of the Admiral's oldest daughter, was a career diplomat, serving posts in cities such as Budapest.

The Ords had a history of military service, with education at West Point. They also went early to California (E.O.C. Ord surveyed Los

Angeles in 1848), and held military and business posts in Mexico. My mother was born in Mexico in 1895 and grew up bilingual in Spanish and English. As a young women my mother lived for some years in Europe where her brother was serving in government posts. When she married my father, a civil engineer, they lived for a year in Turkey. Then, after the Second World War, we lived in Athens, Greece (1947-9), where my father was in charge of reconstructing the railroads, and clearing the Corinth Canal, destroyed in 1945 by the departing Nazis. I went to a French school in Athens while my sisters were educated in Switzerland and France.

My mother's family were Roman Catholics, of English and Austrian roots. My mother cultivated an intellectual Catholic tradition of philosophical spirituality, reading classics such as the writings of Meister Eckhart. She had a quiet disregard for bigoted or "vulgar" forms of Catholicism. I remember her and my older sister laughing when I told them that the nun who was principal of my Catholic high school in Washington was shocked when she discovered that, at the age of fourteen, I was sketching nude men and women in a life-drawing class. At that time I was committed to becoming a fine artist. How else can one learn to draw the body except through life drawing? By implication, such narrow-mindedness on the part of the nun was to be ignored as unsophisticated. My mother's style of culture gave me permission from childhood to think for myself and to feel guilt-free toward religious authorities, priests or nuns, who taught ideas that didn't make sense to me.

My father's family were Episcopalians of old English stock. They carried their religion lightly, more as a class identity than a religious commitment. The story was told of my great grandfather who, with his family, were then members of the oldest Episcopal Church in Georgetown, St. John's. One Sunday, when the rector denounced dancing into the sabbath (Sunday), the Admiral took it as a personal criticism of a party at his house where his daughters had danced past midnight the night before. Gathering his family around him, he marched out of the church and joined Trinity Episcopal Church in Georgetown. This is the church my father attended when I was a child, on the occasions when he went to church, usually Christmas and Easter. My mother let me go to church with him sometimes, a marked departure from the attitude of Catholics in the 1940s who were expected to shun Protestant churches.

My mother's Catholicism was much more serious. We went to mass every Sunday and on holy days of obligation. She prayed regularly, and

in her older age was a daily communicant. She went to lectures by inter-
nationally recognized theologians. While bigoted religiosity could be
bypassed, religion was not a trivial affair. It pointed to deep and profound
matters about ultimate meaning, the deepest level of human soul development. But one had to find one's own way into these depths; they could
not be imposed from outside by rote observances. This was her unspoken
message to me, taught more by example than by words.

My favorite uncle, David Sandow, was from a New York Jewish family. Uncle David, himself childless, was our surrogate father and mentor
in the arts and music in our family. My father was absent through much
of my childhood, being away during World War II, and then in Athens
(before we joined him there) where he died in 1949. Uncle David aspired
to be an opera singer and had a fine tenor voice. He also was a good artist
and painted in the style of the old Dutch masters, Rembrandt and Frans
Hals. Lacking the courage to pursue these loves as careers, he spent his
life as an architect and pursued art and music as leisure cultures, impart-
ing them particularly to us, his nieces. By the age of ten I knew Western
art history well, from many trips through the National Gallery and
perusal of the arts books at my uncle's home.

Uncle David did not go to synagogue, as far as I know. His Judaism
was more of a nostalgia for an old European culture. Rembrandt's etch-
ings of Bible stories based on the old Jewish quarter of Amsterdam were
particular favorites. My mother once told me that he considered becoming a Catholic, attending Fulton Sheen's classes at Catholic University,
but decided against it. Her sad tone of voice when she told me this suggested that she regretted that he had not taken this step. I remember feeling spontaneously proud of him that he had resisted the "temptation" to
leave his own tradition. I was then about fifteen years old. Looking back
on it, I find it interesting that I parted with my mother's assumptions at
this point. It did not occur to me to believe that he ought to become a
Catholic or a Christian in order to be "saved."

My particular family background gave me some perspectives on class
and gender which may seem odd to some Americans, although they seem
natural to me. These perspectives might be labeled, "the fragility of class"
and the "illusion of masculine superiority." My family had some of the
characteristics of what might be called American aristocracy in their
proud memories of ancestors. But this sense of "class" was not associated
with wealth. The main reason for this was that my male ancestors made
their mark mainly in military and government service in which capacity

they either disdained or failed to accumulate inheritable wealth. In this they perhaps belonged to an old fashioned and more innocent concept of service to one's country.

Illustrative of my family's tendency to fail to accumulate wealth is a story about my great-grandfather, General Edward Otho Cresap Ord (always called E.O.C.), who did the survey of Los Angeles in 1848 when it was a sleepy Mexican town. When asked if he wanted to be paid in a tract of land in what would have become prime L.A. real estate, he turned it down, asserting that the area "would never amount to anything, because it had no water." He received payment in cash instead.

This failure to use their opportunities for inheritable wealth was coupled with the early death of men, women, and children. My family history is a story of children dying in infancy or in their teen years. General E.O.C. Ord had thirteen children, seven of whom died in infancy or childhood and another three in their twenties. My father had two sisters who grew up and three siblings, a boy and two girls who died in infancy. His mother died shortly after the last birth. More frequently, along with the death of children, the father and husband died while the remaining children were young, leaving the wife to cope. When my great-grandfather Admiral Radford died in 1890 he not only left his own wife a widow, but a widowed daughter with four young children, another widowed daughter (Sophie D'Meissner) just returned from Russian where her husband and son had died, and a widower son with three children. For a time this whole extended family made do by living together in Washington.

My grandmother Ord returned from Mexico to California about 1905 as her husband was dying, with five young children to raise alone. My mother, in turn, came back from Greece in 1948, where my father had died, to raise three children in Washington. My father's sister, a social worker, moved in with us to help out. While not deeply impoverished by these deaths, these widowed women were considerably reduced in circumstances. My mother made do by going back to work as a secretary and an accountant, reusing the skills she had learned as a young woman to make a living. She sent me to college on a part of her widow's pension. I supplemented that by my scholarship and work as a waitress.

Thus I grew up with a sense that great family stories do not correlate with high economic means. Economic status is fragile, particularly on the female side. Losing one's husband means precipitous downward mobility, and women must be ready to pick up the pieces with their own income producing skills. But this experience also gave me a strong sense that it is women who pick up the pieces and carry on. Three widows made a home for their widower brother and six children in the 1890s. A spinster sister with my widowed mother created a home for us in 1948. In California I experienced a network of my mother's female friends from her early years in San Diego, mostly widows, who bonded together in mutual support.

These older women were creative, highly literate, and socially engaged. My mother's best friend, Helen Marston Beardsley, was a founder of the Women's International League for Peace and Freedom. When I was a teenager she was heavily involved in working with the Farm Workers and the War Resisters. Her claim to fame was that she had been included in Nixon's Enemy's List, when this list revealed after his death. It was she who took me to my first civil rights and anti-war marches. Thus my mother's female friends were also important role models for independent, cultured, and socially engaged women. They shaped my own political radicalization in the 1950s to early 1960s.

Coupled with this sense of strong, cultured, socially engaged women was a sense of the fragility of men and of male power. We grew up with the swords and medals of our male ancestors on the wall, but the reality was that they were absent, dead or away at war. Or those who remained home were mostly "failures," men who were supposed to have succeeded to the military prowess of their ancestors, but who could not do so, and lived in the shadow of strong mothers, sisters, and wives. This gave me a sense that male power was three-fourths bluff, a façade of great strength, but with a fragile interior. It was women who actually sustained everyday life.

I think these experiences made it easy for me to discard male for female God-language. My intuitive sense from my late teens was that there was no powerful, white, male King in the sky. The real divinity that sustains the world is female and looks more like a collective of older women friends. This community of women who sustain the everyday world is my model for my idea of God as the divine sustaining matrix of creation, or what I call Holy Wisdom.

In 1952 my mother, my older sister, and I moved to La Jolla, California, returning to the area where my mother had spent her teenage and young adult years, leaving behind the Radford house in Georgetown, emptied of my father's presence by his death. In South California I became aware of my mother's own world, her fluency in Spanish, her ties to Mexico, as well as her network of friends. There I attended public rather than Catholic schools and then went to Scripps College in Claremont, California. My intention was to pursue the fine arts as my major, but instead I became fascinated by the ancient Near Eastern and Greco-Roman worlds through the Humanities program of the college. I turned from fine arts to the study of religion, philosophy, and history, with a focus on Greek and Roman classics.

My mentor in this program was Robert Palmer, a specialist in Latin classics. Palmer was the translator of Walter Otto's work on Dionysus, and he taught us to take the Greek gods seriously as expressions of religious experience. I remember him expounding the Greek experience of the divine by saying: "First there is the god, then the dance, and then the story." I quickly came to take for granted the History of Religions approach to the religions of the ancient Mediterranean world, the religions of the Greeks and Romans, the Egyptians and Mesopotamians, and also Judaism and Christianity.

Palmer himself was not fond of Christianity and saw the turn of the ancient world to Christianity in the fourth century as a distinct "downer." When speaking of the pagan rhetor, Libanius, who sought to expound a platonic understanding of the ancient gods, I remember him saying with genuine sadness, "It had everything. Why did it lose?" This became a guiding question for my graduate studies, through which I would earn Ph.D. in Classics and Patristics in 1965. How did Christianity, an unlikely Palestinian Jewish apocalyptic movement, manage, between the first and fourth centuries, to gather up all the highly diverse religious and philosophical trends of late antiquity and synthesize them into a winning formula, presenting itself both as the true faith against falsehood and as the culmination of two thousand years of the quests for wisdom in Mediterranean culture? This was and remains a fascinating problem to me.

That I turned into a Christian theologian out of this study, rather than a classicist like Palmer, owes much to other experiences I developed through my studies. Our humanities program included the history of the Jews and Christians, Hebrew scripture, rabbinic writings, the New Testament, and the Church fathers, not as "truth" against pagan falsehood, but simply as one of the expressions of antique culture. This meant that I read Hebrew Scripture and the New Testament with fresh eyes, independent of Christian exclusivist assumptions.

As I read the Jewish and Christian writings, I became fascinated with the Jewish vision of justice enunciated by the Hebrew prophets and Jesus. Here was a religiosity that stood in ethical tension with the social world of its day and against its political and religious authorities, denouncing them for their injustice to the poor while envisioning a new world of justice to come. This was a spirituality and ethic that seemed to be lacking in the mythologies about the Mesopotamian and Greek gods.

This did not mean that they were false and the Biblical world had the "true" understanding of God. Rather it meant that they had different ideas of divinity. The Mesopotamian and Greek gods were cosmological, pointing to a spirituality that sustained and sanctified the natural world as it is. The Hebrew spirituality operated in a different dimension, one of ethical tension with the human social systems and of hope for a transforming alternative. Both these spiritualities are true and important, but the second became increasingly attractive and empowering to me. As I turn to ecological questions today, I again ask how these two spiritualities need to be harmonized.

In 1964, as I was completing my doctoral degree, I became increasingly aware of the struggle for racial justice sweeping the nation. I became involved in the civil rights and peace movements under the leadership of the campus college chaplains. In the summer of 1965 I traveled from Claremont, California to Beulah, Mississippi, with other students and chaplains from the colleges, to be volunteers for the Delta Ministry. Then for the first time I experienced what it was like to be on the Black side of the American racial divide. We imbibed the history of Jim Crow and lynching from its victims and identified with it.

Each night we prepared ourselves to watch for white nightriders that might sweep through the former college campus where the Delta Ministry was housed and shoot at our windows. We blacked out the side windows of our van so that white police would not see that we had whites and blacks riding together and pull us over. One Sunday we tried to go to a white church with a "mixed group" and were barred at the door by the church officers who handed us a flyer proclaiming that racial segregation was God's intention for the races. We were welcomed at the Black Baptist church, but were quietly told that they expected us to dress in Sunday best and not in jeans. We came to assume that we were safe in the Black world, but that the white world was dangerous to us as civil rights workers.

After my summer in Mississippi and my graduation with a doctoral degree, my family (by then I was married and had three children) and I moved to Washington, D.C., where I took up a teaching position at the School of Religion of Howard University, a historically Black University. I would teach at Howard for the next ten years during a particularly volatile time in American society. During my years at Howard I was actively involved in the Civil Rights and Peace Movements and was arrested more than once in protests at the White House or the Pentagon. I would also become aware of the Latin American world and the beginnings of Latin American liberation theology. The feminist movement would arise in the late 1960s, empowered by the Civil Rights and peace movements, but repelled by the sexist chauvinism of our male colleagues.

My involvement in these movements was deepened by the theological reflection that was springing from them. I became interested in Black and Latin American liberation theologies. Then I realized that there needed to be theological work on gender, as well as race and class relations. My first talk on feminist theology (1968) was somewhat modeled after the Black power style of the time: "Male Chauvinist Theology and the Anger of Women." I still remember being fascinated by the fright on the faces of white male churchmen in the audience as a woman dared to voice the topic of women's anger! One of my first books that brought these various essays in Black, liberationist, and feminist theologies together was *Liberation Theology: Human Hope Confronts Christian History and American Power* (1972).

My theological thought at that time was deeply shaped by the prophetic mode of spirituality. My colleagues in these movements and I felt empowered by a religious vision that allowed us to denounce the structures of violence and injustice as contrary to God's will, and to envision a transformed world of justice and peace. Knowing that no system of injustice, including injustice to women, was of God, one felt no need to submit to those religious or political authorities that sought to justify such structures of unjust power by assuming that indeed God had created such systems. Two theologies, a liberation theology and a theology of the patriarchal, racist, classist status quo were in conflict, and continue to be in conflict in the churches today, although the voice of the first has been muted while the voice of the second has regained power.

In the late sixties I also became concerned with two other areas of deep contradiction in Western religious and social culture. One of these was anti-semitism. My relationship with my uncle had long disposed me to be open to the Jewish tradition as an autonomous path of spiritual life. I also remember vividly the newsreels of 1945 that displayed the terrible images of corpses and living skeletons from the Nazi death camps, opened up by the victorious Allied armies. These experiences impelled me to research the history of Christian anti-Judaism that lay behind the vicious anti-semitism of the Nazi ideology. The result of this work was my 1974 volume *Faith and Fratricide: The Theological Roots of Anti-Semitism.*

Awareness of the ecological crisis was also dawning. I remember reading of the Club of Rome report in the Washington Post in 1966 and incorporating the question of ecology into my theological lectures. How has the religious concept of "pollution" actually contributed to creating "pollution," rather than alleviating it by recycling our wastes, I asked? I began to wonder how the subjugation of women and the subjugation of nature had been symbolically and socially interconnected in Western religion and culture. This question would later be called "eco-feminism," although the term did not exist at the time. My beginning thoughts on this were published in my 1975 volume, *New Woman, New Earth: Sexist Ideologies and Human Liberation.*

My background in ancient near Eastern and Greco-Roman religious histories was invaluable to these explorations. In effect, each social crisis was recognized as having ancient roots, roots that went back through Christian history, into deep beginnings in the ancient Mediterranean worlds that had shaped the rise of Christianity. My methodology of dialogue between contemporary crisis and ancient roots in my various writings was to try to plumb these historical roots and how they developed. I was still asking, "How did it happen this way?"

Some may be surprised that in the midst of this journey into liberation and feminist theologies, which involved increasingly deep criticism of Catholic Christian history as a path of many injustices, I remained a Roman Catholic. Why didn't I leave it for some other form of Christianity or perhaps some other religion? I am often asked at lectures, "Why don't you leave the Catholic Church?" as though such a trajectory of criticism would naturally lead to such a conclusion. The questioners often seem to assume that I am somehow too timid to come to this conclusion or it has simply not occurred to me to realize the incompatibility of my theological stance and Roman Catholic Christianity.

A better answer lies in my religious roots and journey, as I have tried to summarize it here. From childhood I had been allowed to assume that Christianity has both superficial and deeper levels of meaning. One was called to seek the deeper meaning. This meant the superficial and even falsifying levels could, indeed should, be disregarded as not the "true" meaning. Secondly, I have become empowered in this critical and transformative vision, not through the other religions I explored, although I also saw them as having truths, but primarily through the Biblical prophetic tradition of Jesus and the Prophets. Moreover, the religious leaders that spoke more powerfully and engaged most deeply in this struggle for justice were, for the most part, Christians, many of them Catholics. These Christians themselves had discovered and were transformed by the prophetic liberationist vision.

The sources of my theology and spirituality were unquestionably Christian, not against other faiths, but out of the distinctive movements of human religious inspiration that were rising with new voice in the 1960s in Black, liberation, and feminist theologies. Early on I realized that I was not much interested in a "sideways" move within Christianity. My own roots and development disposed me to an ecumenical understanding of being a "catholic" Christian. I didn't need to join the Episcopal Church to worship there when I was eight years old. Nor to join the Quakers or Methodists in order to enter into their worship at later stages of my life. In effect, these diverse traditions of Christianity are already mine. Roman Catholicism is, for me, one segment of a diverse and quarreling history of Christians. I don't think that any one of them is significantly "better" than another, at least not enough to justify leaving one to join another.

But also the Catholic community remains "mine" in a special way. My experiences of it have generally been good and not oppressive. My mother had helped to see to that. I had been nurtured in a more mature spirituality by the Benedictine monks of St. Andrew's Priory in Valyermo, California, in the early sixties. The inner circle of my colleagues in liberation and feminist theologies were Catholics. My relation to this community put me in a special relation to Catholic feminists in Europe, in Latin America, in Asia, and Africa. These women looked to me for courage to voice the criticisms that I seemed to be able to say so easily, with so little burden of fear from oppressive authorities.

The fact that my own trajectory of development coincided with the opening up of Catholicism in the Second Vatican Council (1962–65) and the development of liberation theologies and the birth of feminism in Catholic circles, was an important factor in this. Had I been trying to pursue this path of critique ten years earlier there might have been a different outcome. I am the product of a particular moment in both the American and the Catholic histories of those who came of age in the 1960s.

While I have long since outgrown the idea, if I ever really believed it, that Catholicism was the best faith, within which I must remain confined and dependent, what replaced this idea is a recognition that I have a special responsibility to this community. Alongside many sisters and brothers, I have a special responsibility to help, to keep a deeper vision alive, to empower the struggle against the forces that ever try to reinstate oppressive narrowness. The frightening efforts of the present papacy to re-impose a monolithic patriarchal church does not impel me to depart, but rather to redouble my commitment to this struggle.

I don't expect to "win" this struggle, in the sense of making a liberationist, feminist view the sole expression of Catholic Christianity. A two thousand year shaping by patriarchy precludes this possibility. Moreover, I value the diversity in Christianity, if this is understood as many facets of a larger truth that none of us possesses wholly. Rather what is vital both for Catholics and other Christians, and indeed people of many faiths, is to keep the patriarchs from winning. Our modest hope is simply to maintain pluralism in Catholicism and in Christianity generally; to keep the feminist, liberation vision as a vital option, and prevent it from being illegitimated and drowned out by the patriarchs.

One might say that my religious journey, like Rita's, involved a conversion to "another religion," although unlike her I was never expelled, but rather embraced anew by some of those in the institution in which I grew up. My conversion to another religion took the form of a discovery of another option (or options) within Christianity, options that are more authentic and life-giving. My career as a feminist liberation theologian has developed out of joining these other options in Christianity, and exploring them as a base of struggle against the oppressive patterns in Christianity.

In the process of my studies and social engagements I have become involved in several kinds of interreligious dialogue. My 1972 book, *Faith and Fratricide*, brought quick endorsement from the Jewish community that saw it as a break-through in Christian critical self-consciousness. It was officially promoted by B'nai Brith, and I received many invitations to speak at synagogues or in Jewish-Christian dialogues. The Christians involved in the dialogue were less enthusiastic about the book, seeing it as too critical of the New Testament. They preferred to see anti-Judaism as a later corruption, not something deeply rooted in Christian origins.

I learned a much greater appreciation of the Jewish tradition from these discussions. But I also came to the painful realization that I was being politically manipulated in them. I remember one woman in a synagogue where I was speaking coming up to me and whispering, "you are being used." My book focused on the Christian tradition and its development particularly in the West. It made proposals for deep rethinking of Christology to free it of its exclusivist and supercessionist relation to Judaism. I still fully endorse the ideas of this book. But the book was not about the politics of the Middle East, Israel, and the Palestinians, a topic about which I then knew little.

However I began to realize that the Jewish-Christian dialogues had a hidden agenda. Once Christians were fully convicted of their guilt for anti-semitism, they were to become uncritical cheerleaders for the policies of the state of Israel. Above all, they were not to ask about justice to the Palestinians. Indeed they should not mention the Palestinians at all. As I sensed this agenda, I began to read about the history of Zionism, the state of Israel, and the Palestinians. In 1980 I accepted an invitation to go on a trip to Israel organized by some Jewish women from Montreal, who billed the excursion as an opportunity for dialogue between Jewish, Christian, and Muslim women.

The trip proved to be carefully constructed to give us only the Israeli point of view. The one Muslim woman in the group, a Canadian from Egypt, became so upset that she left the group. With several other members of the group, I quietly slipped away on our one free day to cross over to East Jerusalem. There we met with Raymonda Tawil, a Palestinian woman journalist, who set up a quick tour of the Palestinian side of things: a refugee camp, Palestinian women's organizations, and a talk with the mayor of Ramallah, whose legs had been blown off by Israeli terrorists. The world that our organizers did not want us to see became painfully clear.

After that experience I began to attend meetings of the Palestinian Human Rights Campaign, where I met Jews, Christians and Muslims involved in a very different and much more authentic dialogue—or rather solidarity—around a common agenda of creating more just relations for Israeli Jews, and for Christian and Muslim Palestinians in Israel-Palestine. In 1985 I spent a Sabbatical with my husband, Herman Ruether, an expert on Islam, at Tantur, a Christian study center which stands at the half-way point between Jerusalem and Bethlehem. The results of our work during that period was the book, *The Wrath of Jonah: The Crisis of Religious Nationalism in the Israel-Palestinian Conflict* (1989).

I was now a pariah in the official Jewish-Christian dialogues. Speaking invitations for Jewish-Christian dialogues were cancelled. Some reviewers tried to suggest that I had either changed my mind about my first book criticizing anti-semitism or else I had never been sincere in this criticism. The assumption was that any critique of the mistreatment of the Palestinians was anti-semitism. I also became aware of a whole campaign of intimidation that had gone on for years, attacking those who were critical of Israel's treatment of Palestinians. Many Christian leaders have told me privately that they do not dare to speak out on this subject for fear of being vilified. Jewish critics often suffered the most. Marc Ellis, a Jewish liberation theologian, with whom I have worked closely in recent years, was blocked from academic appointments for several years, and almost despaired of finding a job.

My involvement, together with Herman Ruether, in Middle East issues, has also led us into Christian-Muslim dialogues. Some of the most interesting and rewarding of these dialogues have been shaped around the issue of women in both Christianity and Islam. I find these dialogues worthwhile because they involve self-critique on the part of both Muslims and Christians in regard to the patriarchal shaping of the two religions. Other Christian-Muslim dialogues carried out mostly between men have seemed more manipulative to me. Christians are asked to repudiate the remnants of Christendom in the United States and to work for non-discrimination against Muslims in American society, a goal I fully endorse. But Muslims are not willing make a parallel critique of the idea of an Islamic state. For them, the idea of an Islamic state is their tradition and it is not to be questioned.

From this background I was invited to become a part of the International Buddhist-Christian Theological Encounter by my teacher from Claremont days, John Cobb. I first refused this invitation, explaining that I was not an expert on Buddhism, and, besides, I was already spread too thin between my involvements in feminism, Latin America, and the Middle East. But Cobb returned a couple of years later with an insistent renewal of the invitation. I realized that part of the urgency lay in the need for women in the dialogue. The organizers had been severely criticized at the first meeting for having no women.

I reluctantly accepted, but on the condition that Herman Ruether also attend, since he is a political scientist and cultural historian who is a student of Buddhism and other Asian religions in our family. Thus my entrance into Buddhist-Christian dialogue did not start too auspiciously. It was hedged about with several bad experiences of how dialogue can be manipulative and bear hidden agendas. Given the bad histories between the religions one should not expect otherwise. But the real question is whether members of both sides of the dialogue can really speak truthfully, or whether one side, today usually the Christians, are asked to repent of their sins, while the other side admits nothing.

I have been happy that Buddhist-Christian dialogue, as I have experienced it, has been much more honest. Although Buddhists certainly have bad historical experiences of Western Christian imperialism and missionizing, nevertheless Christians and Buddhists seem to meet more as equals. We are able to compare and contrast similarities and differences between these two major world cultures and faiths on a more even playing field. The fact that our dialogue includes both Western and Asian Buddhists, as well as Asian (not enough of them) and Western Christians, also helps. The questions of culture and religion can be somewhat differentiated.

The meetings of the International Buddhist-Christian Theological Encounter have become an important learning experience for me. It has become a model of what a more authentic dialogue should be. Members of the dialogue have learned from each other and enriched their understanding of their own traditions. We have become good friends. In December of 1999, five members of the dialogue took their experience to the meeting of the Parliament of the World's Religions in Cape Town, South Africa. We each presented our experience of the dialogue and what it had meant to each of us. We were gratified by a large, attentive audience, many of whom told us that this was the kind of experience of dialogue that they had been looking for when they came to the Parliament.

The second meeting of the World Parliament in Chicago in 1994 produced a global ethic in which representatives of all the major world religions agreed on basic principles concerning what makes for a just and good society. The third meeting of the Parliament in Cape Town sought to develop the Global Ethic and apply it to concrete projects. To me this is the best fruit of authentic interreligious dialogue. It is crucial that the world's faiths and historical cultures not only end their wars against each other, but enter into the kind of deep mutual understanding that can lead to solidarity in creating a just, peaceful, and sustainable world. Buddhist-Christian dialogue is a crucial part of that process, particularly when it roots itself in joint work on issues such as gender relations, ecology, war and peace, and economic justice.

As I will explain in a later essay, this kind of solidarity in social concerns is the focus of our current work in the International Buddhist-

Christian Theological Encounter. In the years of the encounter Rita and I have particularly been the spokespersons for the issues of women in the two faiths. Our collaboration in a dialogue at the Grail in Loveland, Ohio, in the fall of 1999, the basis of this book, is the fruit of those years of collaboration together in Buddhist-Christian feminist dialogue.

PART II

What Is Most Problematic about My Tradition?

3. Where Are the Women in the Refuge Tree? Teacher, Student, and Gender in Buddhism

Rita M. Gross

WHEN I DID the practice of a hundred thousand prostrations, which involves going from a standing position to being flat out, arms and legs completely extended horizontally for each prostration, the visualization accompanying the practice was of a large tree just beyond a pleasant lake in a grassy meadow. It is called a "refuge tree" because all the Buddhist "objects of refuge,"[1] including all the gurus of the lineage, sit in the spreading branches of the tree. The sense is that one is prostrating to all these figures, surrendering self-cherishing and expressing one's commitment to do whatever it takes "to attain enlightenment for the benefit of all sentient beings." Though this practice is demanding and difficult, both physically and psychologically, it is important to understand that in Buddhism the practice of prostrations is not about self-abnegation and expressing feelings of worthlessness or inferiority. Prostration practice is about reverence for the teachers, gratitude for the teachings, and longing to actualize one's own inherent Buddha-potential, as the gurus sitting in the branches of the refuge tree have already done. While I was more than willing to prostrate and to express these feelings, one aspect of the practice always bothered me and still bothers me. Though there are females

---

1. In all forms of Buddhism, there are three "objects of refuge": the Buddha as example, the dharma as teachings or path, and the sangha as community of fellow travelers. Though Buddhism is non-theistic, it does afford these refuges. They are so central to Buddhism that the ceremony for formally becoming a Buddhist is to "take refuge in the Three Jewels." In Vajrayana Buddhism, the objects of refuge are extended to include the gurus of the lineage, the meditation deities, and the dharma protectors.

among the trans-human, more "mythological" figures inhabiting the refuge tree, there are no women among the human gurus who are the main focus of this visualization. This is not the case for all the various refuge tree visualizations in the various teaching lineages of Vajrayana Buddhism, but it was the case for my specific practice.

In my discussion of what is most problematic for women about traditional Buddhism, I will focus on one issue—the relative lack of women gurus, lineage holders, or primary teachers—because I would argue that all other problems women may encounter in their practice of Buddhism derive from this one major deficiency. I will also focus on this issue because nothing is more central to Buddhism than the teacher-student relationship. Finally, I will focus on this issue because the practice of favoring men over women as teachers so fundamentally contradicts the Buddhist view that all beings contain the spark of indwelling Buddhahood.

I have lived for years with the riddle, "If all sentient beings are characterized by inherent, indwelling Buddhahood, why are there so few women teachers?" as my personal koan.[2] To realize why this question provokes such puzzlement, one must understand the Buddhist point of view about our basic being or our basic nature, though those terms are somewhat inadequate to explain what "Buddha-nature" is. Over the years, I have come to experience that one of the most profound points of divergence between Christianity and Buddhism concerns Christian teachings of original sin versus Buddhist teachings about the inherently enlightened quality of all things, which is sometimes called "basic goodness." According to Buddhism, confusion rather than evil is the basic problem that needs to be solved, and that confusion is not original or inherent. It is an acquired deficiency that never destroys or diminishes inherent enlightenment or Buddha nature. The traditional analogy is that of the sun of Buddha-nature obscured by clouds. The sun is shining; it's just that we can't see it. Furthermore, Buddhism unequivocally teachers that all beings, not merely all human beings are inherently enlightened. Those who teach the dharma need to have uncovered their Buddha-nature to

---

2. Koans are well-known in Zen Buddhism. They are puzzles or riddles that cannot be solved rationally or discursively upon which a student meditates to seek awakening. One koan which many people have heard is, "What is the sound of one hand clapping?"

some extent; teachers cannot be appointed to fulfill quotas. Being a teacher in Buddhism, like liberating oneself from suffering and samsara is not a matter of intellectual knowledge, helpful as that is on the path, but of personal experience.

But if all beings are characterized by Buddha-nature, why is it that so many more men than women have uncovered their Buddha-nature sufficiently to be recognized as teachers? Over the years I have asked various teachers that question and received various answers, none of which has fully satisfied me. The traditional answers tend to invoke the karma of beings reborn as women, whereas I tend to answer the question by pointing to social, cultural, and religious situations of male dominance. My interpretation of this puzzle is backed up by the fact that nothing equivalent to the Christian sacrament of priestly ordination, with its metaphysical need for maleness, has ever been part of Buddhism. The term *ordination* in a Buddhist context means taking on the vows of a monk or a nun, and there is no correlation between being a monk or a nun and being a teacher. And there have been women who were recognized as teachers and lineage holders throughout Buddhist history, especially in Vajrayana Buddhism. It's just they have been a very small minority.

Some contemporary teachers have translated "Buddha-nature" as one's "enlightened gene," a translation I find accurate. But the Buddhist teachings have never said that the enlightened gene is dominant in men and recessive in women. The Buddhist tradition itself has admitted that women face more obstacles than men but it has been very reluctant to investigate the origin of these obstacles faced by women. The only answer consistent with basic Buddhist teachings is that the enlightened gene has been nurtured more carefully in men than in women and so more men have become teachers and gurus. Or, more likely, men have probably been more prone to notice that certain men have ripened their enlightened gene than that women have ripened theirs.

Faced with persistent questions about the role of women in Buddhism from Western students, male teachers have also begun to give more feminist answers to my koan. Many of them encourage students to differentiate between the dharma, the timelessly applicable teachings of Buddhism, and relative cultural situations. Of Buddhist male dominance, they often say, "Oh, that's just culture; that's not the dharma." The Dalai Lama has responded with the slogan "That's history! Now it's up to you." One of my own teachers replied to me "It's because you haven't become a teacher yet!" But those answers are double-edged in a context in which, even among Western Buddhists, men are more likely than women to be promoted as major teachers in many cases. If and when we women do uncover Buddha-nature, will we be recognized so that history could change?

This issue is so crucial for Buddhist women because of the centrality of the teacher-student relationship in Buddhism. As a non-theistic religion, Buddhism teaches that there is no external savior or vicarious atonement. People are not originally damned, needing external intervention to rectify their spiritual status nor can anyone perform the brain transplant that would be required to clear away the confusion that keeps people bound to their human-caused suffering. Each being must perform the spiritual disciplines of morality, meditation, and the pursuit of wisdom required for making the transition from confusion to enlightenment. Nevertheless, fortunately for most of us, we do not have to reduplicate the Buddha's journey of self-discovery completely unaided. Teachers, traditionally known by several titles, including "guru" and "roshi," are considered to be, if not necessary, at least extremely helpful in finding one's way through the vast collection of dharma texts and practices that have come into existence during Buddhism's twenty-five-hundred-year history. This way of understanding what the spiritual quest involves helps explain why a teacher must have some realization herself; if she did not, she could easily misguide students through that welter of texts and practices, thereby possibly delaying the student's realization.

My own personal experience with Buddhist teachers has borne out this Buddhist understanding of the teacher-student relationship and has been quite different from my experience with academic teachers. Initially, I sensed that my Buddhist teachers were the only teachers I had ever met who were aware of something that I had been trying to discover all my life but that I was unlikely to discover on my own. After more than twenty years of practicing Buddhist spiritual disciplines, I still feel that way. That is why I was willing to do a hundred thousand prostrations and why I was willing to become involved in Buddhism at all, despite its patriarchy.

To make the situation more intense for me personally, my karmic "fit" among the various forms of Buddhism is with the one that most stresses the teacher-student relationship, Vajrayana Buddhism. The word *devotion* is part of the vocabulary of this form of Buddhism, despite its traditional emphasis on non-theism. This term, used to describe the student's relationship with the teacher, is troubling to many outsiders to Vajrayana Buddhism, especially feminists, as is the whole notion of hierarchy in the teacher-student relationship. Yet devotion and the experience that goes with it have never bothered me, nor has the natural hierarchy of the teacher-student relationship. After having checked out a teacher and what becoming a student of that teacher would involve, a student who wishes to learn very difficult esoteric material has little choice but to agree to follow the instructions of the teacher. To say, "I'm interested in receiving the highest Vajrayana teachings, but I don't want to do a hundred thousand prostrations" would be the equivalent of saying "I want to receive a Ph.D., but I don't want to write a doctoral dissertation." Such a person would simply be told to leave graduate training, at least in that field. If one receives good training, loyalty, which may be a more neutral term than devotion, to the teachers who give such teachings is not an unreasonable or far-fetched attitude. In this context, it is not possible to consider these issues at greater length, but I have elsewhere discussed them in some detail.[3]

The problem is not with devotion to one's teachers or with a natural hierarchy between student and teacher but that, depending on the lineage, most or all of the teachers are men. I don't mind prostrating to my teachers, but I do mind prostrating only to male teachers and a lineage tree that does not include female teachers.

Because of the importance of the teacher-student relationship in Buddhism, the male near-monopoly of the teaching role can be compared to the male monopoly of the deity role in traditional monotheism. Buddhism, of course, posits no deity as an external creator or savior; the ultimate is not separate from oneself and Buddhism is thoroughly non-dualistic. Nevertheless, the comparison is apt because the most important reference point in each religion—God for Christianity and other forms of monotheism, the teacher for Buddhists—is most likely to be male, and not female. I would claim that most or all of the negative social and psychological repercussions that stem from a male monopoly on the deity figure are also found in Buddhism: low self-esteem among women, opinions that women are not as capable or as worthy as are men, and the sociological endless loop that the reality of male dominance in the present creates the expectation of further male

---

3. For a fuller discussion of these points, see Rita M. Gross, *Soaring and Settling: Buddhist Perspectives on Contemporary Social and Religious Issues* (New York: Continuum, 1998), pp. 60–74.

dominance. This observation is of critical importance for Buddhism. Buddhists take pride in their non-theism, which is regarded as a courageous and realistic outlook. It would be a shock to many Buddhists to realize that, inadvertently, by cultivating and recognizing only men as teachers, they have let in through the back door some of the negative features associated with theism.

On the other hand, the fact that most gurus have been men represents a sociological problem for Buddhists, but not a metaphysical problem. Few Buddhists react to the possibility of female gurus with the shock and horror that many Christians or Jews experience when it is suggested that one could imagine the deity in female pronouns and analogies. The more typical Buddhist reaction would be to agree with the observation that there haven't been many female gurus in the past, but to go on to state that this historical fact does not stem from a fixed, immutable women's nature or men's nature and that there is no particular reason why there couldn't be more women gurus. (Many groups within Theravada Buddhism would be an exception to this generalization.)

In my previous work on this issue, I have emphasized three reasons why female teachers are central to Buddhism. The first is that, given Buddhist teachings about inherent, indwelling Buddhahood, the presence of female teachers would indicate that Buddhists are taking these teachings seriously, rather than fostering the enlightened gene in men and ignoring it in women. Second, female gurus would be important role models for both women and men. Finally, the experience of women who speak for and on behalf of the tradition is important in the task of articulating the spoken dharma, (basic Buddhist teachings) more fully.

The first argument has already been partially discussed. Buddhist teachings have never posited an essential "female nature" and an essential "male nature." Such assertions would fundamentally contradict teachings about *tathatagarbha*, to which I have already alluded. Given that there is no essential female nature limiting women, the disappointing Buddhist historical record indicates that something else has happened so that there are far fewer women gurus than men. The tradition itself has often suggested that beings reborn as women have inferior karma, which limits how much they can accomplish in their life. However, I believe that these traditional teachings can be rather easily refuted and that the more cogent explanation for women's lack of achievement is found in the *present* male-dominated institutional set-up of the Buddhist world rather than in the past misdeeds of beings presently reborn as women.[4] In part because of the conflict between the view of indwelling Buddhahood that pertains equally to all and the practice of institutions that favor men, I have concluded that the fundamental gender problem in Buddhism is a conflict between view and practice, rather than problems with the view. In traditional Buddhism, view and practice should be in accord with each other, and the practice should be a way to realize the view more fully. Therefore, this contradiction at the heart of Buddhism is quite serious. On the other hand, training, cultivating, and recognizing female gurus would demonstrate that Buddhists are serious about the view of indwelling Buddhahood, of the universally present enlightened gene.

As for the need for role models, feminist pedagogy has thoroughly demonstrated that subtle, unconscious clues communicated by imagery and example are often more powerful than explicit messages. This is also the point at which the problems deriving from the male near-monopoly on teaching roles in Buddhism intersects most closely with the monotheistic practice of imaging deity as male. In both cases, certain public explicit aspects of the tradition state that there is no gender discrimination, that both women and men are endowed with Buddha-nature or are created in the divine image, but the less explicit, often non-verbal and unconscious cues of imagery and example contradict those assertions. How many women can act out the gender-free and gender-neutral implications of the teachings on Buddha-nature when all the examples of realized beings that they see just happen to be male? How many women can act out the doctrine of being created in the divine image when that divine is most often imaged in masculine terms? In Buddhism the issue is even more urgent because of Buddhism's non-theism. Humans cannot look to an extra-human force for liberation; it is up to each human to untangle the knot of suffering and conventional existence with only the teachings and the models of those humans who have done so before. And if most of those models are men, what is the message for women? Thus the presence of female teachers is important for women in providing inspiration that the female human body is up to the task of making significant progress on the path. In a cultural situation in which women and men have both been taught to

---

4. For a fuller discussion of this argument, see Rita M. Gross, *Buddhism after Patriarchy: A Feminist History, Analysis, and Reconstruction of Buddhism* (Albany, NY: State University of New York Press, 1993), pp. 142–46.

believe that women are inferior, only the example provided by women who have achieved the goals of the tradition and have been recognized and honored for their achievements will counter deeply rooted cultural attitudes about gender. General or theoretical claims about the irrelevance of gender in the face of massive evidence to the contrary will not be sufficient.

While it is important to emphasize the importance of such role models for women, it is also important to understand that men, too, need to learn from the example and presence of women teachers. One of the greatest popular misperceptions about gender issues is that these are women's issues; men's reaction to the topic of gender is often something like, "That's not about me. I'm just a normal human being. Gender pertains to someone else." Partially perpetuated by the women's movement itself, with its rhetoric that women are equal to men, this misconception, in my view, bears much of the responsibility for the current unwillingness to further engage the topic of gender and for the reality that materials on gender are read or listened to by women but not by men. But, obviously, men are as fully gendered as are women, and part of their gendered reactions often include being uncomfortable with powerful, highly accomplished women. Therefore, they need very much to relate with and learn from women dharma teachers, precisely because of the aura that surrounds dharma teachers. Because this is a sacred rather than a secular role, powerful women teachers are less easily dismissed and diminished than their secular counterparts, at least by people who take their spiritual practices seriously.

In the Buddhist context, the first two of the Four Noble Truths, the most basic teachings of Buddhism, are often called the truths of samsara (cyclic existence) because they are about suffering and the origin of suffering. The last two truths are often called the truths of nirvana (release) because they are about the possibility of liberation from suffering and the path to such an accomplishment. The traditional gendered division of labor assigned women the teaching task of introducing people to the first two truths, in their role as early care givers who preside over the discovery of frustration and dissatisfaction in young lives. Men then take over at a certain point to teach about the later two truths, about release and the path to liberation. One can make the case that this division of teaching labor accounts for a great deal of the fear and hostility that women often receive in traditional religious contexts.[5] As a way of

---

5. Ibid., pp. 232–40, 252–55.

undoing these negative attitudes toward women that are often pre-rational and rooted in early experiences of frustration and dissatisfaction, nothing would be so powerful as the example of women teaching the truths and the practices that untie this knot of self-perpetuating dissatisfaction, for in the Buddhist context, nothing is more valuable than these teachings. People, both men and women, need the example of women who have untied that knot and can teach others to do the same. Nothing would more powerfully undo their own internalized fear and scorn of women, especially accomplished women. (Of course, it is also important that men do their fair share of the teaching tasks involved in working with very young children.)

Finally, I suggest that women teachers are important because it is unlikely that, in cultures characterized by significant sexual division of labor and strong gender roles and stereotypes, men have said everything that needs to be said about dharma, the basic liberating teachings of Buddhism. Out of their experiences as women living in such circumstances, women teachers are very likely to notice and lift up certain critical dimensions of human existence that men are likely to underemphasize, simply because their experiences are less likely to be steered in those directions. I cite the evidence of Christian feminist theology as indicative that the same process is likely in Buddhism. I will discuss only one example of this process in Buddhism. This example concerns really comprehending the centrality of relationship and community as the Third Refuge, the Refuge of sangha. There undoubtedly are other examples of the difference to the articulated dharma that could be make by women dharma teachers.[6]

It is important to understand two critical qualifications that accompany this claim that women teachers could have something significant to say about dharma that has not already been said. First, it is often said that the dharma is beyond gender, neither male nor female and the same for both women and men. I am often asked what difference it makes whether those teachings are presented by a man or a woman. The dharma as dharma is beyond gender. It is also beyond words, a basic, commonly agreed upon point in dharma discussions. But the dharma that is written and spoken is another matter. As is the case for all religious contexts, language

---

6. For an example of a more technical suggestion relevant to the symbolism of Vajrayana Buddhism, see Gross, *Soaring and Settling*, pp. 211–22.

is always limited and conditioned by its cultural contexts. Second, when I talk about women's experiences as women, I am not talking about some timeless female essence that conditions and predisposes women to think thoughts that men cannot think. I am talking about cultural conditioning that occurs in situations of highly ingrained gender norms. Thus, given that men and women inhabit somewhat different cultures in traditional settings which have strong gender roles and expectations, women working out of their experiences as women are very likely to notice and articulate things that men have not.

But these teachings are not relevant to women alone. I have always defined feminism as "freedom from the prison of gender roles." Paradoxically, in a tradition in which both women and men lead role-bound lives, certain insights may be more readily available to women, or to men, because of their socialization as males or females. But, to transcend the prison of gender roles, both sexes need to incorporate the virtues traditionally deemed primarily the domain of the other sex. Thus, at present, certain insights or virtues may be more readily available to women than to men, but they are relevant to both men and women, to the whole cultural and religious setting. This is perhaps the most important reason why it is so important that women articulate their insights and that they are able to do so in their roles as dharma teachers, not merely as secular commentators. That women take on this role is all the more urgent because the virtues and insights of men's cultures, having been publicly written and spoken about for so long, are readily available, whereas the insights and virtues of women's cultures are far more private and hidden. One can easily see that this is the case by noting that it is far more acceptable today for women to take on aspects of the traditional male role and men's culture than for the reverse to happen. But, if anything, the culture needs the virtues typically associated with women to become much more public and generally practiced. Thus, while it is important for women that women become dharma teachers, it is, if anything, even more important for men and for the whole culture.

Traditionally, the tasks of relationship, of nurturing, and fostering connections between people have been assigned to women. Therefore, they have been considered private virtues, not part of the wider arena of public concern, and have been relatively undervalued. Even in some Buddhist cultures, which posit a very strong ethic of caring in the bodhisattva ideal, in practical, everyday ways, nurturing and caring for relationships are low priorities compared to practicing meditation and studying dharma texts. I have long criticized the North American Buddhist *sanghas* with which I am most familiar for not really taking *sangha* or community, the third of the Three Refuges, very seriously and I discussed what would be involved in taking the Refuge of community more seriously.[7] In particular, I have emphasized that, as everyone in society flocks to take on the traditional masculine role, work and family take up far too great a portion of peoples' time, leaving seriously insufficient time and energy for community and friendship—for sangha and for relationships in a wider, rather than a merely private, context.[8] When I first voiced these concerns, fellow Buddhists suggested that I was undermining basic Buddhist values and that somehow, life wouldn't be tough enough if people actually tried to care for and nurture each other psychologically in the sangha through friendship and community life. Fortunately, in the sangha with which I relate most closely, the lineage holder has also begun to emphasize that sangha is absolutely central to Buddhism and that people need to take that Refuge as seriously as they take the Refuges of Buddha and Dharma.

Nevertheless, there is no question that in North American culture at least, women are the relationship experts, the people to whom caring and nurturing relationships are of critical importance and the people who put the most effort into the task of taking care of relationships. This is a problem, not because relationships and nurturing are unimportant but because they are too central to human well-being to be relegated to the private sphere as the speciality of only half the human population. One could argue that much of the malaise of contemporary North American society has to do with the facts that nurturing is severely undervalued, not important in public policy and public discussions of what directions we need to take as a society, and not rewarded. The solution is not to continue to assign these tasks to women and the private realm alone, but to regard them as central to human competency for both men and women. For this to happen, however, given the traditional gendered division of labor, women, who are more likely initially to notice and emphasize the centrality of nurturing and relationships, need effective public forums from which to teach this message. This would be the case for both secular and religious teaching and policy-making contexts, though my concern is primarily within the context

7. Gross, *Buddhism after Patriarchy*, pp. 259–69.
8. Gross, *Soaring and Settling*, pp. 94–107.

of North American Buddhism. If the message of the centrality of nurturing and relationship for human well-being is taught by dharma teachers with teaching authority, I expect that North American Buddhists would take that message seriously. And, under current conditions, those teachers are more likely to be women than men; additionally, given the traditional gendered division of labor, people may well initially hear that message more clearly if it comes from women dharma teachers.

What of women teachers in the past? On the one hand, the rules of monastic Buddhism have always curbed women's teaching roles and been more conducive to men's practice than to women's practice, though they have never limited women's spiritual achievements. On the other hand, women fare much better in the traditions of non-monastic forest or cave-dwelling yogis. Because this style of practice has been especially important in Tibetan Vajrayana Buddhism, the Buddhist denomination with which I am most familiar actually has some examples of very powerful women teachers.

The rules of monastic Buddhism, from earliest times, preserve the gender hierarchy that was prevalent in ancient India, even though the Buddha did not honor any of the other traditional hierarchies. Indirectly, these rules meant that women never became major teachers, despite the impressive accomplishments of the early Buddhist nuns, because, though they could teach other women, they could not easily teach men. Every nun, no matter how long she had been ordained, was junior to the most recently ordained monk, and nuns could not reprimand monks. Such rules make it difficult for women to function as men's teachers. Nancy Falk has shown how detrimental this inability was for the long term survival of the nuns' order. Lay patrons wanted to donate to the most prestigious monastics, all of whom were men. The women's orders were impoverished as a result and eventually died out in India.[9] Today, the full ordination for nuns (as opposed to the novice ordination) remains only in Chinese, Korean, and some Vietnamese lineages.

In the hazy beginnings of Vajrayana Buddhism, however, women seem to have been important and they have retained some influence throughout the history of Vajrayana Buddhism, which includes very

---

9. Nancy Auer Falk, "The Case of the Vanishing Nuns: The Fruits of Ambivalence in Ancient Indian Buddhism," in *Unspoken Worlds: Women's Religious Lives*, ed. Falk and Gross, 3rd edition (Belmont, CA: Wadsworth, 2001), pp. 155–65.

strong lay and yogic elements, as well as a monastic tradition. One of the earliest recorded circles of Vajrayana practitioners was an eighth century Indian group, including both women and men, led by Princess Lakshminkara. In the following centuries, many such groups developed, and women continued to take leadership roles in them.[10]

When Vajrayana Buddhism entered Tibet in the eighth century, the same pattern continued, at least according to some accounts. Stories of how Buddhism entered Tibet always include narratives about the great Indian yogi, Padmasambhava, who was summoned to tame the local deities when their opposition to the new religion made it impossible to complete the construction of Samye, the first Buddhist monastery in Tibet. Western historical accounts and Tibetan legendary accounts, however, are quite different. Western accounts claim that Padmasambhava had little lasting influence in Tibet, that he stayed only a few years, lost favor at the court and returned to India. Tibetans, however, revere him as Guru Rinpoche (Precious Teacher), a second Buddha, and the founder of the Nyingma order (one of the four main teaching lineages). According to Tibetan accounts, he stayed in Tibet for many years and taught many students. Tibetan accounts also always include stories about Yeshe Tsogyel, his foremost student and consort who became an important teacher in her own right, whereas Western accounts never mention her.[11] To Tibetans, Yeshe Tsogyel is not a minor or an esoteric figure. She is very well-known and Padmasambhava is often portrayed with her. I find this difference fascinating and instructive. Was there a historical women behind the legends of Yeshe Tsogyel? If not, it reveals a keen sense of the need for balance between the masculine and the feminine principles that Tibetans saw fit to create legends about such a women in their narratives about the origins of their religion. It also reveals something about Western perceptions that the legends about Yeshe Tsogyel are not even mentioned in Western histories of Tibetan Buddhism.

---

10. Richard H. Robinson and Willard L. Johnson, *The Buddhist Religion: A Historical Introduction*, fourth edition (Belmont, CA: Wadsworth, 1997), pp. 130–32.

11. For a full account of her life, see Keith Dowman, *Sky Dancer: The Secret Life and Songs of the Lady Yeshe Tsogyel* (London: Routledge and Kegan Paul, 1984). For a feminist commentary, see Rita M. Gross, "Yeshe Tsogyel: Enlightened Consort, Great Teacher, Female Role Model," in *Feminine Ground: Essays on Women and Tibet*, ed. Janice Dean Willis (Ithaca, NY: Snow Lion, 1987), pp. 11–32.

Another famous Tibetan woman teacher is Machig Labdron, an eleventh century woman who was the originator of Chod practice, an esoteric practice in which the meditator visualizes her or his body being fed to hungry sentient beings. These teachings were so powerful and popular that they actually traveled from Tibet to India, the only set of teachings to reverse the normal flow of Buddhist teachings from India into Tibet. Indian pundits so doubted the authenticity of her teachings that they traveled to Tibet to test her, but after numerous tests and debates, they were convinced that she was, indeed, a genuine teacher. Her teachings and practices have been transmitted to the present day and are still practiced by many important leaders of Tibetan Buddhism.[12]

A final historical and contemporary example is that of the Mindrolling lineage, a Nyingma family lineage that has always been somewhat independent. Today, the Mindrolling lineage is represented by two sisters, one of whom has been recognized as a tulku, as an incarnation in a famous lineage of women teachers that goes back, ultimately, to Yeshe Tsogyel. She teaches throughout Asia, Europe, and North America as a Rinpoche, a fully authorized lineage holder. These sisters take great pride in the heritage of the Mindrolling lineage, in which, from its beginnings, the daughters have been as thoroughly educated as the sons. They rarely, if ever, were the heads of the lineage, but on at least one occasion, the sister of the lineage holder, who had been defeated and killed, was able to rescue the lineage and restore the full teachings to the next generation because of her own education and accomplishments.

In the contemporary Buddhist world, both Asian and Euro-American, more attention is being devoted to women's education, the status of women in Buddhism, and, especially in North America, to women becoming teachers. Despite all the criticism that Western feminism is a middle-class North American movement that does not address the issues of women or men in the rest of the world, I am convinced that these improvements in Buddhist women's situations worldwide owe a great deal to Western feminism. North American Buddhists, especially women, were the first to become outspoken and articulate in their questions and critiques of traditional norms regarding women, and these articulate critiques have been heard throughout the Buddhist world.

---

12. Jerome Edou, *Machig Labdron and the Foundations of Chod* (Ithaca, NY: Snow Lion, 1996).

There is now an international movement for Buddhist women, with regular publications and regular international conferences. The movement is concerned with many issues in addition to the presence of women teachers; in fact, other issues, such as restoring the nuns' full ordination and women's education in various Buddhist countries, probably receive more attention than the issue of women teachers. For many Buddhists, the expectation is still that teachers will be monastics rather than lay people, and the emergence of teachers is impossible without high standards of education for women. Thus the issues in the forefront of the international Buddhist women's movement are integral to the long-term project of fostering women teachers.

In North American Buddhism, the question of women teachers has been explicit almost from its beginnings. I attribute this explicit awareness of the need for women teachers to the fact that Asian Buddhist teachers began to arrive in North America and teach widely at about the same time as the feminist movement became strong, a turn of events that I have labeled "the auspicious co-incidence of Buddhism and feminism in the West." ("Auspicious co-incidence" is a technical term used to designate that two lines of karma or cause and effect have come together in a fortunate way. The most usual and important auspicious co-incidence is the meeting of teacher and student.) Coming to Buddhism in the era of feminism, rather than in the fifties, for example, women who were attracted to Buddhism simply assumed that Buddhist teachings and practices were meant for them as well as for men. Unlike women of the postwar baby boom generation in the fifties, they did not assume that their role was to be enablers and caretakers who did the child care and ran fund-raising suppers while the men studied and practiced. As already noted, they questioned Asian teachers about why there were no women teachers among their ranks, and studied and practiced side by side with the men. As a result, serious practice and study is more equitably shared by both men and women in North American Buddhism than in any previous form of Buddhism.

With so many women engaged in serious study and practice, it was inevitable that, as teaching roles became available to North American students, women would take on such tasks. In most North American Buddhist contexts, at least those made up mainly of Euro-Americans, meditation instructors and teachers who teach the on-going classes at dharma centers are as likely to be women as to be men. With head teachers, who have much more independence in their teaching and teach nationally rather than locally, the situation is sometimes different. It is also difficult to make generalizations because there is so much variation from one lineage to another.

Nevertheless, the Euro-American Buddhist world is generally said to involve three main sets of lineages, the Vipassana movement originating in South-East Asia, the Zen movement, originally associated with Japan but now also involving lineages from Korea, China, and Vietnam, and the various Tibetan Vajrayana lineages. The Vipassana and Zen movements are, at this point, much more independent of their Asian ancestors than are the Tibetan lineages. It is also the case, that, though there are exceptions, many more women have received dharma transmission, teach independently, and hold the highest teaching rank in these movements than among North Americans who practice Tibetan forms of Buddhism. Thus, one could suggest that the degree of relative independence from Asian Buddhist authorities is an important indicator, at present, for the likelihood that there will be independent women teachers.

One could then ask why the Zen and Vipassana movements are so much more independent in North America than are the Tibetan lineages. I will suggest two hypotheses, though these are somewhat tentative. First, the complexity of advanced Vajrayana practices is notorious; mastering them seems to require training almost from early childhood and extremely long periods of intensive training, which relatively few Westerners have undertaken. But, I suggest the more important reason may be that the Tibetans have lost their homeland with its numerous practitioners and thus are both more dependent on their Western students for the survival of the tradition and more free to teach in the West than are their East Asian or South-East Asian counterparts. Tibetan teachers have little reason to boot their Western students out of the nest onto their own resources.

Within Tibetan Buddhism itself, the mechanisms for empowering new teachers is quite unusual. Most frequently, young children are chosen as the rebirth of a recently deceased teacher. I would contend that it is only culture that predisposes those doing the selecting, at present Tibetan men, to consider only boys. More infrequently, adults are declared to be such incarnations whose status was not noticed earlier in their lives. Some Westerners have been chosen in this way, including one woman, but these appointments have received a justifiably skeptical response from many Western Buddhists.[13]

---

13. Martha Sherrill, *The Buddha from Brooklyn* (New York: Random House, 2000).

Women were among the earliest Vipassana teachers who trained in Asia for years and then founded the North American Vipassana movement when they returned to North America. The first generation of North American Zen students to receive dharma transmission, who trained under Asian teachers in North America, consisted mainly of men, but as many more Zen students receive transmission, many women are among their ranks. In the Tibetan Buddhist lineages, there are few such examples, though some women teachers have achieved national renown nevertheless. The best known is perhaps Pema Chodron, a nun who heads Gampo Abbey in Nova Scotia, a meditation center and abbey within the Shambhala Vajradhatu network, and writes very popular books on Buddhist practices of loving-kindness and compassion.

Shambhala Vajradhatu, founded by the famous teacher Chogyam Trungpa and now headed by his son, who now goes by the title "Sakyong Mipham Rinpoche," is the largest Tibetan Buddhist organization in the Western world, and one of the largest and most famous and successful Western Buddhist organizations. Because it is also the Buddhist organization to which I belong, I am quite familiar with its practices concerning gender and women teachers. The organization presents a very interesting blend of conservatism and impeccably gender inclusive practices—up to a certain point. I have long been regarded as the lightning rod for feminist issues in this sangha and have sometimes been taken seriously for this reason and at other times dismissed. The official line tends to be that feminism is unnecessary because gender is irrelevant to the dharma and women "do everything" anyway. However, the language of the chants still uses the generic masculine, and I have had some interesting, not wholly peaceful encounters on this issue over the years. In the summer of 1999, when I taught at Vajradhatu Seminary, the premier teaching environment in Shambhala Vajradhatu, I was asked to give a talk on gender. I brought up the issue of the language of the chants and the students responded in droves by signing a petition to have the language changed. (Some chants have already been changed to gender inclusive language and I have been told that the rest are in the process of being changed. But things change very slowly.) Interestingly, the Sakyong himself is very careful in his use of language and routinely uses feminine pronouns and images in his teaching.

Regarding teachers within Shambhala Vajradhatu, there will probably always be only one Rinpoche, one head lineage holder, the current Sakyong Mipham Rinpoche. This situation is more in accord with the

Tibetan style, in which there are relatively fewer completely independent teachers and lineage holders than in the Zen tradition, for example. However, many senior students are authorized as teachers and they, in fact, do the vast majority of the teaching within Shambhala Vajradhatu.

Among these teachers, there are various ranks as well. There is a national body of "Senior Teachers," who can teach somewhat independently at the various Shambhala centers around the world. This group includes many women, many of whom are very highly regarded as teachers. However, a much smaller group of eighteen among thousands of practitioners within Shambhala Vajradhatu has been selected as *Acharyas*, whose prestige and teaching authority far outranks that of the Senior Teachers. Of these *Acharyas*, six are women, four of whom were appointed very recent to this writing (June 2000). This imbalance has been widely criticized but, so far, has not been rectified. It is not that there are not sufficient numbers of women who could be appointed as *Acharyas*, at least according to most observers. For example, at the 1999 Seminary, ten of the fifteen Senior Teachers were women. This gender discrepancy between the two most prominent groups of teachers within Shambhala Vajradhatu occurs frequently.

To compound the problem, with one exception among the *Acharyas* and very few exceptions among the senior teachers, women who are authorized to teach within Shambhala Vajradhatu do not usually discuss gender issues in their teaching. Many of them regard feminism as irrelevant and have regarded me as either naive or unnecessarily divisive for my openly feminist teaching. Thus, the issue of women acting as teachers is being addressed to some extent, but the reasons why it is so important that women teach, discussed earlier in this chapter, are not being recognized. It is a common tactic in many circles to respond to feminist critiques by promoting non-feminist women. But it is still disappointing and does not address many issues central to the dynamics of teacher, student, and gender in Buddhism.

IN READING RITA'S essay on gender discrimination in Buddhism as it affects the lack of women teachers in the tradition, I realized that I did not have this same experience in Catholic Christianity. Despite the ban on women's ordination, in my actual experience of growing up in Catholicism, women teachers abounded. This is because Catholicism has a strong female monastic tradition that is unbroken from the early centuries. While some female religious orders are cloistered contemplatives, teaching has been the major role of nuns, particularly in the United States. I was taught by nuns in Catholic schools until my junior year in High School, when our family moved to California. There I attended public school and then a private college. It was in these schools that I experienced a dearth of women teachers.

There were occasional experiences of narrow-mindedness—such as the women principal who was shocked that I was in a life drawing class as a teenager, a story I recounted in my biography—an event that was received more as amusing that threatening, due to the culture of my family. But, by and large, I did not experience these religious women as threatening my freedom of thought. Perhaps if I had stayed in Catholic education longer, this would have been the case. But what I got from them was a solid foundation in grammar, writing, and logical thinking, which have stood me in good stead ever since. Often when I read the wandering sentences of my students, I wish that they had had my fourth grade nun who had made us diagram sentences and thus learn to visualize sentence structure—an exercise that I loved.

In my Catholic school all the students, teachers, administrators, and principals were women. Women owned the whole operation. Male authorities were elsewhere, deferred to if they were around, but usually not present. There was an implicit feminism in the culture. The sisters sometimes dropped the suggestion that they much preferred teaching girls to boys, an ambiguous statement. But there was no special emphasis on femininity as a limitation of our abilities. We were expected to play hard in hockey, basketball, and baseball and work hard in studies. For a year or two I entertained the idea of becoming a professional baseball player and practiced my pitching assiduously. It did not occur to me that gender was any barrier to this goal. When I went out for the debate team and won for our school against the public high schools of the District of Columbia, the nuns were there in the front row. The principal enfolded me in her robes in a big hug—something that I found slightly embarrassing at the time!

Male symbols for God also were distant. They were there, but not stressed at the expense of women. The central object of devotion in our religious practices was Mary. Female saints also abounded. But the big religious event of the year was May Day. We got out of classes for days to practice for this event. On the day itself we were dressed in white dresses with different colored sashes and flowers according to our grade. After a procession circled through the gardens, we ended at a statue of Mary. The top student got to crown Mary Queen of the May, while we all sang, "O Mary, we crown you with blossoms today, Queen of the Angels, Queen of the May." (We would also have assumed that angels were female, but even if they were male, Mary ruled over them.) God the Father and Jesus were male, of course, but they did what Mary told them to do. If you had Mary on your side, God the Father and Jesus would be no problem. This female centered religious community gave me a strong sense of self-confidence as a woman, reinforcing a female centered family.

In public high school, this changed radically to a co-ed world in which men were in charge as teachers and administrators, where the ideal boy was a football player and the ideal girl a cheerleader. I ran for student president and was treated as a pathetic oddity because I imagined that a girl, especially one who wasn't even popular, could aspire to this office. I decided instead to write for and soon to edit the high school newspaper, where I found a small community of marginal fellow students who liked to think and write. Our sponsor was the French teacher (a male) and most of us also studied French, not a popular option at the school.

I went to college at Scripps College in Claremont, and was again in a women's school where female brains were valued. But here too the teachers and principal were male. The only women teachers taught languages; there was an implicit message that this was a second class teaching field. Although we were given the impression that there was no ceiling to our aspirations as women, there was a covert message at work. Teachers and fellow students alike assumed we should marry soon after graduation and use our education for volunteer community work, not a professional career. My own professor of Latin classics, Robert Palmer, who had mentored me through my doctorate, astounded me when I was finishing my thesis. When he discovered that I was leaving Claremont for a teaching job in Washington, he rebuked me angrily, declaring that he had expected me to stay around as his teaching assistant. "We just get someone who is well trained, and they leave," he complained. I was outraged, but said nothing since I still had to pass my orals on the thesis.

Meanwhile I had reconnected with the female Catholic world through Immaculate Heart College where I studied Greek patristics with an Irish priest. I taught there in the last year of my doctoral work. Here I encountered Catholic women religious deeply transformed by their appropriation of the Second Vatican Council, and on their way to becoming self-conscious feminists. The artist Sister Mary Corita was their star teacher, and her art work was central to the new art and spirituality of the Immaculate Heart sisters. Here too May Day was big, but they celebrated it by dropping huge Corita posters of tomatoes down in front of the college, reading, "She is the juiciest tomato of them all," and having a star student do a dance of the seven veils (clothed) in front of her statue.

But Cardinal McIntyre, the archbishop of Los Angeles, was not pleased. In my last year there (1964–65) the sisters were engaged in a prolonged struggle with him over their independence, which ended with them dissolving their community as a canonical religious order and reorganizing themselves as a free standing religious institute. In the Spring of 1965 this struggle was still unresolved, and the principal regretfully told me that she couldn't rehire me for the next year. I already had a reputation as a feminist. (I had written an article on birth control that was published in the *Saturday Evening Post* and then reprinted in the *Reader's Digest*.) I told her not to worry since I was moving to Washington and had a job there (in a Black Protestant seminary, Howard University School of Religion).

I have kept my ties with the Immaculate Heart Sisters and taught in their Master's program in Feminist Spirituality many times (a program they created after their order became independent). Every time I see the former principal (whose has been writing a book about the struggle of the IHMs with the Cardinal), she apologizes once again for having had to tell me in 1965 she couldn't rehire me. I tell her once again not to worry. I had other options. This experience with the IHMs taught me two lessons. One is that Catholic sisters are at the forefront of creativity in Catholicism and the second is that their freedom is circumscribed as long as they remain tied to the Catholic institution as part of canonical orders.

This drama of struggle between feminist nuns and male church authorities has been played over and over in the last thirty-five years. No order has gone non-canonical as dramatically as the IHM's, but many skirt the edges of a terminal conflict by keeping male church authorities at arm's length as much as possible. Many women have left orders, with a considerable number continuing as lay affiliates of their communities. Religious women in the United States have become both highly educated professionals and the avante-garde of the progressive wing of the church. In every struggle for justice in society, they are at the forefront among Catholics. Many have ceased to go to Mass regularly, and have substituted feminist liturgies in their own communities.

Feminist nuns are my own most constant supporters. I have given numerous lectures and short courses through the sponsorship of Catholic nuns at places such as Mundelein College in Chicago (where Matthew Fox began his Creation Spirituality program, before moving it to Holy Names College in Oakland, California, a place where I now teach regularly as well). My more recent work with religious women is in the Goddess/Gate program in Mexico City, sponsored by Franciscan sisters. This program boldly breaks the boundaries of Christian exclusivism by inviting women (men are welcome but only a few attend) to explore their spiritual journey in the light of the ancient pre-Hispanic goddesses of Central Mexico.

The program typically ends with the Misa Mujer, a radical feminist adaptation of the mass led by the Mexican women who authored it. In the confession we confess that we have not always resisted patriarchy, but at times have capitulated to its silencings. In the offertory, we celebrate the struggle for life of many women, including those of despised groups, such as lesbians and prostitutes, and affirm our identity as "transgressors." Although women from many walks of life attend this program, its most faithful attendees are other religious women, an indication of how radical the split between church authorities and nuns has become.

The response of Protestants and others to this split is often to ask "why don't they leave?" The answer quite simply is that these women are strongly loyal to Catholic Christianity as they understand it (as a liberating, feminist message) and also are deeply attached to their female religious communities. It is here that they have their primary identity as church. Many people outside the Catholic church also regard the refusal to ordain women as the intolerable central keystone in the arch of ecclesiastical patriarchy. They can't understand why any woman would remain in a church that doesn't ordain women.

Catholic feminists, lay and religious, of course, support the ordination of women. Some are active in the Women's Ordination Conference, the main advocacy organization on this issue. Many see the rages of the Vatican against this change as the last cries of a dying system. But many, myself included, are not especially eager to be ordained in the present system. Ordination would link them to a hierarchy of control that they presently somewhat evade through the quasi-independence of their religious order. They do not believe they would have this freedom as priests. For them ordination of women must come as part of a larger process of changing these structures of control.

Women in Catholicism, especially nuns, are teaching and leading other women in a network of programs and conferences in feminist spirituality and social justice issues. Few Catholic men are participating in these programs. Moreover, the Vatican is acting to eliminate women teachers in seminaries and is trying to exclude them from religious studies departments in Catholic colleges. The work of Catholic feminists continues to be read, however, covertly. I have heard from male seminarians that they have taken my work as central to their studies, even in Rome. But obviously I am not invited to teach or lecture there openly. A few men have defied this ban. The Jesuits as an order have chosen to support Catholic feminists and especially feminist theologians, and have invited me to speak at several of their colleges.

Yet generally a deep split—always latent—between male church authority and religious women has become ever deeper and wider. Many Catholic women are moving forward, while some Catholic men, especially the priests and hierarchy, are re-entrenching themselves in male-only ghettos. Bad karma for the future is being built up.

4. Oppressive Aspects of Christianity

ROSEMARY RADFORD RUETHER

IT IS HARD to speak in a few words about what I find oppressive in Christianity. Analyzing the oppressiveness of Christianity for women and other marginalized people has been the lifework of myself and many other feminist theologians for more than thirty years. I am tempted to exclaim, "How can I count the ways!" For me the oppressive force of Christianity for women and other subjugated people comes, not primarily from this or that specific doctrine, but from a patriarchal reading of the whole system of Christian symbols. Yet these same symbols can be liberating, read from a prophetic, liberationist perspective. So what I will to do in this chapter is demonstrate how the Christian symbols have been read in a patriarchal framework. In the next chapter, on what I find liberating in Christianity I will show the potential for reading these same symbols from a feminist liberationist framework.

What is the patriarchal framework for reading theology? Obviously this derives from patriarchal hierarchical slaveocracies, the social framework in which Christianity was born. The patriarchal reading of Christianity repressed the beginnings of prophetic, liberationist understandings of the gospel message in early Christianity. It polemicized against female leadership in early Christianity and gradually succeeded in largely eliminating it. It sought to integrate Christianity into the dominant imperial Greco-Roman society of the second century and to delegitimize the subversive aspects of the Christian movement.

The New Testament was written in the context of this struggle. It contains the remnants of a subversive Christianity which has been overlaid by a patriarchal understanding. Thus, the New Testament is the major source for canonizing the patriarchal reading of Christianity, but also for reconstructing the nascent, suppressed, alternative forms of Christianity that significantly featured female leadership. Some of the documents of this alternative Christianity, such as the Gospel of Mary, have also been preserved outside the New Testament.

In this Gospel, written sometime at the end of the first century, Mary Magdalene is understood as the "apostle to the apostle" who has a special relation to Jesus, as the one who best understands his teachings. She is portrayed as conveying these secret teachings to the apostles, amid controversies over the authority of women. The Gospel vindicates this authority of Mary as the true intention of Christ, against Peter and other apostles who decry her authority.[1] Such writings give us insight into the conflict that raged within early Christianity over women's leadership.

In this chapter I will summarize the patriarchal reading of Christian symbols as it was shaped into the dominant synthesis of Christianity between the second and the fifth centuries, with further elaborations occurring in medieval scholasticism. I will summarize this synthesis under five headings: anthropology, sin and grace, God, Christology, and the Church. By looking at the patriarchal reading of these symbols, it will become evident that this was constructed, not simply as particular "prejudices" of specific theologians, appearing here and there in Christian thought, but as a comprehensive system and worldview.

1. ANTHROPOLOGY

HOW IS FEMALE gender related to humanness? Early Christianity saw a close relation between the human soul, specifically the mind or reason, and the divine *Logos* or *Nous*, which was seen as the divine nature of Christ. They interpreted the idea in Genesis 1:27 that God created humanity in the image of God to refer to the mind or soul in each human person. The human soul as mind or reason mirrors the divine Reason/Christ. As a reflection of the divine Mind, the soul partakes in a created fashion of God's spiritual nature and hence is immortal and capable of eternal life.

But do women possess reason and hence the image of God, or only men? The Greek philosophical tradition, exemplified by Aristotle, saw women as lacking autonomous reason and being inherently inferior to and dependent on the male. The Jewish tradition was ambivalent about

---

1. "The Gospel of Mary," in *The Nag Hammadi Library in English*, ed. James M. Robinson (San Francisco: Harper and Row, 1977), pp. 471–74.

whether women were made in the image of God.[2] Some rabbinic teachers saw women as equally in possession of the image of God and some saw Adam alone as the image of God. This ambivalence is reflected in chapter eleven of St. Paul's letter to the Corinthians. Here Paul says, "But I want you to understand that Christ is the head of every man, and the husband is the head of his wife and God is the head of Christ."

Paul goes on to argue from this cosmic hierarchical order of the headship of God over Christ, Christ over man, and man over woman, that the woman should cover her head, but the man should not: "For the man ought not to have his head veiled, since he is the image and reflection of God, but the woman is not so, but is the reflection of man."

Some contemporary Christian feminists have juxtaposed this patriarchal text from First Corinthians with Paul's statement in Galatians 3:28 that "There is no longer Jew or Greek; there is no longer slave or free, there is no longer male and female, for all of you are one in Christ." This is read in modern feminism as a proof text that race, class, and gender hierarchies have been overcome in Christ. While such hierarchies may have existed in a fallen, sinful world, they have been abolished in the new redeemed order of Christ, and hence are no longer to exist in the Christian community.

But these two texts exist in a more complex relationship in Paul's own thought. In First Corinthians, gender hierarchy is seen, not as part of a system of fallenness or sin, but rather as the original, continuing normative cosmological relationship of God, Christ, male, and female. The Galatians 3:28 text was probably cited by Paul from a pre-Pauline baptismal formula. But Paul himself in Galatians was primarily interested in the part of it that referred to overcoming the distinctions between Jew and Greek. When conflicts arose in the Church of Corinth about women claiming spiritual equality by departing from marital relations with their husbands, Paul was ambivalent. His preference was to see the hierarchies of male over female and master over slave as still intact within the present world, although they may disappear when Christ returns and inaugurates the Kingdom of Heaven.

----

2. See Mary Rose D'Angelo, "The Garden Once and Not Again," in *Genesis 1–3 in the History of Interpretation*, ed. Gregory A. Robbins (Lewistown, PA: Edwin Mellen Press, 1988), pp. 1–42. For discussion, see Rosemary R. Ruether, *Women and Redemption: A Theological History* (Minneapolis, MN: Fortress Press, 1998), pp. 24–30.

The baptismal formula that Paul cites, which included the phrase, "no longer male and female," seems to have been drawn from a cosmology of gender origins that believed that humanity originally existed in a spiritual pre-gendered state. Making humanity into male and female is then a secondary stage that anticipated the fall into the body and sinful corruptibility. The Christians who crafted this text believed that in Christ, those who had been baptized had returned to the pre-gendered spiritual state and thus had overcome the secondary state of being created "male and female."

The view of gender implied by this cosmology allowed Christian women to claim spiritual equality with men, but in a framework that identified such women as having abolished their femaleness altogether; they would no longer be wives who engaged in sex and produced children. Thus, equality in Christ was linked to celibacy and a concept of spirituality identified with negation of sex and femaleness.[3] Clearly, this is very different from the modern feminist understanding of gender equality.

However even this idea of spiritual equality became too threatening to Paul and his successors, particularly as women in their congregations claimed the freedom to preach and travel as evangelists by renouncing marriage and family. Later writers in the New Testament insist that equality in Christ is *only* spiritual, in a way that does not change the actual power of masters, husbands, and fathers over slaves, wives, and children. "Wives obey your husbands, slave obey your masters, children obey your parents" becomes an insistent theme in the later strata of the New Testament, repeated in several epistles (Ephesians 5, 6; Colossians 3; 1 Peter 2–3). The repetition of this demand itself testifies to the extent to which those traditional power relations in the family had been challenged by the incipient liberationist tradition in early Christianity.[4]

The Epistle to Timothy, written in the generation after Paul, seeks to give a definitive basis for women's continued subordination in the church and to refute any thought that this subordination has been changed by Christ. Women are said to have been created second and also to have been the guilty originator of humanity's fall into sin. "For Adam was formed first and then Eve, and Adam was not deceived, but the woman was deceived and became the transgressor" (1 Tim. 2:13–14). This text

---

3. Ibid., pp. 22–24, 29–30.
4. Ibid., pp. 30–43.

locates women's "place" in nature and society as both secondary to the male in creation and also as punishment for being the only one of the primal pair who had been deceived and who transgressed. The consequences of this status are made clear; women are to exercise no authority in the church: "Let woman learn silence in full submission. I permit no woman to teach or to have authority over a man. She is to keep silent…Yet she will be saved through childbearing, provided they continue in faith, love and holiness, with modesty" (1 Tim. 11–12, 15).

Yet Christianity was committed from its beginnings to women's capacity to be redeemed, to be baptized equally with men and to attain eternal life. Contrary to popular claims by many feminists that the Medieval Church taught that women did not have souls, this thesis was never taken seriously by the church.[5] How then could women be in the image of God? For if she is not in the image of God, how could she have a redeemable soul? St. Augustine, in his commentaries on Genesis, sought to resolve these contradictions. His solution was to distinguish between a spiritual capacity in woman's inner soul and her psychological and physical nature as female.

Augustine affirmed that the spiritual capacity of women's souls was made in the image of God equally with those in men. This inner soul in women (and men) is non-gendered, and redeemable. But women as female, that is, her sexuality and sexual body, is not in the image of God, but images the body which is carnal and sin-prone. Qua female, even in Paradise, woman was created by God to be subject to the male in her sexual roles as wife and child-bearer.[6]

This split view of woman as redeemable human soul and inferior femaleness made subject to the male was extended by Thomas Aquinas. Thomas adopted Aristotle's theory that women are biologically defective and inferior. For Aristotle the relation of male and female is parallel to the relation of mind and body, spirit and matter. The male alone possesses procreative power, while women contribute only the material substance that is formed by the male seed. In procreation the potency of the male

---

5. That Thomas Aquinas and the Medieval Church taught that women don't have souls is a commonplace of popular feminist critique of classical Christianity. See, for example, the article by Mary Beth Lang, "Trying to Keep the Faith in a Female-phobic Church," *Chicago Tribune*, WomanNews section, October 13, 1999. But this claim is a misunderstanding of the complexity of scholastic thought on women.

6. See discussion in Ruether, *Women and Redemption*, pp. 69–77.

seed shapes the female matter in the women's womb, like an artisan shaping a piece of clay.

When the seminal power of the male seed is able to shape the female matter fully, the result is a male. If some defect occurs in this process, so that the matter is incompletely formed, a female, characterized by lack of full capacity for rationality, moral self control, and physical strength, is produced. The product of an incomplete gestation, women are inherently inferior in body, mind and will and must be under male subjugation, due to their incapacity for autonomous existence. They are to be ruled and are not capable of holding leadership in society.[7] Thomas took this Aristotelian anthropology into his theological system and applied it to his view of male and female humanity. This view also shaped his view of Christology and priesthood, as we shall see in the later sections of this chapter.

This traditional view of woman as second in creation but first in sin, subordinate by nature and not permitted to exercise public leadership in church and society, was inherited by and continued in the teachings of the magisterial Protestant Reformers, Luther and Calvin. Both Luther and Calvin repeated the main lines of the Augustinian argument that woman, while possessing a non-gendered redeemable soul, was nevertheless under male subordination in the original order of creation.[8]

However the Reformers discarded the Aristotelian concept of woman's defective nature. Subordination is a matter of a social order decreed by God to establish proper relations of authority between the genders (and classes), not a matter of the inherent inferiority of some humans to others. Women's acceptance of this subordination to the male is a matter of obedience to divine command, not of biological defectiveness.

In the eighteenth and nineteenth centuries, the anthropology of gender hierarchy was gradually reshaped to be about complementarity. Instead of thinking of the male as having the fullness of human nature—capacity for reason, moral will, and physical strength—while women have only a defective portion of this human nature, the anthropology of complementarity divides humanity into two halves; each half has some essential human capacity and is complemented by the other half. Men as masculine still are seen as possessing the capacities of rationality, moral will, and physical power, but women are now ceded the qualities of intuition, moral altruism, poetic feeling, and motherly nurturance.

---

7. Aristotle, *Generation of Animals*, pp. 729b, 737-8b, 775; *Politics*, p. 1254
8. Ruether, *Women and Redemption*, pp. 117–26.

These feminine qualities come to be associated with religiosity and the Christian ethic of altruistic love. Women's piety and altruistic service to others are needed to lift men from what would otherwise be brute power and egoism. Thus, women can be lauded as more moral and spiritual than men, but only in a framework that privatizes morality and spirituality, locating these in the home, rather than the world. If women leave the protected place of the home, they will lose their higher moral qualities and fall into a debased state of "masculinization." Men can accept women's nurturing upliftness, but only so long as they don't cede their own headship and become "feminized." Thus the anthropology of complementarity depends on each sex remaining distinctive, men as masculine and women as feminine, in their separate spheres.

This anthropology of gender complementarity, based on a white, middle class split of home and work, private and public, into feminine and masculine spheres excludes women from public leadership in church and society as effectively as did the old Aristotelian system, but in a framework that idealizes woman as guardians of a privatized morality and piety. This is the anthropology preferred by twentieth century patriarchs, such as "pro-family" Protestant fundamentalists and Pope John Paul II, in his encyclicals on women, such as his 1988 *Mulieris Dignitatem* (*On the Dignity and Vocation of Women*). These men argue that keeping women "down" is really keeping them "up" in their special dignity and virtue.

2. SIN AND GRACE

THE CLASSICAL CHRISTIAN doctrines of women's inferiority as female and subjugation to the male were worsened by presupposing her primacy in sin. The New Testament *locus classicus* for this doctrine, as we have seen, is Timothy 2:13–14, where it is said that woman was formed second in the order of creation, but took primacy in sin. Therefore, she is to keep silent. She is not to teach or have authority over the male. She will be saved by childbearing, but only so long as she fulfills this role submissively and in modesty.

Augustine understood this to mean that woman, while created subordinate to the male in creation, was now in forced subjugation as divine punishment for her primacy in sin. She was created subordinate, but became insubordinate, and so was punished for this by having the pains of childbirth worsened and being placed under what now becomes coercive subjugation to her husband. This coercive subjugation is to be continually enforced by church and social authorities, both to restore women's original dependent place in the order of nature and to punish her for her sin.

The medieval scholastics and the Reformers continue this Augustinian line of thought. Luther expresses it frankly:

> This punishment too springs from original sin and the woman bears it just as unwillingly as she bears those other pains and inconveniences that have been placed on her flesh. The rule remains with the husband and the wife is compelled to obey him by God's command. He rules the home, and the state, wages war, defends his possessions, tills the soil, plants, etc. The wife, on the other hand, is like a nail driven into the wall. She sits at home . . . In this way Eve is punished.[9]

This theory amounts to a victim-blaming view of women's subordination. Women deserve this subordination both by nature and as punishment. This theory implicitly encourages men to reinforce their coercive punishment of women whenever they see them "getting out of hand." Any resistance by women to male demands for submissive obedience can justify coercive measures, including hard blows, in order to punish women once again for their insubordination and to return them to their "place." Wife beating is implicitly sanctioned by this theory that women's punished status rooted in her disobedience should be continually reinforced to prevent further insubordination.

Redeeming grace for women, in this theory, does not overcome subordination, but rather reinforces it. "She will be saved by childbearing, as long as she continues in faith, holiness and love, with modesty." The good Christian woman demonstrates her converted mind and soul by interiorizing her secondary and subordinate place in God's creation and her deserved punishment for Eve's sin. She quietly and submissively accepts her husband's rule over her, even his harsh words and blows. By redoubling her submission under his abuse, she shows herself worthy of redemption and presumably wins her husband's care and affection. This is a formula for the battered wife, who collaborates with her dominator through her redoubled submission, which she understands as her means of redemption.

---

9. Ibid., p. 120.

3. GOD

THE DOCTRINE OF God reinforces a patriarchal reading of Christianity and, indeed, becomes its capstone by understanding God as a patriarchal male who created the world as a system of male hierarchical rule of men over women, masters over slaves, rulers over subjects. Although no form of Christianity except Mormonism sees God literally as a physical human male, the patriarchal male metaphors for God are read as expressing God's spiritual nature. God rules as one with sovereign authority to dominate and punish. Rationality, ruling power, and the spiritual are read as male qualities possessed primarily by men and inappropriate for women.

This also means that female metaphors are inappropriate for God, since femaleness symbolizes that which is creaturely, servile, carnal, and sin-prone. The dualistic symbolism of male to female as God is to creature and as mind is to body makes divine masculinity central to the patriarchal reading of Christianity. This symbolism also reinforces the idea that woman, qua woman, is not in the image of God, since the divine nature is not appropriately imaged in female terms. This essentialist reading of male gender metaphors lurks behind the strong resistance by Christian leaders to accepting inclusive language for God. God cannot be imaged in terms of the female, because femaleness by definition images the non-divine, the bodily and the sinful, both ontologically and morally.

4. CHRISTOLOGY

THE DOCTRINE OF Christ reinforces the dominant Christian victim-blaming view of woman by reading its Christology out of its masculinist view of both humanness and of God. On the one hand, Christ is God, the son of God, the manifestation of God's *Logos* or Word/Reason. These divine qualities are read as essentially male and not female. Christ as the incarnation of the divine *Logos* must be male to represent the masculine nature of God.

On the other hand, Christ is perfect man, the complete, sinless human being who represents the original and redeemed potential of the human. Woman is an incomplete or misbegotten human with imperfect humanness, lacking fullness of bodily power and mental capacity, and hence cannot represent the human ideal, while the male possesses the fullness of human nature. Hence Christ, in order to be both fully man and fully God, must be male. This rationale for Christ's necessary masculinity, developed by Thomas Aquinas, was based on his Aristotelian anthropology. Christ's maleness was not simply an "accident" of his identity, like his ethnicity, time, and place. Rather it was necessary in order for Christ to represent humanity in its fullness, as the Head and representative of the human race. Since only males possess normative humanness, Christ had to be male.

This same argument of Christ's necessary maleness is continued in the argument for exclusive male priesthood in Roman Catholicism today. In the 1976 "Declaration on the Question of the Admission of Women to the Ministerial Priesthood," the Vatican document declared that women cannot be ordained because the priest represents Christ. Maleness is intrinsic to Christ's nature, and so in order to represent Christ, the priest also must be male.

However, significantly, the Declaration avoids the Thomistic tradition that argues that Christ had to be male in order to represent the fully human. This Aristotelian view of woman as a defective being who lacks full humanness is no longer acceptable in the modern world. So the Declaration leaves unexplained why Christ had to be male, while Thomas understood maleness to be necessary for his full and normative humanness. The Declaration simply claims Christ's maleness as a "natural fact." But this natural fact also remains essential for representing Christ sacramentally.

The Declaration claims that the whole sacramental economy is in fact based on natural signs, on symbols imprinted on the human psychology. "Sacramental signs, says Saint Thomas, represent what they signify by natural resemblance. The same natural resemblance is required for persons as for things. When Christ's role in the Eucharist is to be expressed sacramentally, there would not be this 'natural resemblance' which must exist between Christ and his minister if the role of Christ were not taken by a man. In such a case it would be difficult to see in the minister the image of Christ, for Christ himself was and remains a man" (Declaration 5:27).

5. ECCLESIOLOGY AND MINISTRY

THE ABOVE MAKES clear the close connection in the patriarchal reading of Christianity between normative maleness, Christology, and ordained ministry. The exclusion of women from leadership, specifically ordained ministry in the church, follows from these views of humanness, God, and Christ. If Christ had to be male in order to represent both the fullness of humanity and the nature of God, it follows, as Thomas Aquinas reasoned, that only the male can be ordained. The view that maleness is necessary in order to represent Christ in the person of the priest continues to be enforced by official Catholic teaching, but it has grown incoherent from having lost its anthropological presuppositions that women lack full humanness. Rather, it bases itself somewhat lamely on a sacramental theory of "natural signs" whose necessity is unexplained.

One wonders why the priest should not also be a Jew, a first century Galilean, to be swarthy and bearded, in order to have a "natural resemblance" to the historical Christ. Clearly there is some unexplained reason why maleness is essential if the priest is to have this "natural resemblance" to the human Christ while these other particularities are not necessary. What remains in this argument is a deep conviction that women are not, and cannot be Christomorphic, by their very being as female. But the earlier presuppositions of this assertion that women, as women, lack the image of God and are not fully human, have been concealed.

The exclusion of women from priestly roles is also reinforced by the symbolic analogy of Christ and the Church as bridegroom and bride, found in Ephesians 5:22–24: "Wives be subject to your husbands as you are to the Lord. For the husband is the head of the wife just as Christ is the head of the Church, the body of which he is the Savior. Just as the Church is subject to Christ, so also wives ought to be subject in everything to their husbands." The symbolism of mind over body, as analogous to male over female, is assumed here. Women lack headship over their own bodies because they lack rationality and autonomy. They therefore are defined legally and physically an extension of their husband's "dominion," over which he rules as head.

An analogy is made between the male as the head of his wife, who is an extension of his body, and Christ, who is the head of the body of the Church. Ephesians does not actually extend this analogy to the priest as representative of Christ in the Church. At the time when Ephesians was written, there was no such sacerdotal leadership caste that was understood to be hierarchically elevated, as representatives of Christ, over the laity, who represented the church as Christ's body. But after this kind of priesthood developed, the analogy of Christ being over the Church, as the head is over the body and as the male is over the female, was extended to include priest over laity. Thus, the male priest or clergyman come to be seen as the representative of the male headship of Christ over a feminized laity.

The priest becomes the ecclesial counterpart of male headship over the wife who is his body/property in the marital relationship. Hence, for a woman to be a priest is to subvert this entire social and cosmic order. One group of conservative Anglicans who opposed the ordination of women even argued that women priests represented a "spiritual lesbianism!"[10] Behind this extraordinary claim is the assumption that the relation of priest to laity duplicates a heterosexual hierarchy of male over female. A woman priest represents a homosexual relation of a female to another female, the laity!

Women who desire to be ordained are typically accused of lusting after power, with the implication that it is inherently wrong for women to exercise power. (Presumably it is fine for men to view the priesthood as a power role!) Lurking behind this charge is still the assumption that for women to seek leadership is a repetition of the sin of Eve, that proneness of the woman to insubordination that expresses her rejection of her divinely appointed place in creation. Ecclesiological hierarchy duplicates and reinforces, rather than countering, patriarchal hierarchy in society.

This fundamental ordering of the Church as a patriarchal hierarchy of priest over laity and male over female is then extended in a hierarchy among male clergy: priests, bishops, Patriarchs, or Pope. Each higher level of hierarchy concentrates power and authority over the lower levels. In Roman Catholicism, this view of the Church as a hierarchy that culminates in the Pope, as representative of Christ on Earth, has taken the form of a long struggle by the Papacy to concentrate jurisdictional and doctrinal authority in one man, and to suppress remnants of collegiality and democratic decision-making of bishops together, bishops with priests, priests with laity.

This trend toward papal centralization culminated in the First Vatican Council (1870) in the doctrine of papal infallibility. The Pope elevated himself above the human condition of fallibility and defined himself/had himself defined as participating in divine inerrancy and indefectibility. This, of course, itself depends on a definition of God as

---

10. This claim that women's priesthood was spiritual lesbianism was made by opponents during the 1975 convention of the American Episcopal Church that voted for women's ordination.

absolute and unchanging power and truth. Although the Second Vatican Council tried to restore elements of collegiality, the Vatican, under Pope John Paul II particularly, has carried out a continual counter-revolution that seeks to restore and even heighten papal jurisdictional and doctrinal absolute monarchy, and to put papal teachings beyond discussion or question.

Ecclesial patriarchy ends in idolatry. As God is the ultimate patriarch, so the ultimate patriarch is God. The fundamentalist Protestant theory of Biblical inerrancy, which was also shaped in the late nineteenth century, is an effort to shield traditional Christianity from modern historical questioning. While it doesn't divinize the preacher or minister himself, it divinizes the Bible as God's Word incarnate in a way that somewhat similarly puts beyond question the words of those who wield the Bible as a weapon against critics.

Traditional Christianity created a tightly knit and devastatingly effective system of theological symbols to enforce the belief that patriarchal hierarchy is the "order of Creation," God's intended social order. To acquiesce to it is to be obedient to God. To rebel against it is to repeat the primal sin of Eve's disobedience to God's command that caused evil to enter the world. This system kept women in their place for centuries and punished those who rebelled against it.

It is only in the last two hundred years and effectively in the last thirty years that a shift of consciousness has allowed a critical questioning of that system. Alternative visions of women's original equality, restored in Christ, began to revolutionize society. These ideas are rooted in the repressed liberationist elements in the Christian tradition that have arisen and empowered a struggle to create new relations between men and women, races and classes, based on partnership and mutuality rather than hierarchy.

But the forces that seek to reinforce patriarchal hierarchy in Church and society are not yet defeated. They have remobilized in the churches, in politics and in the media to re-inscribe patriarchal hierarchy as the normative world view. Christian fundamentalists, Protestant and Catholic, play a leading role in this patriarchal backlash. Once again they seek to paint feminists who criticize patriarchal hierarchy as demonic, rebelling against their divinely appointed place in the family, the church and society, and thereby undermining the social order and unleashing all manner of social evils upon the world. As daughters of Eve, women who persist in insubordination become witches, the handmaids of the Devil.

As Christian Right leader Pat Robertson put it, in a letter which he sent out to raise funds to combat a state Equal Rights Amendment in Iowa, feminism causes women to "leave their husbands, kill their children, practice witchcraft, destroy capitalism, and become lesbians."[11]

---

11. This statement by Pat Robertson was reported in the article by Maralee Schwartz and Kenneth J. Cooper, "Equal Rights Initiative in Iowa Attacked," *The Washington Post*, August 23, 1992, A15.

Response by Rita

I NEVER GOT to the point of considering Christianity as a feminist, as is clear from my autobiography. By the time I began consciously feminist explorations of religion, I had long since been excommunicated and had ceased to have any interactions with Christianity. However, I did live and practice as a feminist Jew for just under ten years, and in those years, I explored a symbol system somewhat akin to Christianity, or at least more akin than Buddhism. Though I have never discussed Christian feminism as an insider, it is safe to speculate that I would have focused upon the same issues in Christianity that I had focused upon in in the few articles on Jewish feminist theology that I did write.

For me, the first issue that emerged in my Jewish practice was the extremely limited role of women in traditional Jewish ritual and scholarly life. No amount of telling me how much Jews honored women as wives and mothers could satisfy me, for I wanted to be fully included in the worlds of synagogue and school that for me were the only reason to be Jewish. As narrated earlier, in the environment of the University of Chicago Hillel foundation in the middle and late sixties, that longing was largely fulfilled, and I had a leadership role in instigating the changes made by the "Upstairs Minyan."[1]

The more serious issue for me—exclusively male God-language—did not emerge until after I had left the University of Chicago. Early on, I was unconvinced by feminist arguments that addressing the deity in feminine terms made any difference. As someone well versed in comparative studies in religion, I was only too familiar with the co-existence of goddesses and patriarchy. However, during my first year in Eau Claire, 1973, memories of the angel story, narrated in my autobiography, came to the surface and I began to believe that, despite many examples of goddesses co-existing with patriarchy, god-language did matter for twentieth-century feminists. Though the presence of female imagery of the divine certainly did not correlate one for one with appropriate, humane treatment of women, the absence of such female imagery always correlated with patriarchal religious patterns. Furthermore, since that lack of female

---

1. For a discussion of this Jewish congregation, see Marian Henriquez Neudel, "Innovation and Tradition in a Contemporary Midwestern Jewish Congregation," in *Unspoken Worlds: Women's Religious Lives*, ed. Nancy Auer Falk and Rita M. Gross, 3rd edition (Belmont, CA: Wadsworth, 2001), pp. 221–30.

divine imagery was often used to justify male dominance and male superiority, as had been done in the angels story of my autobiography, it
became utterly clear to me that Jewish and Christian monotheism could
not and would not foster the full humanity of women until it was normal, rather than scandalous, to refer to the deity in female terms.

The following summer, 1974, I finished my doctoral dissertation. The
first piece I wrote after that was the essay "Female God Language in a
Jewish Context."[2] Clearly, from a very early stage of my career, I was
engaging in cross-over work. What was a historian of religions doing writing a theological essay? When I wrote that essay, I was still fully and only
Jewish in my religious identity, though I was finding Jewish life in a town
in which the synagogue held services only once a month and most people
were Jewishly illiterate to be quite trying. That essay discussed only *language*, not *imagery*, for my mind simply stopped or fell into an abyss when
I tried to think of feminine imagery for deity. Not too much later, my
imagination led me to familiar and beloved Hindu goddesses as models
for feminine imagery of deity and I wrote several articles on that topic.[3]
(It should be noted that I was not suggesting that Jews or Christians adopt
Hindu goddesses, as those articles have sometimes been misinterpreted,
but that they learn from those examples.) By the time I wrote those articles, I was much less sure I wanted to remain in a Jewish, a monotheistic,
or a theistic context, but I was extremely interested in what it would take
for any of these options to work. I was convinced then and remain convinced now that theistic and monotheistic symbol systems must include
feminine imagery of the divine and that such imagery is at the center of
the changes that traditional religions must make. I remain very interested
in the topic of Goddesses and am currently writing a book on them.

However, I have become quite disaffected with the traditional
monotheistic idea of the deity, whatever gender imagery may accompany
it, as an entity ontologically separate from the world and human beings,
and with the myth or sacred story of creation, revelation, and redemption
that typically accompanies that idea. Now, when I return to a church or

---

2. *Womanspirit Rising*, ed. Carol Christ and Judith Plaskow (San Francisco:
Harper and Row, 1979), pp. 176–73.

3. "Steps Toward Feminine Imagery of Deity in Jewish Theology," in *On Being
a Jewish Feminist: A Reader*, ed. Susannah Heschel (New York: Schocken, 1983), pp.
234–47, and "Hindu Female Deities as a Resource for the Contemporary
Rediscovery of the Goddess," *Journal of the American Academy of Religion* 46:3 (Sept.
1978), pp. 269–91.

a synagogue, I can delight in the poetry of the ritual and liturgy, but if I were asked to take its contents as anything more than fiction (and there's nothing wrong with fiction), I would have to say that I find that impossible. I do not object to anthropomorphic imagery when imagining what ultimate reality might be like, for the meditation deities of Vajrayana Buddhism are highly anthropomorphic and gynemorphic. It is reifying these images as ontologically existing entities that makes no sense to me. In Vajrayana Buddhism, the meditation deities are personifications of enlightened mind, and thus a device for gradually wearing away dualistic misperceptions and misconceptions as one works with these images in visualization practices. But I know that Jews and Christians would be offended if I were to think of their deity in that way, and so I see no point in trying to do so, even though I frequently listen to the Christian classical sacred music that I love so much as I write and study.

Most troubling of all to me are Christian versions of the story of the fall and redemption, sin and grace, and the need for vicarious divine atonement because of the deity's displeasure with human beings. Probably I never have done any mature theological thinking regarding that story, for its equivalent really isn't found in Judaism. At this point I also sense the greatest difference between Christian and Buddhist thought. I have already emphasized Buddhist idea of tathagatagarbha or inherent Buddhahood, which for me profoundly contrasts with ideas like original sin and vicarious atonement. It is difficult for me to imagine a feminist version of a story that I find inherently unsatisfactory and troubling.

I have sometimes commented that Buddhist feminists have at least one good fortune, in that we do not have to deconstruct and reconstruct the deity of monotheism, do not have to deal with creation, sin and grace, Jesus, or the God of monotheism. To me, the all-encompassing web of the patriarchal reading of Christian symbols and widespread acceptance of the reading are completely daunting. Nevertheless, during my many years of teaching Christian feminist thought to a largely Christian student body, I eagerly sought out and presented the various feminist accounts of Jesus in particular and Christian theology in general, including those by Rosemary. I am grateful that my spiritual journey has made it unnecessary for me to personally re-imagine these symbols and stories. I am equally grateful that people like Rosemary have taken as their life's work the successful re-imagination of these symbols and stories, given that Christianity and monotheism are likely to be major forces in our world for the foreseeable future.

PART III

---

*What Is Most Liberating
about My Tradition?*

5. What Keeps Me in Buddhist Orbit? Silence, Contemplation, and the Dharma

RITA M. GROSS

UNDOUBTEDLY, ONE OF the most radically freeing aspects of Buddhism for me has been its meditation practices. Equally important has been an emphasis on a traditional Buddhist way of learning—contemplation. *Meditation*, as I am using the term, is technique or practice that is not about pursuing ideas but about resting the mind. It is usually done seated, in silence, returning one's focus or attention to a neutral reference point or object of meditation, usually the breath, when distractions occur. Contemplation, as I am using the term, is a way of working with ideas that seeks to let insight into their genuine meaning arise, rather than grasping after intellectual fixes and large amounts of information. One looks into the pith teachings of the dharma slowly, coming back to them again and again, rather than assuming that one has "gotten it" with the first understanding that arises. Meditation and contemplation are what have made Buddhism something more primordial in my system than simply some ideas that sound good intellectually—an ideology that I "believe in" and use as a weapon. Thus, I am suggesting that what is most liberating about Buddhism is not *this* idea as opposed to *that* idea, thought I find the ideas, the teachings of Buddhism quite compelling, far more compelling than the ideas of monotheism. But beyond any ideas, any intellectual content, is a way of working with mind itself that I find radically freeing, and that I would also suggest has implications and utility not only for individual comfort but for social well-being.

Meditation and contemplation are what have brought me what stability and equanimity I have, what ability I have not to be tormented by the silliness and greed I see all around me. Though, like every meditator, I can kid myself that I don't have time today, can experience intense boredom and frustration in some meditation sessions, and can get too caught up in projects and busyness to do sufficient contemplation. Nevertheless meditation and contemplation are and have been the polestar of my universe for some time now.

Disciplined silence, it seems, was what was missing from Jewish spiritual disciplines that I tried to take on as a daily practice. I remember very keenly my frustration with the wordy daily liturgy. I tried to do it in Hebrew because I understood it better in graceful Hebrew than in a stilted, uninspired English translation, but I had only recently learned Hebrew and it did not flow easily. What frustrated me most was that even the so-called "silent prayer" was a long series of words, said sub-vocally rather than out loud, whether alone or in congregational worship. I had also already worked my way to a sort of *via negativa* theology, for I regarded Truth as something well beyond what words could capture. I was more than ready for practices promoting reverent, receptive, and inquiring silence. So when the truth of the Four Noble Truths hit me that fall day of 1973, I was receptive to all four truths, including the requirement for meditation, not just the first three more intellectual or philosophical truths.

Disciplined silent meditation practice was the one religious option that had never before been offered to me in all my religious training within Christianity and Judaism, and contemplation was the one mode of learning that had not been introduced to me during my extensive academic training in the world's religions. For me, they are what I had been looking for that other religious systems, in the midst of their concern for doctrinal correctness and detailed codes of behavior simply did not offer. Therefore, I tend to see mediation as something distinctively Buddhist, even though the most basic practice of *samatha* or stabilizing the mind is pre-Buddhist and pan-Indian. I also now know that both Judaism and Christianity do have contemplative traditions, though they had been largely lost to the general public due to the European enlightenment and the forces of modernity.

Now, when I teach meditation, I am careful to point out that a lifelong practice of basic *samatha*, mindfulness of the breath, does not require one to be or become a Buddhist. Other meditations, such as visualization practices and mantra recitation do require that one be a card-carrying Buddhist, but not basic *samatha*. I would claim that the way in which various mindfulness practices have become widely available in the past thirty years is one of the more positive spiritual or religious developments of our time.

But when *I* sought out meditation practice, I already knew Buddhism reasonably well academically. Without that *knowledge*, I doubt whether I would have become a meditator. For me, willingness and desire to meditate came as the result of seeing the cogency of Buddhist ways of talking about reality, especially, at first, the Four Noble Truths. This fundamental set of teachings describes, first, the reality of suffering; second, the cause of suffering; third, the possibility of the cessation of suffering; and finally, the eightfold Noble Path. Later, other Buddhist teachings began to hit me with the same cogency and personal knowledge of their truth. Because I already knew a lot about Buddhism, when I began to meditate, it was like taking a match—meditation practice—to straw, my own academic familiarity with Buddhism. Therefore, whenever I teach Buddhism in a Buddhist context, I always emphasize the helpfulness of an early, thorough grounding in Buddhist teachings. The teachings themselves are very powerful, though relatively remote without contemplation and meditation, but what can one contemplate if one does not know the teachings, and why would one meditate without some understanding of what is the point, the fruition or result of meditation practice? Together, all three are like a three-legged stool or tripod—very stable if you get the proportions right. Knowledge of the teachings sparked willingness to practice and practice deepened understanding of the teachings. This process of endless layering between academic knowledge and the experiential deepening brought about by practice has not yet ended for me.

It is very difficult to talk about contemplation and meditation and their results. What could be the utility of thinking about a short passage or a basic list of dharma terms for hours, only to realize that its depths still elude one? What could sitting in good, disciplined posture, focusing on the breath, and returning the focus to the breath when thoughts intervene (without passing judgement on the thoughts) possibly have to do with anything? Though the techniques specific to contemplation and meditation are somewhat different, together they effect subtle but profound changes in one's state of mind. Because their resultant transformation is the most liberating dimension of Buddhism for me, from this point in this chapter, I will speak of them together as practice.

Despite the difficulty of talking about the cause and effect relationship between practice and personal transformation, I would say unhesitatingly that meditation and contemplation are what transform a set of intellectual ideas into visceral reality, what change remote data into the lifeblood through which one knows that certain things are true. They are also the keys to a certain lightness of mind that makes dogmaticism impossible, or least very uncomfortable. This is a very interesting combination: certainty without ideology, without self-centered investment in what is certain. "Freedom from the hot torment of the *klesha*-s (conflicting emotions)" is a traditional phrase that expresses well, to me, this state of mind.

The best place to begin an explanation is with the standard Buddhist diagnosis of the cause of all suffering—ego, in the sense of self-cherishing and self-clinging. However, saying that does little to make the issues immediately clear; the English word *ego* is loaded with emotional, intellectual, and religious connotations which do not readily correspond to Buddhist usages of the term, which are themselves somewhat varied. Fundamentally, Buddhists mean by *ego* the false, but deeply rooted belief that we exist as separate and eternal entities, which makes us evaluate everything we encounter as either "for me" or "against me." Therefore, clinging to or aggression against others, in defense of that ego, are the primary emotions (*klesha*-s) of the untrained mind. But it is not the thoughts and emotions themselves that are the problem; it is the extremely close identification of ourselves with those thoughts and emotions, the uncontrolled way in which they dictate what our lives and our actions will be. Because we cling so desperately to this non-existent self that we believe is separate from and independent of the rest of reality, our reactions to others, that is to say our own thoughts and emotions, become the puppet master; we do little but jump around reacting to them and identifying completely with them. That is why ideology and aggression are often so strong in unpracticed people. That is the "hot torment" of the *klesha*-s.

I do not believe that there is any way to unwind and relax this intense knot without some practice, some kind of spiritual discipline. Simply reasoning about the counterproductivity and falseness of ego, as understood by Buddhists, by itself, will not undo ego, though it will lessen ego's hold. Intellectual knowledge of the fact that suffering is caused by attachment does not, by itself, bring detachment, though it is more useful that the belief that attachment and desire are the sum and substance of the good life. I know of no more cogent demonstration of the claim that the master's tools (thoughts and emotions) will never dismantle the master's house (ego).[1] Practice works because it is not one of the master's tools; it

---

1. This phrase in the title of a celebrated essay by Audre Lorde has been used many times to claim that feminist thought must depart from the models inherited from the male establishment if feminism is to be truly liberating. Audrey Lorde, *Sister Outsider: Essays and Speeches by Audrey Lorde* (Freedom, CA: The Crossing Press, 1984), pp. 110–13.

does not attack ego directly but simply refuses to operate on its terms; It is an entirely different method.

However, practice will not untie this knot quickly or easily. Practice is by no means a quick fix; it is agonizingly slow and frustrating. No reliable meditation instructor would promise students otherwise. Nevertheless, most people with a longstanding practice would say that it has brought some relief from the "hot torment of the *klesha*-s" that would not otherwise have happened. It is not that the same thoughts and emotions no longer occur: the popular idea that meditation puts an end to troublesome, disturbing thoughts and emotions is a misconception. The difference is that, though the same thoughts and emotions may occur, the necessity to believe in them no longer occurs. Instead, something unwinds and relaxes. Thoughts and emotions occur and then there is a gap, some space in which one can bid the old familiar pattern hello and good-bye without buying into it. There is good reason why one of the traditional analogies for the process of waking up is "like a snake uncoiling."

One also begins to see that thoughts and emotions by themselves, no matter how uncomfortable, are not the problem. Practice is not about condemning thoughts and emotions as the "bad guy," as is so often thought, or about trying to substitute "good thoughts" for "bad thoughts." The problem is attachment to thoughts and emotions, belief in them, identifying with them, whatever their content may be. Unwinding and relaxation occur because practice is not a direct attack on the source of suffering, the thoughts and emotions with which ego secures itself. Rather, it is a patient, ongoing refusal to buy into ego's enticements that gradually wears ego out. That result is always described as freedom. The mind is much more alert, open, flexible, and accommodating without being in any way zombie-like. It is very difficult to describe the change because it is so subtle, but it is such a relief.

For me, this transformation first happened regarding feminist rage, anger, and ideology, at all of which I was quite proficient. I was heavily invested in them emotionally; they defined me; they were my ego. Like many people with a just cause, I also felt completely entitled to my anger and to self-righteousness about my anger, because I had been and was being wronged. As my autobiography narrates, I had been involved in feminist scholarship for some years before I started to meditate and became a Buddhist. When I began to practice, I fully expected that it would have no effect on my feminism. How could it? The feminist cause is so clearly just! In fact, if anyone would have told me that my mode of feminist expression would change radically, I may well have decided that practice was too dangerous. Who would I be without my justified feminist anger about injustice? I was sure that feminism would be one track in my life, and Buddhist practice another; if one were to affect the other, surely feminism would challenge Buddhism, but not the other way around. But I really didn't expect these parallel tracks to impact each other, probably because I had been taught for so long that scholars should keep their religious or spiritual views private. Being a feminist scholar was part of my public work; that I happened to do Buddhist meditation was irrelevant to everything else. Of course, things didn't happen that way. Being a Buddhist practitioner became part of my public scholarly identity, which is a grave heresy for someone who studies world religions in a comparative perspective.

Since then, I have written feminist critiques of Buddhism and Buddhist critiques of feminism, thus earning the ire of both constituencies. I feel like a bridge trying to get two shores to talk to each other, translating back and forth between them, trying to get feminists dislodged from their Eurocentrism and trying to get Buddhists to understand that they do need to pay attention to gender injustice in traditional Buddhism. For years, many of my feminist colleagues thought I had defected by joining an Asian tradition that is accurately assessed as traditionally male-dominated. They could understand someone who chose to do feminist theology in the context of the Christianity or Judaism into which she had been born, but to convert to a religion that did not have impeccable feminist credentials was, in their view, incomprehensible as well as disloyal. Meanwhile, my Buddhist friends assured me that as I became more firmly grounded in practice, I would put away childish things, become detached, and cease to care about something as trivial and worldly as women's equality. In the seventies, when I first became deeply involved in practice, many American Buddhists were ex-hippies, war protesters, and radicals, who saw how aggressive and ideological much of their previous social activism had been. Most of them then thought that being apolitical and without a cause was essential to being a "real Buddhist."

Perhaps it was lucky for me that I was so isolated in Eau Claire during those years. I didn't have to hear feminists chiding me for being Buddhist or Buddhists chiding me for being feminist too often. Fortunately, both shores of the Buddhist-feminist divide have been more appreciative and less critical of me for some time now. However, many who evaluate my work from a Buddhist perspective see me mainly as a feminist critic of Buddhism, the "Mary Daly of Buddhism," which I do not find accurate or flattering. I am not "post-Buddhist"; people who do not see how deeply Buddhist my work is simply misread me. If I, as a feminist critic of Buddhism, am to be paired with a feminist theologian who has worked and re-worked the Christian tradition, I would prefer to be paired with Rosemary, with whom I have much in common.

When I began this largely uncharted experiment in being a Buddhist and a feminist, I was quite defensive about and attached to everything I then regarded as part of feminism, especially ideology and anger. Buddhism was not going to change that! Ironically, especially in view of how I am sometimes regarded as a Buddhist heretic because of my feminist critique of Buddhism, practice affected the kind of feminist I was long before I could formulate a feminist critique of Buddhism. My first articles and talks in which both Buddhism and feminism were discussed were about how much Buddhist practice had affected feminist practice, not about gender problems in Buddhism. I had not expected that result, and, as I have already said, I may have stayed away from practice if I had known ahead of time that practice would affect my feminism. Who would I be without my feminist anger and ideology? Now, I am so grateful no one told me that I would change as a feminist if I practiced. Practice offered me something that simply wasn't available in feminism, or at least something I couldn't find. Today, I would have to say that many of the most valuable and helpful things I have learned, I did not learn from feminism.

After being involved in serious meditation practice for several years, I began to discover that I simply didn't find anger so satisfying any longer. Previously, when I was overwhelmed by misogyny and patriarchy. I always experienced emotional relief through venting verbally, often with extreme sarcasm and cutting intellect. But I no longer found it so appealing to get mad when gender issues arose because the relief was not as reliable, and I began to see that, in any case, my anger was not doing anything to alleviate the general misery brought about by patriarchy and misogyny. I began to realize personally the Buddhist teaching that aggressive speech and actions always produce negative reactions. I began to see that people tuned out when I ventilated my angry feelings, that my fits of aggressive rhetoric only caused further mutual entrenchment, rather than any significant change in those whom I confronted. I wanted to do something more helpful.

These changes were very scary at first because I feared that I was ceasing to care about concerns that had been central to my life for years.

Maybe my Buddhist friends were correct and practitioners are not involved in "causes." But something else was also happening. With practice, the anger that had been so much a part of my feminism had started to transmute. I no longer experienced so much of the time that painful state in which clarity and anger are totally mixed up. The clarity remained but the anger started to settle. My body no longer tensed with hot explosive energy; instead I began to hold a relaxed body state that has nothing to do with giving in and everything to do with furthering communication. As my anger became less urgent, my clarity concerning gender issues and the dharma increased proportionately and my skill in expressing my convictions without polarizing the situation also increased. I was actually becoming a much more effective spokesperson for feminism. I was not ceasing to care about feminism, as my Buddhist friends had been encouraging me to do, but ceasing to nurse my anger. I did not stop saying the same things that I always had, but when I expressed myself less aggressively, people could hear what I was saying. I discovered a middle path between aggressive expression and passive acquiescence.

One does not have to choose between either confronting someone or getting rolled over, even though that's what the conventional world teaches us. Thereby, some measure of victory over violence may be achieved, because one cannot be so easily dismissed when one does not respond aggressively to provocation. This middle path is very hard to maintain. It takes being with each moment, moment by moment, to avoid getting rolled over or becoming confrontational, but that is the magic of the middle way. The point of feminism is not to fight wars but to alleviate the suffering caused by conventional gender roles. Practice can tame the anger and unleash the clarity of feminism or any other cause so that communication is more possible.

Furthermore, practice not only transforms intellectual beliefs into living realities, as discussed earlier in this chapter, But paradoxically, practice also makes it impossible, or at least uncomfortable, to view one's cherished ideology as a one-size-fits-all conceptual fix on the world. This is another example of a middle way available through practice. I think it is largely unrecognized in our culture how aggressive conviction can be unless people also have the detachment and mental calm and coolness that practice brings. Conviction without detachment from those convictions and lack of ego-investment in them only produces a mind-set that is rigid, inflexible, and defensive. It also fuels confrontation and battle with those who may have other convictions.

As one of my main teachers recently said, ". . . *samatha* practice is supposed to make us a little more open minded. If we practice and our *klesha*-s get worse, if we become more agitated and discursive, it's not working."[2]

If, instead, one experiences through practice the hot torment of the *klesha*-s" somewhat less and is less agitated, more calm, relaxed and dispassionate, one is then more able to appreciate how counterproductive more conventional reactions can be. Buddhist psychology includes some very useful teachings about why calmness and lack of agitation are a better basis for social concern than passionate self-righteousness about one's own cause and aggressive, confrontational tactics against the others. Given that we live in a society that not only tolerates, but often justifies aggression, these guidelines are critically important. They apply no matter how moral one's own cause may be or how immoral and oppressive are those with whom one is struggling. All of them involve looking more closely at pain and its sources.

First, it is helpful to look into one's own emotional state when one feels aggression or ill-will toward another, or when one is filled with self-righteous certainty about the evils of one's opponents and would really like to do them in, to let them have a taste of their own medicine. It is often said in Buddhist psychology that being reborn in hell is the result of hatred and aggression toward others, and that, conversely, the psychological experience of the hell realm is intense hatred, aggression, and resentment, which is why the experience is so hellish. There is no worse suffering than to be consumed with aggression and resentment. It does not matter if one is actually being oppressed rather than projecting inaccurately onto one's opponents. The very experience of being resentful or of feeling aggression and anger toward others is very painful. Sometimes it is easy to see this with other people, to see that their resentments and anger cause more pain to themselves than to anyone else. The supposed target of resentment or anger may not even be aware of the intense feelings directed against them, and these feelings may well not harm their supposed target at all, with only the resenter being damaged. Anger or resentment is like a boomerang; it returns to the one who sent it.

---

2. Sakyong Jamgon Mipham Rinpoche, *1999 Seminary Transcripts: Teachings from the Sutra Tradition—Book One* (Halifax: Vajradhatu Publications, 2000), p. 76. Privately circulated publication.

So does practice mean that one never experiences angry thoughts? Not exactly. The difference is that one can say "hello" and "good-bye" to the thought without buying into it, without going into the whole twisted emotional turmoil that getting sucked into rage can cause in oneself or the harm it can lead us to inflict on others. Eventually, after having been greeted and dismissed enough times, some thought patterns do get tired of coming around to visit, and check out for good, but there are no guarantees about how long that process might take.

Second, if someone is being aggressive toward us, yelling and screaming, inflicting psychological and physical harm upon us, why are they doing it? The answer is that they are doing it because of their own pain and suffering. Especially according to Mahayana Buddhist psychology, it is important to look into the source of aggression, whether one's own or another's; when we do, we will always find that behind aggression, anger, and resentment, lie pain and suffering. The aggressor is hurting at some very deep level. Their actions are unskillful, unprocessed ways of dealing with pain, responding to it, trying to get rid of it. If one can remember this basic psychological fact, it is much more possible to respond to aggression with kindness and compassion rather than with one's own aggressive response and the desire for revenge. Compassion, however, can include stopping those who are harming us (and themselves in the process of harming us) from doing any more damage. These teachings about aggression and pain do not mean that we cannot defend ourselves from attack simply because we understand why others are attacking. But compassion also includes looking into the aggressor's pain and seeking to facilitate alleviation of the aggressor's pain and a fundamental reorientation on his or her part. A story from the Buddhist tradition that stands out for me as an example of such actions is the story of how Yeshe-Tsogyel converted her rapists to the dharma, whereupon they became her students.[3] Such skill would truly be difficult to attain and maintain, but it cuts the cycle of aggression in a way that revenge never will.

Because of this subtle relationship between anger and pain, I have always been critical of Buddhists who dismiss feminism as irrelevant, as not needing a response except to be rejected, because feminists are "too angry." The implication is that if feminists would speak nicely, they

---

3. Keith Dowman, trans. *Sky Dancer: The Life and Songs of the Lady Yeshe Tsogyel* (London: Routledge and Kegan Paul, 1984), pp. 118–19.

might listen, but since feminists are improperly angry, in the judgement of these Buddhists, feminists don't deserve a hearing. Even more inappropriate are Buddhists who make hostile comments about feminism or to feminists. (I am only too familiar with that scenario.) Buddhists, of all people, should have more psychological savvy and ask "*Why* are feminists so angry?" Buddhists should wonder in what ways we have been harmed and why that has made us so angry—granting that aggression may not be the best way to handle that hurt. Nevertheless, Buddhists should be wondering, "How have women who are feminists been hurt?" They should realize it must be some major, serious hurt, given how angry feminists are, and work to alleviate that pain, rather than only telling feminists that their anger is "un-dharmic," and that if they were good practitioners, they wouldn't mind patriarchal oppression or would see that that is the way things are.

Third, it is important to investigate what is likely to happen if one responds to aggression with anger, resentment, or the desire for revenge. Responding to aggression or oppression with further aggression will usually result in yet another round of name-calling, fighting, and seeking to inflict pain. Fighting back aggressively, which is different from self-defense to stop aggression, usually does not produce peaceful results or the results that one truly desires. Very rarely do people give us what we want and need because we are angry with them for not giving it in the first place. Once again, the master's tools (further aggression) will not destroy the master's house (the initial aggression). Instead, we need somehow to find the middle path between fighting and acquiescing that was discussed earlier in this chapter. Someone has to be able to stop the endless cycle of aggression and counter-aggression by simply not giving aggression back. It might as well be me—but not by allowing myself to be taken advantage of. I have to come up with something more skillful than that.

Sometimes people express a fear that the calmness, stability, and lack of agitation brought about by practice will make people apathetic, apolitical, and indifferent to the suffering of others. The established logic of Buddhism, however, is that personal calmness and lack of agitation inevitably and naturally give rise to genuine unconditional compassion that is not tainted by self-interest and the expectation of rewards, as well as the willingness and ability to work ceaselessly for universal well-being. This happens because people are energized rather than stupefied by the calmness, detachment, and lack of agitation that characterize a mind processed by practice. These qualities free enormous reservoirs of energy that previously had been used for self-protection, worry, self-recrimination, and self-evaluation. For many North Americans, it is something of a shock to begin to experience that ego-based desires and "self-interest" are not at all necessary to feeling joy and enthusiasm for life and for projects. In fact, the opposite is true. When one is consumed by "the cause" with which one is completely identified, frustrations and failures sap one's energy considerably. When one can tap into what lies beyond this personal identification with the project, even frustrations and failures are not so draining. They are not felt as a personal attack.

While traditional expressions of this compassion might not be activist enough to suit many people who practice engaged spirituality today, it is nevertheless the case that Buddhism always proclaims that individual calmness and lack of agitation lead to universal compassion. Additionally, it is claimed that, in fact, such personal calmness and lack of agitation are the only bases for true compassion. Without them, one's supposed regard for the well-being of others is tainted by one's own needs and expectations of them, which may well set off another round of resentment and aggression. Supposed concern for the well-being of others could be nothing but a projection of one's own version of what is good for everyone. Because such premature desires to solve the world's problems are an ever-present problem for social activists and non-conformists, it is always useful to check how much of one's motivation is ego-based, never to lose openness and flexibility of mind, and to avoid self-righteousness and ideology.

Practice makes it possible to care about people and things without becoming miserable about the stupidity and silliness so often displayed. For example, the selfishness of many North Americans concerning their "right" to and "need" for a large, inefficient personal automobile or truck could easily irritate me considerably. Compounding this selfishness is the fact that it is not uncommon for these huge vehicles to have only one occupant and for every member of the family to have some sort of personal automobile. Meanwhile, public mass transportation is ignored. It is incomprehensible to me how people can be so blind to the negative impact they are having, not only in the present but well into the future. In addition, the drivers of these vehicles are often very discourteous and the vehicles themselves are dangerous to those riding in or driving smaller, sensibly sized cars. This is only one example of the silliness and greed I see all around me which could so easily wear me out and cause me to spend endless amounts of emotional energy reacting to their presence if I had no experience of detachment and mental calm. Or this silliness and greed could easily dissuade me from continuing to care about the future of the planet and just do what is most comfortable and convenient, such as buying an air-conditioned car. (Very recently I gave up my seventeen year old car for safety reasons and replaced it with another small vehicle without air-conditioning.)

I would suggest that lack of personal spiritual discipline and the psychological and spiritual transformation it brings has been the greatest problem in many social movements to date. I will conclude with three reasons why, in my view, spiritual discipline is so necessary for social transformation, why it involves much more than personal comfort. Rather than viewing spiritual discipline as a self-indulgent waste of time that takes away from the real work that needs to be done, a claim I have often heard, I would suggest that the relaxing, unwinding, detachment, and lack of agitation that practice allows are important in ways that go well beyond individual comfort.

First, the results of practice provide staying power for the long haul of caring about a cause that contravenes the wishes and desires of conventional people and mainstream culture. Causes like feminism, environmentalism, economic and racial justice, and peace are not likely easily or quickly to attain their goals. I do not expect to see significant results within my lifetime. If I had not calmed down from the white heat of rage and frustration I felt before I began to practice, I doubt that I could have sustained my work for over thirty years. Or I would have been a lot more miserable about my lack of success and the difficult circumstances under which I work. The notorious side effect of passion for just causes is burnout, simply losing heart and not knowing how to go on. Meditators often talk about practice providing "space" in their minds in which provocations can dissolve. This spacious quality, I would suggest, is immensely helpful to anyone who engages in a lifelong pursuit to challenge convention and change society and institutions.

Second, because aggression cannot fuel lasting social change toward peace and justice, I believe that the way in which practice tames aggression is one of its most important effects. One frequent and accurate comment about many social activists is that they are just as aggressive and combative as those with whom they do battle, even though they have the "right" cause. I have always been horrified by the peace movement symbol of a clenched fist inside a circle. I am equally horrified by the phrase "fighting for" peace, justice, the environment, or any other worthy cause. These symbols and phrases indicate a great deal about the collective psyche of the culture, about its assumptions that only confrontation and overcoming opposition will gain any results. But we have too many examples of fighting only leading to resistance and more fighting. As has already been noted, this is another clear case in which the master's tools (aggression and fighting) will not destroy the master's house (aggression and fighting).

Third, meaningful and lasting social change toward gender, economic, racial, and environmental justice will only come about, I believe, through internal change and growth, individual by individual. Those who oppose legislation that would make various kinds of oppression more difficult often appeal to this cliché true change only comes from within. I am not endorsing that reasoning with my comments on an ultimate need for inner transformation, nor am I suggesting that legal and institutional changes are beside the point. They can provide a push toward meaningful change that would otherwise probably never happen. Nevertheless, peace and justice are more viable and lasting if they are not conditions that are imposed on unwilling people who would rather fight and oppress others if they only could. To return to a previous example, I wish that I could charge people who drive large inefficient vehicles five times as much for gasoline as those who drive small efficient vehicles, because I would if I could. But it would be much more effective if, individual by individual, people awoke to the selfishness and destruction involved in their actions and changed their habits. As a society and a planet, we need to impose conditions that curb the endless growth of consumption and population so that there can be a future, whether or not people like such impositions. But it is more important to emphasize the tools that allow people to realize that it is possible to be truly content with less. For that kind of inner transformation toward peace and contentment, even in difficult or unwelcome circumstances, nothing has been more effective for me than practice—both meditation and contemplation. They are the most liberating aspects of Buddhism.

RESPONSE BY ROSEMARY

RITA DESCRIBES HER experience of meditation and contemplation as the central practices that have made Buddhism the powerful key to spiritual growth in her life. These practices were absent from her experience of Christianity or Judaism. I greatly appreciate this centrality of meditation for her identification with Buddhism. For me too it is practice and not simply some theoretical or doctrinal ideals that are central to my identity as a Christian.

Meditation and contemplative prayer are not, of course, foreign to my tradition as a Catholic. Indeed it was seen as the highest expression of spirituality. Even as girls in high school we were encouraged not only to attend liturgy regularly (Mass on Sunday and Holy Days "of obligation" were required), but also to spend time regularly in silent prayer. But there were few guidelines for such silent prayer. It was assumed that we would pray the rosary, itself a fixed sequence of prayers that involves visualization of the key "mysteries" of the faith.

I experienced a different tradition of meditation in Quaker meetings. Quakers don't accept the Augustinian view of Original Sin. They believe everyone is rooted in the inner presence of the divine or the "inner Light," although this has been obscured by the outward chatter of the "world." Silent Quaker meeting is intended to be a communal meditational experience in which all center themselves in this Inner Light, stilling the "worldly" chatter of their own thoughts. The hope is that as one becomes deeply in touch with this Inner Light, a revelatory message will arise and can be spoken to the assembly. I found this a very moving experience. The testimonies were usually few and only after a long period of silence. Sometimes a whole meeting would go by and no one would speak.

In my doctoral studies I became acquainted with the contemplative traditions of classical Christian monasticism, beginning in the fourth century. As I mention in my chapter on "What I Have Learned from Buddhism," I was affiliated in that period as a lay member of the Benedictine order. My husband and I, together with many progressive Catholics, became Third Order Benedictines in relation to an innovative Benedictine monastery in the high desert of Vallyermo, California, under a charismatic Benedictine, Vincent Martin. The monastery was originally Belgian but was located for years in China and, thus, brought an interesting mix of European and Chinese traditions. They also were active promoters of renewed liturgy and the other reforms of the Second

Vatican Council and were patrons of new liturgical art, such as that of Sister Mary Corita.

In this context I learned to participate in the monastic round of prayer, or the "hours," that consist mostly of chanting the psalms. But I also became acquainted through my studies with a tradition of contemplative prayer that involves a series of stages of purgation intended to culminate in an ecstatic communion of the soul with God. These stages seem to me somewhat similar to that described by Rita in Buddhist mediation. From my studies of Neo-Platonism and Alexandrian Christianity, I expected that there was some common thread of contemplative spirituality that ran from Indian Buddhism into the Eastern Mediterranean world in the third century A.D.

In this patristic contemplative tradition, the person is directed through a "ladder of ascent" in which one begins by stilling the appetites through fasting, sexual abstinence, and vigils. As the appetites are stilled, one then seeks gradually to free oneself from sense knowledge. Sense knowledge is recognized as fleeting outward forms of a deeper reality. As one moves more and more beyond sense knowledge, there comes a series of "dark nights of the soul" in which one wrestles with stray conflicting images that come into the mind. Eventually this issues into an ecstatic experiences in which one passes beyond the realm of words and images altogether into increasing unitary communion with God, dissolving one's ego, but without losing a self distinguishable but not separated from God.

While on retreats at the Benedictine monastery I spent some time trying to experience something of this meditational tradition. But there was little training in how to do it as a lay person. Also, at a certain point, I felt myself impatient with it. I began to feel that it was a delusion. I began to feel that I was not in contact with God, but simply in a circular movement within myself. Maybe this was the point where I needed Buddhism to tell me that there was no objective God out there to experience. I believe now that what I was recognizing was the untenability of the ontological hierarchy built into this tradition of meditation. If I had known a tradition of meditation that affirmed this "emptiness," I could have moved on to another stage. Christian meditational traditions have grown moribund for this reason, but could be renewed through an encounter with Buddhism.

But my response to this experience was to reconceive God as that which is under and around us, sustaining and renewing our lives, not an objective entity "out there." I also turned to social action, feeling that the primary way that one lives out of this grounding in the divine that is in and through all things is to work for just and harmonious relations between human beings in society. I became impatient with a monastic life in which one withdraws from the "world" to spend one's whole life in contemplative prayer. This moment in my life is reflected in the letters that I exchanged with Thomas Merton in 1966–67. In these letters I debated vigorously the virtues of monastic life against the virtues of my own immersion in the struggle for social justice in the world of the Black poor of Washington, D.C.

At that time, Merton himself was struggling with the question of whether to leave the monastery, probably for some more ecumenical form of monastic life that would have involved increasing dialogue with Buddhism. He died accidentally while attending a Buddhist-Christian conference in Thailand in 1968. I never met him personally. At that stage in my life, I had no knowledge of or interest in Buddhism and probably would have seen it as more of the same contemplative withdrawal into the self at the expense of society that I was questioning in the Catholic tradition.

Although I have never gone back to "working at" contemplation, I think this earlier work has had a certain effect on my life. I have a sense of maintaining and cultivating a certain "calm center" in the midst of struggle to which one does not give oneself over entirely. One is simultaneously engaged and detached. One is engaged in committing oneself to justice and doing what one can to make some change for the better, however small, in a particular time and place, but one is also detached from being frustrated or angry at any lack of results. There is no final Kingdom of God or paradise that will be achieved on Earth, although one can hope for moderate changes for the better and the curbing of evils. But commitment, putting oneself on the right side, the risk of reprisal this may bring, refusing to back down, solidarity with communities of resistance, and celebration of the new life this creates—this itself is the practice, the practice of a spirituality of the cross and the resurrection.

Rita would also see Buddhist meditational practice as issuing in compassion, and hence in efforts to further social justice. This is particularly true in the development of Engaged Buddhism, a movement with some parallels to Christian liberating theology. But the relationship between contemplation and action is somewhat different for me. I see the contemplative piece as embedded in the action itself and its practice, rather than seeing action as something that flows out of the contemplation but is separated from it. I also have some problems with the Buddhist stress on changing each person one by one and the worthlessness of social change if individual selves are not changed. I would wish to see a more dynamic interrelation of individual transformation and legal and institutional change.

The emphasis on changing each person one by one, and the assumption that only in this way can one make social change (not necessarily Rita's view, but that of some of her Buddhist critics) reminds me of a confrontation I observed during the Civil Rights movement in the mid-sixties. In this exchange white Southerners were insisting that legal change was unimportant because what counted was for each white person to come to "love" Blacks. The Blacks retorted angrily with something to the effect that "we don't care if you love us or not. What we want is to make sure that you will be prevented by law from discriminating against us and pay the price if you don't obey the law."

To understand this exchange one has to understand that Blacks had had their fill of white claims of love for them. Even during slavery, white slave owners had claimed to love their slaves and to be on the side of their best interests, but these best interests did not include freeing them from slavery, or even punishing slave owners who beat their slaves viciously. What Blacks wanted was strong legislation that would make it illegal for whites to do with them what they wanted, and would punish whites who transgressed these laws.

I believe that both sides of this debate were partly right and partly wrong. In the immediate situation, the legal changes that made it criminal to discriminate against Blacks in public services, the vote, access to jobs, and education were crucial. A new legal culture of equal rights needed to be established. Whites needed to know that they would be brought to justice if they broke these laws. I also believe that a changed pattern of law creates a changed culture. People quickly got used to seeing Blacks sitting at the same lunch counter with them. Soon they took it for granted. They may not have learned to love Blacks anymore than they love anyone else sitting with them at the lunch counter, but they take it for granted they have a right to be there.

This does not mean that it is irrelevant to cultivate the deeper compassion and mutual regard with the other that stirs one to protest when the other is abused. People who have cultivated this deeper compassion and mutual regard for the other are crucial for maintaining and deepening the culture of justice. They are needed to intervene when this culture is violated and threatens to slip back into the older patterns of discrimination, despite the law. But such people are always a minority.

One needs the dynamic interaction of both kinds of change, both the legal changes that constrain the majority and set the parameters of civility and changes toward a deeper compassion experienced by a minority that helps direct the focus toward personal regard for the other.

Let me conclude this response by saying something about the issue of original sin versus original goodness—or primal Buddha-nature—that Rita sees as dividing Christianity from Buddhism. I don't believe this is as big a difference as she does. Perhaps this is because her Christian background was Lutheran, which has one of the strongest theological views of original sin as "total depravity." All forms of Christianity believe that humans were originally created as good, as a part of a creation by God that was "very good." All forms of Christianity also see this as having been changed by "original sin." But what they mean by this change differs. Eastern Orthodox Christianity emphasizes that original goodness is still our essential nature, that we still share in the divine nature of God, while sin is a distortion that covers our essential goodness like distorting clothing. This clothing can be discarded. Contemplative practice is the means for discarding it and thus renewing our original "Christ nature," or image of God, that is our true self.

Classical Protestantism, on the other hand, grounded itself in a radical interpretation of the Augustinian view that we have totally lost this original good nature and are completely alienated from God, and, therefore, dependent on an outside redemptive act from God to save us from this utter estrangement. Their rejection of meditational practices is integrally related to this strong view of original sin. Meditation is seen as based on the assumption that one still has an essentially good nature and can recover it "by oneself," without the help of God.

Catholicism officially accepts the Augustinian view, but not with the radical interpretation of the Reformation. This means that the Catholic view oscillates between more or less radical views of the loss of original goodness, but always retains an assumption that the image of God remains our true nature and is still somehow available as a basis for transformation. No Catholic would talk of "total depravity," a term that sounds humorous to most Catholics. Also for both Catholic and Orthodox Christians, Christ as savior is not set against our inner capacity for goodness, because the Christ of history is the manifestation and renewal of that original goodness in which we were created in the beginning. He is the paradigmatic expression of that Christ-nature that is our true self. Christ mediates to us what we truly and really are. This is perhaps not that different from the idea of Buddha and Buddha-nature.

6. What I Find Liberating in Christianity

ROSEMARY RADFORD RUETHER

THE SYSTEM OF theological oppression of women that I outlined in the preceding chapter is so total that, once one has understood it in all its ramifications, it is hard to imagine how one might speak of anything liberating in Christianity. Indeed, as Christian women have acquired a critical feminist perspective, as they have glimpsed the extent of this system of patriarchal theology, not simply as a theory, but as the justification of a practice to dominate and define their being, many of them have felt no choice but to leave Christianity altogether. I understand that response. If this was the only option for understanding Christianity, no woman, indeed no man with any sense of right relation to women, should be a Christian.

I would argue, however, that there is another framework for reading Christianity, a prophetic, liberationist framework that subverts this patriarchal reading and offers a radical alternative. This prophetic liberationist perspective was partially present in Christianity's beginnings as a subversive movement. Although marginalized and repressed, it never entirely disappeared. Movements that expressed this more inclusive understanding of Christianity continued alongside the triumph of patriarchal Christianity, partly surviving on their own, partly interpenetrating dominant Christianity.

A liberationist vision was so much present in the early Church writings that became the New Testament that it could not be entirely eliminated. Women's movements throughout Christian history have hung on to, rediscovered, and reformulated aspects of this liberating reading. The history of the liberationist tradition includes second century radical Christian movements, such as the Montanists, who clung to the prophetic vision of redemption of the early Jesus movement. They believed that the outpouring of the Spirit dissolved gender differences and liberated women to be prophets of a coming transformation of the world. One of the Montanist women prophets, Priscilla, even declared a revelation to her of Christ in female form: "Under the appearance of a woman, clothed in a shining robe, Christ came to me and revealed to me that this place (the holy city of the Montanists) is sacred and it is here that Jerusalem will descend from Heaven."[1]

The liberating tradition includes elements in women's monastic communities in the Patristic and Medieval periods who believed that women's equality of soul superceded their inferiority of gender and allowed them to be vehicles of God's revelatory visions. Christian women mystics maintained the Jewish tradition of God as female-personified Wisdom. They understood God as beyond literal gender while being able to be imaged as both male and female. The Wisdom tradition overcame the notion that male metaphors for God made males specially godlike, while women lacked this capacity to image God. In Julian of Norwich's famous visions she affirms that "God all Wisdom is our kindly Mother . . . as truly as God is our Father, so truly is God our mother."[2] Julian's writings represent the flowering in Medieval women's mysticism of this fluid and gender-inclusive understanding of God.

One radical humanist in the Reformation period, Cornelius Agrippa von Nettesheim, in a lecture originally given in 1509, challenged the victim-blaming theory of the Fall. He revised the Augustinian view that women were created subordinate as female and had primacy in sin. Agrippa claimed that women were fully equal in God's original creation and, indeed, that they have a special affinity with divine Wisdom that gives them spiritual and moral superiority. The subordination of women is not due to either women's inherent inferiority or divine mandate, but is simply an expression of male tyranny: "Women are forced to yield to men like a conquered people to their conquerors in war, not compelled by any natural or divine necessity or reason, but rather by custom, education, fortune and tyrannical device."[3]

---

1. See Ronald E. Heine, *The Montanist Oracle and Testimonia* (Macon, GA: Mercer University Press, 1989), 49.1. Also Rosemary R. Ruether, *Women and Redemption: A Theological History* (Minneapolis, MN: Fortress Press, 1998), p. 52.

2. Julian of Norwich, *Showings*, ch. 58, 59; Edmund Colledge and James Walsh, trans. (New York: Paulist Press, 1979), pp. 159–61.

3. See Barbara Newman, "Renaissance Feminism and Esoteric Theology: The Case of Cornelius Agrippa," in her *From Virile Woman to Woman Christ: Studies in Medieval Religion and Literature* (Philadelphia, PA: University of Pennsylvania Press, 1995), p. 241; also Ruether, *Women and Redemption*, pp. 129–30.

Agrippa's treatise represents a basic paradigm shift in the Christian reading of the relationship of creation, fall, and gender. For the first time, as far as I know, women, in their original nature, are seen as fully capable of all human faculties, including political leadership. Instead of women's subordination being justified by some combination of original subordination and punishment for sin, men, as usurpers of domination over women, are seen as the culprits. Subordination itself is identified as sin and wrongdoing, rather than God's intention. Women rightfully claim full equality in all spheres with men. The early sixteenth century was hardly ready for such a message. It would not be heard again with this kind of directness until the birth of modern feminism in the nineteenth century.

The Quaker tradition paralleled elements of Agrippa's rereading of Genesis and affirmed an original unqualified equality of men and women. They saw the subordination of women, and other forms of domination, as themselves expressions of the primary sin, which they defined as the "usurpation of power of some over others." They believed women's original equality was restored in Christ. This equality continued in the true prophetic church, restored in the Society of Friends, while the established churches had betrayed it.

In the Quaker community, women were not only allowed but mandated to preach and to minister in the Society. Margaret Fell, in her 1666 treatise, "Women's Preaching Justified, Proved and Allowed of by the Scriptures," argues that Christ commissioned his women followers to be the emissaries of the good news of his resurrection, so that men could only receive the gospel by simultaneously accepting the legitimacy of women's preaching: "What had become of the redemption of the whole of mankind if they had not believed the message that the Lord Jesus sent by these women, of and concerning his resurrection?"[4]

This Quaker rereading was inherited and developed by nineteenth-century feminists, such as Sarah and Angelina Grimké and Lucretia Mott, themselves members of the Society of Friends. In twentieth-century feminism, these earlier egalitarian rereadings of the Christian traditions are reclaimed and find for the first time a full theological

---

4. Margaret Fell, *Women's Speaking Justified and Other Seventeenth-Century Quaker Writings about Women,* ed. Christine Trevett (London: Quaker Home Service, 1989), p. 8; also Ruether, *Women and Redemption,* p. 139.

development. A feminist, liberationist reading of Christianity recovers this alternative line of Christian tradition from the margins and shadows of Christian theological history. Rather than being silenced, unknown, or condemned as heretical, it assumes centrality as a normative memory of the liberating potential in Christianity, betrayed in its beginnings, but never entirely lost.

The liberationist paradigm in Christianity is rooted in the Jewish prophetic tradition. Here God stands on the side of the poor and the oppressed, rather than representing the mighty, the kings and rulers of the earth. Through the prophets God denounces those who oppress the weak and vulnerable, and announces a new world to come in which "the mighty will be put down from their thrones and the poor lifted up." This is a radical shift in the social location of God from where it had been in state religions, as these had existed in the Ancient Near East. Now, the Kings, the mighty, are not seen as the incarnations or representatives of God vis á vis their subjects. Rather, they are called to account for their oppression of the poor, whose advocate God becomes, speaking through the prophet.

This prophetic critique represents a creative revision within Israelite religion in the eighth through the sixth centuries B.C.E. It was applied primarily to class relations within Israel, to the oppression of poor farmers, and to their disenfranchised heirs, widows, and orphans in Israel, against the political and economic elite that was robbing them. The prophet recalls this elite to their proper role, which is protection of the poor. In the fourth through the second centuries B.C.E., this critique was extended to include the oppressed condition of the nation of Israel over against the great empires that were dominating it, seizing its land and exiling or enslaving its people.

Christianity began as a movement rooted in this Jewish prophetic tradition. It began to further extend the liberationist paradigm to include those subjugated within families, women and slaves, as well as to the ethnic division that separated Jews, as God's elect people, from gentiles. This trend reflects universalist movements within the Judaism of the first century as well as in the Greco-Roman world.

Some early Christians experienced themselves as a new kind of community in which marginalized people from various ethnicities, women, and former slaves came together as a brothers and sisters. This led them to explore the idea that redemption overcame gender, ethnic, and socio-economic divisions. As we have seen, this was expressed in the early

Christian baptismal formula quoted by Paul: "In Christ no more male and female, Jew or Greek, slave or free." But this nascent insight failed to be translated into a clear questioning of gender, race, and class hierarchy in society. The culture of antiquity was too deeply convinced that these hierarchies were rooted in the structure of the cosmos. This culture could understand women becoming equal only by assuming that such equality meant that women would somehow transcend the cosmic system itself, thereby anticipating a genderless, spiritual world to be found only before and beyond the present cosmic system.

As Christianity separated from Judaism and became a new religion, it distorted its universalism into a triumphalism of Christianity against Judaism, which became the seedbed of the Christian anti-Judaism that would bear evil fruit in the Nazi Holocaust. Slavery and male domination of women were also reaffirmed by spiritualizing the vision of liberation while reinforcing the social consequences of patriarchal slaveocracy. Yet the subversive potential of the prophetic, liberationist readings of ethnic, class, and gender divisions continued to be rediscovered in successive forms of Christian renewal, of which feminist, black, and third world liberation theologies are modern expressions.

In the rest of this chapter I will outline a kind of feminist mini-systematic theology, showing in summary fashion how one can read the symbols of anthropology, sin and grace, God, Christ, and church from a feminist liberation perspective.

1. ANTHROPOLOGY

THE FOUNDATION FOR an egalitarian understanding of theological anthropology starts with a rereading of the foundational text, Genesis 1:27: "So God created man in his own image, in the image of God he created him, male and female he created them." An egalitarian reading claims that the male pronouns in this text are intended to be inclusive, generic references to a human species identity that is shared equally by men and women. As humans who possess the same humanness fully both men and women partake equally in the image of God.

But what does it mean to be in the "image of God"? Classical Christianity read it as referring to a spiritual quality that reflected the divine *Logos*. It allowed that both men and women possessed this spiritual quality in some non-gendered way. But the concept of the "image of

God" in Jewish thought referred to human representation of divine dominion over the "lower" creation, over animals and land. Dominion was always understood to be held solely by males—specifically the ruling class males, the patriarchal class. Women were never accorded a share in this dominion, but rather were understood as included under it.

These two meanings of the "image of God" are the root of the ambivalent reading of this text. If women are included equally in the image of God in the sense of equally shared dominion, then this would undermine the idea that women are included under male dominion as part of the lower creation and open up the possibility of women's equal political, economic, and legal rights. These were unthinkable conclusions in classical patriarchal societies, but an eco-feminist perspective questions the whole concept of dominion itself, the special power of humans to rule over the rest of creation.

Paul's denial of women's equal possession of the image of God in 1 Corinthians 11:7 is based on his assumption that the term "image of God" entails dominion, in which men possess "headship" over women. But the Church Fathers read the term "image of God" primarily in terms of the possession of a redeemable soul. Since they believed that women must have a redeemable soul if they are to be baptized, they had to claim that women were created in the image of God in this sense. But they also assumed that women were under male headship. They did not have any dominion over property, persons, or things, but were themselves included in such property.

Augustine combined the affirmation of women's possession of the image of God, in the sense of possessing a redeemable soul, with denial of their capacity for dominion by distinguishing between the gender-neutral soul in women created in the image of God and women's subjugated femaleness. Among the Reformers, it was Calvin, with his legal mind, who best understood the double meaning of the term *image* and the need to distinguish between these meanings. He affirmed that woman was created in the image of God, in the sense of having a spiritual capacity for redemption of the soul, but not in the sense of possessing dominion.[5] In the original order of creation, which was then

5. See John L. Thompson, "Creata ad Imaginem Dei, Licet Secundo Grado: Women as the Image of God according to John Calvin," *Harvard Theological Review* 81, no. 2 (1988), pp. 137–38. Also Ruether, *Women and Redemption*, p. 124.

reinforced as punishment for sin, women are excluded by God from exercising rule; rather, they are included among those persons and things over which the male is given rulership.

The Quaker tradition rejected this distinction between image as spiritual capacity for redemption and image as dominion. For them, creation in the image of God means that men and women have equal spiritual capacity, but they also claimed that a dominion which put women under the rule of men was not set up by God in the beginning. No hierarchy of some humans over others was established by God in the beginning, no subjugation of one to the other. On the contrary, the domination of some over others is the beginning of sin.

The early nineteenth-century feminist theologians, Angela and Sarah Grimké, inherit this critical paradigm shift. For them, possession of the image of God by all humans, male and female, means not simply equal spiritual capacity, but also shared dominion. If all humans share dominion equally, then there can be no dominion of some humans over others. Slavery and male dominion over women are thereby both illegitimate. The Grimké sisters first developed their argument about equality in the image of God to delegitimize slavery. They then realized the need to apply this argument to gender equality.

Sarah Grimké expresses this link between personal equality and shared dominion dramatically:

> We must first view woman at the period of her creation. "And God said, let us make man in our own image, after our own likeness; and let them have dominion over the fish of the sea, and over the fowl of the air and over the cattle and over all the earth and over every creeping thing that creepeth upon the earth." . . . In this sublime description of the creation of man (which is a generic term including man and woman) there is not one particle of difference intimated as existing between them. They were both made in the image of God; dominion was given to both over every other creature, but not over each other. Created in perfect equality, they were expected to exercise vice-regency entrusted to them by their Maker in harmony and love.

After detailing what she sees as the destruction of this original equality by male usurpation of power over woman, Grimké declares: "But I ask no favors for my sex. I surrender not our claim to equality. All I ask of our brethren is that they will take their feet from off our necks and permit us to stand upright on that ground which God has designed us to occupy."[6]

This paradigm shift in the interpretation of women's equality in the image of God has important consequences. It reflected a shift away from a spiritualized view of an inner equality of souls that would be realized only after the end of this world, when the present gender hierarchies of the order of creation have been dissolved. The focus of redemption now becomes this-worldly, overcoming social systems of slavery and male domination that have established wrongful systems of the power of some over others. Such power over others is now understood as sin, as usurped, illegitimate, power. Redemption is not to be seen as a flight to a gnostic a-cosmic heaven, but as restoration of the original equality of creation by reconstructing social relations on earth so as to overcome hierarchy and develop a society based on legal, economic, political, and social equality.

Twentieth-century feminism inherits this paradigm shift in the understanding of redemption. Equality in the image of God means both the equal value of all humans as persons as well as equity in power relations—shared power—rather than the right of men to rule over women, masters over slaves, whites over blacks. The focus of redemption becomes this worldly justice rather than an other-worldly escape from history. Third world feminist Christian theologies of Africa and Asia also see this equality in the image of God as foundational to their liberation vision. Asian Christian feminists have named their journal *In God's Image* to signal their claim to this idea.

Two trends in later twentieth-century European and American feminist theories and theologies, however, have introduced new complexity into this claim to stand foursquare on women's equality with men in the image of God. One involves new movements that champion feminine "difference," and the other consists of post-modern anthropologies that question the idea of any "essential" human nature.

In post-modernist thought humans are so different as members of distinct cultures, histories, and societies, as persons in many contexts, and even as individuals who change from moment to moment, that it is impossible to speak of any universal or essential qualities that can simply

---

6. Sarah Grimké, "Letters on the Equality of the Sexes and the Condition of Women," in Larry Ceplair, *The Public Years of Sarah and Angelina Grimké: Selected Writings* (New York: Columbia University Press, 1989), pp. 205, 208: also Ruether, *Women and Redemption*, pp. 163–34.

be understood as human per se, the same in all humans. Contemporary feminist theory and theology is deeply conflicted with respect to these contrary trends and challenges. In this short chapter there is not room to do justice to these conflicting views. Instead, I will briefly summarize my own approach to each of them.

The stress on feminine difference is rooted in the anthropology of complementarity that we discussed in chapter two. Men and women are not "the same" but have different "natures." Femininity and masculinity point to the predominance of compassionate relationality in women, egoistic separateness in men. Feminists who champion women's difference do not do so in order to accept women's confinement to the domestic sphere. Rather, they wish to assert the superiority of women's qualities and to refuse what they see as a debasing reduction of women on a model of humanity based on masculine qualities of questionable value.[7]

I believe the best solution to this problem is not to essentialize gender difference, but rather to recognize that these differences are socially constructed and maintained through socialization and culture. The social construction of both masculinity and femininity limits and distorts both men's and women's larger human potential, and also distorts their relation to one another into sadomasochistic power relations. Both men and women need to grow into their larger potential. They need to claim the whole range of capacities that have been assigned to one or the other gender, but in a new relationship of mutuality, rather than competitive power. Equal humanness thus points us to an evolving vision of "right relations," not reduction to the sameness of men and women modeled on what it has meant to be men in patriarchal societies.

Post-modernism stresses difference in another way.[8] Every culture, every person is so different that there can be no commonality by which we can talk of a normative humanness, even as a vision of our unrealized potential. But I think that this cannot mean that humans are so different from each other that as a species they don't have roughly equivalent potential for learning and skills. Science has shown the remarkable similarity of

---

7. A key writing for difference feminism is Carol Gilligan, *In a Difference Voice* (Cambridge, MA: Harvard University Press, 1981).

8. Jacques Derrida's writings are any important source for this post-modernist anti-universalism. For a feminist expression, see Mary McClintock Fulkerson, *Changing the Subject: Women's Discourse and Feminist Theory* (Minneapolis: MN: Fortress Press, 1994).

all humans to each other in biological endowments. Global inter-cultural exchange has shown that, while there are individual differences in creativity, no human groups are so different from each other than they cannot learn to speak each other's languages and attain similar skills.

We need a language that can affirm this deep commonality of humans as a species, while at the same time acknowledging and celebrating the multi-contextualization of this common potential in a great variety of cultural expressions. Difference is neither a hierarchy of better and worse nor a specialization in some capacities which others lack completely, but variety in commonality. Hope for liberation means both allowing every person their full potential and relating all persons to each other in mutually enhancing, rather than oppressive, ways.

2. SIN AND GRACE

TO CLAIM GENDER equality in the image of God as both equivalence in human capacities and mutually shared power transforms the basic meaning of sin and fallenness in the Christian tradition. Instead of woman being seen as the transgressor responsible for sin through disobedience to her original subordination, domination itself is now seen as the meaning of sin and the cause of a human "fall" into distorted relations with each other. The Quaker tradition and its nineteenth-century feminist daughters pioneered this reinterpretation of sin and the fall. Sin is "the usurpation of power of some over others." In this usurpation of power of some over others lies the basic sinful impulse that distorts God's original creation, generating many forms of violence and oppression—men over women, lords over subjects, rich over poor, masters over slaves. These distorted relations are summed up in war, hence, the close connection in this tradition between egalitarianism and pacifism.

A feminist rereading of sin and the fall questions three assumptions of Augustinian tradition: the fall as a historical event at the beginning of history; loss of human goodness and freedom of will through the fall; and the fall meaning a fall into carnality characterized by sexual concupiscence. The fall is not a once-for-all historical event back in some moment of the primordial past. A modern understanding of earth history and human evolution within that history precludes literalism about this mythic story. Rather we must think in terms of a basic tension in human existence between "is" and "ought," between our sense of our larger potential and our present partial existence, between egoistic selfishness and community-building relationality.

These tensions can be translated into social structures and ideologies that institutionalize domination, whether the expropriation of wealth and power in the hands of a ruling elite at the expense of the majority of humans or dominion over the earth itself. But these tensions can also give birth to critical, transformative movements that question such ideologies and promote an ethic of justice and mutuality. Human history is not a tale of a primordial loss of the potential for goodness and harmonious relationality. Rather, as the Jewish tradition has claimed, human experience is a continual struggle between these two tendencies. The potential for goodness and mutuality is not lost in some original cataclysm that leaves humans with only a self-enclosed egoism.

But structures of privilege and oppression and our socialization into them can dim our awareness of our larger potential. "Conversion experiences" are breakthroughs to this larger potential that enable us to question and free ourselves from the grip of the systems of dominating power and to name these as wrong. Conversion experiences are facilitated by critical epistemic communities that validate such questioning and nurture liberating transformation. To be converted all alone is humanly impossible, even though it may sometimes seem to those with dissenting views that they *are* all alone.

The distortion of our good potential is not a fall into concupiscence or sexual pleasure. Such a distorted self, one that denies its own vulnerability, cannot find genuine delight in others. Sexual pleasure itself becomes distorted into objectification and abuse of the other. Sex becomes sinful, not because it gives us pleasure, but when we take pleasure in a non-mutual and abusive way. The Christian view of sexual pleasure as the essence of evil has enhanced this abusive distortion of sexuality into a dichotomy of puritan repression and exploitative libertinism.

Liberation frees us to be open and mutual with one another. This includes healing our capacity for sexual pleasure by enjoying mutual delight in one another. Creating another human person is not a necessity that "allows" us occasional, guilty moments of sexual pleasure. Rather, procreation should be a responsible choice to be distinguished from sexual pleasure. The normal purpose of sexuality is to delight in one another; its occasional and intentionally chosen purpose is also to participate in the creative capacity that humans share with the rest of nature, to produce another member of their species.

Redemption is the process of liberating transformation by which we free ourselves from constricting ideologies that justify systems of domination and alienation. It is often experienced as "grace," as something that comes to us from "beyond" ourselves, not because it is beyond our own potential, but because we have lost touch with this potential. This potential is awakened in us by others who communicate to us better possibilities, help us questions constricting systems and allow us to grow. This in the deepest sense is what "education" should be, not socialization into constricting systems of self-defense, but the communication of liberating power to grow and transform ourselves. Such communities of liberating growth are what church and redemptive communities should be all about.

But institutionalizing educational or religious communities distorts their purposes. These institutions may continue to use the language of education or redemption, but they become a means to impose systems of domination and to socialize their members to accept them. Liberating community, like our good potential itself, has to be continually rediscovered. Liberating community is the essential means for discovering our larger potential for goodness and mutuality and, in the process of rediscovering it, we also renew or reinvent liberating communities.

3. GOD

FEMINIST LIBERATION THEOLOGY draws on the Christian tradition that taught that all our metaphors for God are only partial pointers to a spiritual reality of God that transcends all our terms. The *via negativa* or apophatic theology in Christian tradition emphasized the need to deny the appropriateness of all our images for God in order to express God's transcendence. To take any images of God literally is idolatry; to use language for God's power to make God into the sanctioner of oppression is blasphemy.

But divine transcendence is not best understood as infinite separation or spatial distance between us and a God who rules over us from beyond. This model of transcendence is based on masculine ego development that separates mind from body, male from female, disconnected transcendence and static immanence. Rather, we should think of divine transcendence as God's radical freedom from all our systems of lies and oppression. But this also means that God is closer to us than we are to ourselves, grounding and renewing our freedom to transcend oppressive patterns, while at the same time putting us back in touch with our good potential. The God who frees us at the same time nurtures our growth into our good potential. In Julian of Norwich's language, she is our "very mother."

Feminists reclaim the fluid, dynamic gender language for the divine in the Jewish and Christian tradition, particularly the sapiential tradition which images God in the female metaphor of Wisdom, the cosmic creator, sustainer and redeemer in whom "we live and move and have our being." A feminist liberation reading of God-language involves a double transformation. It privileges metaphors for God that are gender inclusive and liberationist. God may be imaged as female, as Holy Mother Wisdom, who nurtures our good potential.

God also is the Liberator who sides with the poor and puts the mighty down from their thrones. This includes women, the oppressed in patriarchal societies, as those with whom God sides. Third World feminist theologies point particularly to poor women, to Black and Third World women, as the oppressed of the oppressed, whom God is empowering to become liberated liberators. In putting the mighty in all these systems of power down from their thrones, God empowers us to seek the peaceful kingdom where all humans and the earth itself are in harmonious partnership.

But feminist theology must retain an element of the via negativa that remembers that no image for God can be taken literally. Feminist theologians must eschew a female chauvinist reversal in which women are established as morally and spiritually superior, as "goddess-like" against men who are seen as the moral brutes. This temptation can all too easily become a self-fulfilling prophecy! The goal of redemption is both liberation from oppression and inclusion of all beings as images of God, as places where God can be encountered. In an eco-feminist theology, this also means displacing the anthropocentrism that reads only humans, but not the rest of nature, as images of God. We are not called to rule over, but to enter into life-sustaining mutuality with all nature, as we do with one another as humans.

4. Christ

A FEMINIST LIBERATIONIST Christianity moves away from the high Christology of the patristic tradition to Jesus as a Jewish prophet of liberation as described in the gospels. Jesus represents God as one who heals and affirms the poor, particularly the poor and despised woman. He affirms the most marginalized women—the woman with a flow of blood, the Samaritan woman, the prostitute—as those who best understand his message. He denounces the teachers of the law, the clerical class who oppose his good news to the poor. To follow Jesus is to follow him in this mission of liberating the most oppressed, affirming the despised of the dominant society and religion. But this also means following him into risky witness, one that might even mean death at the hands of those who seek to shore up the present systems of power and their religious ramifications.

5. CHURCH

FOR A FEMINIST liberation Christianity, church means recreating redemptive communities, inclusive communities of equals—men and women together across all classes and races. Not only male domination but also clericalism must be dismantled. In liberating churches, ministry and community are dynamically interconnected, rather than being set up as a clerical caste ruling over a silenced, disempowered laity. The church is called to be a place where the redeemed community of equals is tasted and celebrated in nascent form. It is also called to be a place where the struggle is carried out against the continuing systems of domination that rule the world of society and church, and a place where we can heal from our own inner compulsions to empower ourselves only by dominating others.

In this mission, the church as redemptive community continues the risky witness of Jesus. It risks retaliation and must sustain its liberating and celebrative energy in the midst of hostility and counter-attack from the powers that be. Again and again, it fails and becomes a collaborator in domination. But the memory of Jesus and the power of divine Wisdom empower it to rise again and again.

RESPONSE BY RITA

I FIND IT interesting that Rosemary has dealt with the same material, the same story of creation, sin and grace, and redemption (God, Christ, and the church), interpreted in two different ways, in her chapters on what is oppressive and what is liberating in Christianity. By contrast, I have not told a Buddhist "grand narrative," nor have I dealt with the reverse of what is most problematic about Buddhism in my chapter about what is most liberating about Buddhism. Altogether, my focus has been less doctrinal than Rosemary's. I have not taken to task root symbols of the Buddhist tradition nor suggested that the longstanding mainstream interpretations of the Buddhist tradition are what have been limiting and damaging to women.

This is because I would claim that the most basic problems in Buddhism are not with the view but with the practice. I have proposed that, regarding women's full participation in Buddhism, an intolerable contradiction between view and practice is found throughout Buddhist history. The view is gender neutral and gender free, but the practice has favored men over women, and men's advantages have rarely been questioned. The Buddhist tradition itself has usually solved this contradiction by reference to standard interpretations of Buddhist belief in rebirth combined with the belief that the particularities of any specific rebirth are due to cause and effect (karma) extending over countless lifetimes. Buddhism has usually conceded that women have more difficult lives than men, regarding female rebirth as unfortunate, but attributes this misfortune, not to women's nature or men's nature, but to actions taken in past lives that result in the unfortunate situation of being reborn as a woman in a cultural situation that advantages men. Everyone who is now a man has probably been a woman in a previous life, and there is a good chance that the reverse is also true; since women can change into men and vice versa, positing a fixed men's nature or women's nature would make no sense. Furthermore, Buddhism, in its doctrines of egolessness and emptiness, has firmly denied that any phenomenon, not merely humans beings, whether men or women, has a fixed, immutable, independent, and changeless nature.

As I have already said, I am not convinced that traditional Buddhist explanations of women's present difficulties are adequately explained by appeal to karma inherited from past lives when there is so much evidence of *present* male dominance that is self-serving rather than necessary. But I would also claim that the solutions to this problem lie, not as much with further doctrinal developments as with attention to Buddhist practices, scrutinizing carefully to see if current practices really are in accord with the most basic Buddhist teachings—egolessness, emptiness, and indwelling Buddha-nature. Therefore, I have focused on two practices. One of them, the infrequency of women teachers, is problematic, both for women and more generally. The other is the practice of meditation and contemplation, which I regard as even more liberating than Buddhism's basic doctrinal messages because it is the vehicle for actually *realizing* that message. Interestingly, in my chapter on Buddhist practices, I did not focus on changes necessary to Buddhism, but on changes that I experienced through Buddhist practice and how Buddhist practice could help social activists and non-conformists. Buddhist practice itself has nothing to do with whether one is a man or a woman, but it is a method that would help both women and men transform themselves away from the damaged selves that result, at least in part, from harmful gender norms and practices and toward a more genuinely human mode of being.

In reflecting on the story and categories that Rosemary uses in both her chapters on liberation and oppression, I was hard put to imagine what equivalent story I could tell. It certainly wouldn't be the story of the life of the historical Buddha. (Note that Rosemary did not talk much of the life of Jesus either.) In each case, she begins with the category of anthropology and discussions of human nature deriving from the Genesis account of creation. The fact that there is no equivalent to creation in Buddhism is, I suspect, why I cannot come up with a parallel story. How would things begin, in Buddhist perspective? That, we are told is one of the great unanswerable questions. Thinking about them may be interesting, but it is not salvific. Things start with primal ignorance, but not in the sense that first there was nothing and then there was a "big bang" of ignorance, after which the rest unfolded. Buddhism talks of "beginningless time," of endlessly repeating patterns; ignorance is the origin only in the sense that each spinning of the wheel is set in motion by ignorance. Ignorance of what? The textbook answer is "things as they are," something well beyond words and concepts, except for the things we can eliminate. Most important to eliminate is duality, especially duality between a created and limited human nature and ultimate reality. As stated many times already, according to Buddhism, human beings already contain the seed of Buddhahood, which is their true nature and is not separate from ultimate reality. Thus, primal ignorance could also said to be a mistaken identity in which we simply do not realize our true nature. Why are people (and all other creatures) ignorant? There is no moment at which everything was okay and then ignorance reared its ugly head. There is no equivalent narrative to the narrative of the fall. Furthermore, Christian and Jewish narratives of the creation and the fall are highly gendered, and the meanings of those stories about gendered beings for contemporary men and women has been highly contested, as Rosemary shows. Accounts of ignorance simply are not gendered in Buddhism in the way in which accounts of creation and the fall are gendered in Christianity. Nor is ultimate reality gendered in Buddhism, unlike the assumption and argument that only male analogies were dignified enough for the Creator that held throughout most of the history of monotheism. Thus, my claim that in Buddhism, the most serious problems for women occur with the practices, with the institutional set-up of the religion, rather than with its view, its basic "theology."

I am not thereby trying to suggest that somehow Buddhism is better and requires less fixing. In fact, it is more difficult to explain how the practices of Buddhism surrounding gender could be so far off, given its gender neutral and gender inclusive view, than it is to explain why Christianity is institutionally male-dominated. Christian theology and its basic narratives are highly gendered and lend themselves somewhat easily to patriarchal interpretations if those with the power to interpret desire to use the texts in that way. The case for a feminist re-working of traditional Christianity is so obvious because its male-dominance is so pervasive at every level.

By contrast, many Buddhists are seduced into thinking that Buddhism simply does not require a feminist critique because of the even-handedness of Buddhist views of gender and the fact that it does not engage in women-blaming to explain the human situation. Furthermore, many Buddhists regard attempts to change political, economic, or social structures as doomed to failure because current arrangements are the outcome of karmic patterns so complex and so intertwined as to be unfathomable. Nor, as many people see it, is there much urgency to change present oppressive structures and institutions, given the inevitability of future lives. If I am forced to miss opportunities and experiences that would help me on my path in this life because I am a woman, I will get those opportunities at some point in the future. "Not to worry!" I am told. I will be reborn as a man and then will be able to do all those things that were denied to me in this life because of my sex.

Some people, I am sure, genuinely believe that such views support the idea that gender is irrelevant in the long run. To me it sounds like a glib "better luck next time," combined with smugness that "I must have done something right because I'm a male. That smugness, of course, justifies and perpetuates the status quo of a practice of male gender privilege combined with a belief that gender is ultimately irrelevant. This version of male privilege is more subtle than that presented by monotheistic religions, and, therefore, perhaps more tenacious.

PART IV

What Is Most Inspiring about the Other Tradition?

7. What I Have Learned from Buddhism

Rosemary Radford Ruether

L ET ME START out by making clear that my experience and knowledge of Buddhism are limited. I am not a scholar of Buddhism. I have read few of its classical texts. My experience of Buddhism has come primarily from some recent experiences of dialogue with Buddhists. For some twelve years I have participated in the International Buddhist-Christian Theological Encounter, founded by John Cobb, a Methodist theologian teaching at the Claremont School of Theology, and Masao Abe, a Japanese Buddhist scholar. Rita has also been a member of this dialogue. I have also attended international meetings of the Society for Buddhist-Christian Studies. I have read a few modern Buddhist writings, such as the work of Sulak Sivaraksa, a founder of the Engaged Buddhism movement. I also attended a key conference of the movement for Engaged Buddhism in Bangkok in 1997, which Sulak helped to organize.

The International Buddhist-Christian Theological Encounter does not assume that its participants are scholars of the other religious tradition. We meet as scholar-practitioners of our own traditions, who speak out of our traditions and dialogue with others speaking from their traditions. I have not tried to read classical texts or become a scholar of Buddhism, not because of any aversion to doing so, but primarily because I feel my plate is too full already with my present commitments.

But, as I have indicated in the chapter on my autobiographical roots of dialogue, for as long as I can remember, I have been averse to any form of religious exclusivism. I come from a family that brought together Catholics, Protestants, and Jews, in which my mother's best friends tended to attend the Friend's Meeting, as did I in my teenage years, while also attending Mass. Religious pluralism and inclusivism was the context of my developing interest in religious studies in college. My teachers in college and graduate school were of a world religions perspective and my earliest studies took me out of Christianity into other religions of the ancient Mediterranean world. These studies were based on the assumption that these religions were equal bearers of truth.

At a point in my intellectual development in my late twenties, I decided to recommit myself to a Catholic Christian religious identity. This decision was facilitated by the second Vatican Council in the early sixties and by the development of renewed and feminist liberation forms of Christianity among Catholics. This remains my primary religious community, not because I see this as the best or only place to be, but simply because it is my place to be. I believe in the finitude of all of our cultural identities. It is impossible to be all things. Each of our religious cultures is limited and partial, but we can and should expand our horizons to include insights from one another's religious cultures, and we should participate in them to some extent, just as we should become bi-lingual or multi-lingual.

But we can't learn all possible languages and cultures or live out all possibilities. Eventually we have to come down to some limited expression of cultural identity and focus on particular communities as primary places where we live and take responsibility for our group's well-being. It is in this spirit that I attend Mass in the Catholic university parish to which I belong and worship in the chapel services at the Methodist seminary where I teach. It is in this spirit that I have been a part of Jewish-Christian, Christian-Muslim, and Buddhist-Christian dialogues. Each of these dialogues has been quite distinct and has brought me different experiences of religious insight. In many ways I have found Buddhist-Christian dialogue to be the most insightful in terms of a transformation of my own world view.

These learnings from Buddhism have been gradual. As I indicated in my autobiographical chapter, I did not initiate entrance into Buddhist-Christian dialogue. Rather I was somewhat dragged into it by my former teacher John Cobb, in part so there would be more female participants. So I entered it with some question as to whether I wanted to spend my time in such an endeavor. My first couple of meetings with this dialogue group did not entirely assure me that this was for me.

To understand my experience it is important to understand that the International Buddhist-Christian Theological Encounter structured its first cycle of meetings in a particular way. For over ten years the Theological Encounter organized its dialogue as a discussion of parallel theological or doctrinal themes. They chose themes that seemed parallel in the two religious traditions and focused on examining their similarities and differences over a three day period.

The dialogue worked its way through a series of such parallel themes. Among these themes were Ultimate Reality: God or Nirvana; Material Existence: Creation or Maya; the Path of Transformation: Conversion or Enlightenment; the Founder: Buddha or Christ; and Religious Community: Church or Sangha. Each three-day meeting was spaced at eighteen-month to two-year intervals. At each meeting four primary papers were written on the topic, two by Christians and two by Buddhists representing somewhat different perspectives in their respective traditions. There were also response papers, by Buddhists to the Christian papers and by Christians to the Buddhist papers. This method allowed for a comprehensive interchange on the topic.

But this methodology also gave a fairly intellectual cast to the dialogue. Rather abstract metaphysical discussion predominated, but with little sense of what Buddhist or Christian religious experience might be all about. I found myself unsure whether I really wanted to devote myself to such abstract conversation, with so little experiential input. Never, for example, was it suggested that we might share a prayer or meditation experience from the two traditions.

At first Buddhism seemed to me somewhat similar to the traditions of metaphysical contemplation of neo-Platonism with which I was familiar from my studies in late antiquity and patristic Christianity. I remembered that my early teacher of Plotinus, Philip Merlan, a Viennese Jewish scholar, once pointed out in class that the teacher of both Plotinus and the Christian mystical theologian, Origen, in Alexandria, Egypt, bore a name that suggested a Buddhist background. Between India and Egypt in the early centuries of the Common Era lay trade routes that were routes for the transmission of ideas. Thus I was prepared to see a historical affinity between Buddhism and the rise of contemplative mysticism in Alexandrian Christianity in the third century.

During the first couple of sessions, I found myself revisiting some of my own discomfort with this neo-Platonic mystical tradition. For several years in the early sixties my husband and I had a close relationship to the Benedictine Abbey in Valyermo, California. We even became third order Benedictines. I spent some extensive retreat time at the monastery, immersing myself in the ancient Christian traditions of contemplative spirituality. At some point I became disenchanted with this path. On one occasion, while walking in the hills around the monastery trying to "get in touch with God," I had a distinct sense that all these efforts to "talk to God" were really just talking to oneself. I began to wonder whether an exclusive focus on individualized contemplation was not simply a kind of spiritual narcissism. I turned to social action as a more stimulating kind of spirituality, rooted in liberation theology.

Between August, 1966, and February, 1968, I engaged in an extensive correspondence with Thomas Merton (these letters have been published in *At Home in the World* (Orbis Books, 1995). My letters in this exchange have a somewhat aggressive tone that reflected my own disenchantment with monastic life. I felt the need to challenge Merton, as a leading exponent of Catholic monastic life and contemplative spirituality, about the viability of this way of life. I was asking at that time, what is the point of spending one's time focusing on the inner self in contemplative prayer, rather than doing something about injustice in the world?

Today I would see a need for a balance between these two spiritualities, the spirituality of activist engagement and the spirituality of inner renewal. Without prayer and nurturing one's inner self, one readily becomes burned out in social action. But Buddhism, as I first encountered it in the dialogue, seemed to be exclusively inward and monastic. It seemed like the other worldly path of contemplative spirituality whose adequacy I had questioned long ago. Again I wondered, is this enough? Is this a kind of inward-turning narcissism and irresponsibility toward the deep injustices of society. Where is Buddhism's social ethic?

Gradually the balance within Buddhism between the quest for enlightenment and the ethic of compassion became more evident. As the renewal movements of Engaged Buddhism became more prominent in the Buddhist-Christian Encounter, I became more interested in it. I will speak more about Engaged Buddhism later in this chapter. For the moment I want to turn to those patterns of metaphysics and world view that have come to be most inspiring to me, and which have partly reshaped my religious perspective. I don't claim to be stating these themes exactly as a Buddhist would state them, but rather as they have seemed meaningful to me.

First, there is the theme of co-dependent arising, which describes the nature of reality for Buddhism. Buddhism does not believe in a literal God of any gender who exists as an ontological being outside of the world. Their vision, as I understand it, sees reality as arising mysteriously from an ultimate Void and ultimately returning to this Void. What arises and returns to this ultimate Void are not ontologically separated subjects, but phenomena which are contingent and interdependent upon each other.

This view, to a large extent, corresponds with my own intuitive sense of the nature of reality. Whatever I call God is not some ontological being, some ultimate Mind, existing invisibly in a disembodied form beyond the world. Rather, what exists is this very creativity of inter-dependent co-arising, out of which all the inter-related phenomena of contingently existing reality burgeon forth and co-exist with each other, returning ultimately into the Void, to arise in new forms.

This perspective corresponds to my understanding of reality as it has been suggested in modern post-Newtonian physics. Since I first took physics in high school in 1953, I have had a sense of reality informed by the post-Newtonian perspective of an electro-magnetic field that is the basis of what we experience as sensible reality. I remember my high school physics teacher expounding to us the nature of atomic and subatomic particles. As one descends from the atomic to the sub-atomic level, we realize that our very experience of solid materiality is an illusion. The ulti-mate root of reality is the dance of energy in patterns whose nature—and even existence—we cannot definitively determine. The most we can say is that energy has tendencies to exist in certain patterns.

At this level of reality, the split between mind and body, spirit and matter, matter and energy disappears. Matter itself is energy in patterns of movement. As my physics teacher discussed this post-Newtonian understanding of ultimate reality, I felt a kind of thrill, as if we were touching ultimate mystery, perhaps what could be called God. But I also realized that it would be out of place to say this in a physics class. Modern physics is committed to a split between spiritual experience and mathe-matical "facts" that precludes making such connections.

But, more recently, many other spiritual seekers have recognized the similarities between the Buddhist sense of reality as co-dependent arising and post-Newtonian physics. Fritjof Capra expounded this thesis in his popular book, *The Tao of Physics* (1977). Significantly, in this new inter-est in the connection between the two, Eastern thought gives us a way to access experiencing this reality spiritually. This aesthetic, ethical, and mystical experience of the physical has been forbidden in the Western sci-entific dualism of objectivity and subjectivity.

Connected with this view of ultimate reality is an understanding of the self as a non-substantial matrix of experiences held together by our mortal organism and destined to pass away into that great Void of becoming. The Western notion of an ontological eternal soul separable from the body, taken over from Platonism, has never made sense to me. I would allow that there may be mysteries of our fate beyond death of which I am ignorant. Yet my own sense of myself is that of being a non-substantive self-conscious organism contingent on all other sensible phenomenon with which I am inter-related, destined to dissolve into the great Void of coming to be and passing away.

Both Christianity and Buddhism have cultivated a spirituality of "letting go of the ego," but this has meant something different in the two traditions. Christianity has put ultimate value on the immortality of the soul. The Christian understanding of letting go has focused on a self-depreciation that is often confused with antipathy to self-esteem. This has been particularly destructive to women, who have often lacked such adequate self-esteem.

The Buddhist focus on letting go of the ego is more a recognition, on a deeply insightful level, of one's own contingency and interconnection with all things. I think this can be understood as something quite different from an assault on a sense of self-esteem. I believe we are called to affirm the integrity of our personal center of being, in mutuality with the personal centers of all the other beings across the species, while at the same time accepting the transience of our personal selves. This acceptance of both the value and the transience of the self allows us to be awakened to a deep sense of kinship with and compassion for all the other transient beings with which we are interconnected.

Humans, like animals and plants, are living centers of organic life who exist for a season. Then the life force that holds our organism together fails, and we die. Our bodies disintegrate into their material components to enter the cycle of decomposition and then re-composition as other entities. The material substance of our bodies lives on in plants and animals, just as our bodies are composed from minute to minute of substances that were once parts of animals and plants, stretching back through time to prehistoric ferns and ancient biota that floated on the primal seas of the earth. Even before earth history, the material elements in our bodies were generated in the dust of exploding stars. Our kinship with all Earth creatures is global, linking us to all that exists today, to all that has been, and all that will be in the universe.

The Jewish and Christian traditions have cultivated deep fear of this decomposition process, seeing it as evil and the product of sin. To touch the decomposing is to be polluted, alienated from God, who is eternal and immutable. Traditionally, God is thought to be totally other from all mutability, from all coming to be and passing away. I believe we need a new spirituality that reconciles us with becoming, with coming to be and passing away, and that sees the divine as the ground of this process, rather than as alien to it. We need a contemplative process to help us immerse ourselves in our own roots in this process of growth, disintegration, and re-composition, seeing it as a wonderful mystery of life. We need psalms and meditations to make our kinship with all things in this transformative process an experience of wonder and awe, rather than an experience of fear and avoidance.

Such meditations do not in any way relieve us of our responsibility to one another here and now, but rather allow us to value each other all the more, since they are what we are and have now. We are called to live ethically and responsibly in relation to one another (that is, to all beings, not just human beings) within our life span. In that way we pass better possibilities on to our descendants. Conversion to a spirituality of non-striving, of liberation from the compulsive egoism that accompanies belief in one's ultimate immortality, allows a calm center to subsist, even while we actively engage in ethical concern and efforts to better the well-being of those around us.

This sense of contingency and the ethical call to interrelation is also expressed for me by the Buddhist theme of "compassion for all sentient beings." Buddhist spirituality calls for the development of the calm cen-'er through meditation and acceptance of one's contingency and lack of ·ltimate immortality. This does not lead to insensitivity to others' suffering, but to compassion for all sentient beings. Unlike Christianity, which, at best, extends its concern only to other humans, Buddhism calls for us to include all beings which are sentient, which can suffer.

This means compassion for animals as well as humans. Animals' rights and movements to end abuse of animals are, thus, supported by Buddhist sensibility. Christianity has seen humans alone as valuable. Animals are simply instruments of human need. This is based on the notion that only humans have rational, eternal souls. Such a separation of human and animal, based on ideas of who possesses or lacks an immortal soul, has tended to further the abuse of animals.

A key theme in Buddhist spirituality that has become particularly helpful to me is the cultivation of "mindfulness." Mindfulness, as I understand it, is simply a constant reminder to oneself to slow down, to become fully aware of where one is, here and now. Western culture and psychology stress speed and constant anticipation of the future. One is never where one is now, but is always pressing forward to something else that is not yet, but is still to be. This has given Western culture a powerful dynamism for change. While this has precipitated some helpful changes that have benefited many people, such as technologies that increase production of goods, medical innovations and the like, the ecological crisis is now making us aware of the destructive side of this endless pressing toward the "not yet." The world is being rushed, not to a millennial blessedness, but to a destructive breakdown.

We need to rediscover the actual processes by which the Earth renews itself, and reintegrate our own human processes into this slower and more sustainable pattern of change through disintegration and recomposition, the rhythms of day and night, summer and winter. We need to learn to live fully and deeply where we are at the moment, rather than endlessly rushing forward, which leaves us unfulfilled in the long run, because we have never lived where we are.

A great deal of the violence in Western culture is rooted in this rushing toward what is not yet, which combines with a lack of ability to be where we are now. This combination generates a high level of frustration in Western society that again and again leads us to push others out of our way when they impede our rush, and even to kill them. The phenomenon of road rage is an apt and telling eruption of such violence.

The cultivation of mindfulness is a meditation technique that stops this rush forward toward what is not yet and turns us to where we are now. I often try to practice this while driving. Here I am in a car, moving too slowly on the freeway. Instead of becoming angry because the cars ahead of me are moving slowly, impeding my rush to get somewhere else, I turn to where I am now. I become aware of my breathing, of my body sitting in the car, of all the cars, houses, and trees that surround me here and now. I cease to be frustrated, but instead can be where I am, fully in the present.

This practice of awareness of the present is not in conflict with preparing for new possibilities ahead, but makes me more efficient in pursuing them, as I take each moment one at a time. Such a practice of mindfulness seems to me a wonderfully practical mysticism. It is not about some other world. One doesn't have to be in a monastery to practice it. It is about living one's life fully and intentionally wherever one may be in each precious moment.

Cultivating a calm center with which one learns to live mindfully in each moment calms aggression and violence. This is an important component in Buddhist understandings of peace and non-violence. Engaged Buddhism is a movement that particularly has mined these elements of Buddhist spirituality and made the connections between the individual center of experience and all that is interconnected with it, or, to put it in more Western terms, between the individual and society. Society does not just mean human society, but our relations to all living things, to animals and plants, air and water, as well as humans.

Engaged Buddhists have been prominent in movements for animal protection and for peace and non-violence. I have been particularly inspired by the expressions of Engaged Buddhism which have been developing the social aspects of Buddhist spirituality, curbing the tendency for this spirituality to become passive and individualized. A central teaching of Buddhism is that the path of enlightenment is a process of overcoming the obsessions of greed, hatred, and delusion. Sulak Sivaraksa particularly has developed the social reading of these common Buddhist themes.

These three impulses, greed, hatred and delusion, sum up the driven self convinced of its own immortality, and seeking to extend itself infinitely. Greed means seeking to own and control as much as possible. Hatred points to the egoistic self-seeking of competing with everyone else for power and possessions. Delusion is manifested in the egoistic self that denies its own contingency and cloaks its greed and power drives , in the false belief that, denying mortality it can thereby escape its own end.

Sulak sees the global capitalist-militarist system that rules the world as the expression of this ego-driven self writ large. The neo-liberal or free market capitalist system is driven by greed, the desire to extend the egoistic self infinitely to possess more and more consumer goods. It is driven by consumerism, the belief that one can achieve happiness, invulnerability and security from want and need by accumulating and consuming more and more goods. Since goods are not infinitely available, consumerism necessarily creates a system of global injustice while at the same time devastating the Earth. A wealthy elite concentrates more and more wealth in its hands, at the expense of the rest of humanity and the Earth.

This system of capitalist consumerism also generates violence toward and hatred of others. Its greedy egoism assumes competitive relations with all other beings, a belief that one can expand one's control of wealth only by diminishing the wealth of others. From this competitive stance toward others flow violence and warfare. Global capitalism is intrinsically militarist, seeking to monopolize weapons of violence to control one's unjust monopoly of wealth.

Finally, the capitalist-militarist system covers up its own destructive reality with lies. It claims it will bring democracy, justice, and peace to all, when it actually can only fuel injustice and violence. Its lies become a system of delusion, misleading both the victims and the victimizers about the reality of what is actually going on. False ideologies are the cultural underpinnings of the system of global capitalist-militarism. These false ideologies that delude us about the reality of this system dominate the press, the pronouncements of governments, and the teaching of economists and other idealogues who buttress this system of lies and delusion.

Sulak's analysis of the global system of greed, hatred and delusion is very compelling to me and is a powerful complement to Christian liberation theology, to which he acknowledges his debt. In liberation theology and engaged Buddhism, both Christianity and Buddhism offer powerful social interpretations of their traditions that can support each other in a global struggle for a just, peaceful, and harmonious world. The Buddhist version of a social spirituality can supply what is often lacking in social Christianity—namely, the shaping of a calm, and peaceful interior self engaged in freeing itself from the egoistic impulses of greed, hatred, and delusion. So equipped, we are aided in seeking to free society from the collective ills generated by these ego-drives.

This Buddhist path to socio-economic liberation was opened to me especially by my participation, in December of 1997, in a conference on Alternatives to Consumerism sponsored by Sulak's center for Engaged Buddhism, held in Bangkok, Thailand. That event brought together 250 people from 26 nations, most of them from Asia. Although the participants included Christians and Hindus, Buddhist spirituality pervaded the assembly; communities of Buddhist monks chanted at the opening of each morning's session. We met in the Buddhamandala Park in Bangkok. The park is laid out in the shape of a mandala with winding waterways, flower gardens, and temple pavilions, centering around a huge statue of a walking Buddha. We slept, ate, and met together in the pavilions. Some of us imitated the umbrella tents hung on trees that Buddhist monks construct for sleeping in the forests; others laid out sleeping bags in the pavilions.

The conference gave one a taste of the synthesis of spirituality and social organizing. We glimpsed the bringing together of resistance to a destructive global system of consumerism combined with the construction of alternative communities. These communities live a sustainable way of life that is both meditative and practical. Many grassroots groups from all over Asia shared experiences with each other about how they had developed such communal movements of resistance and alternative ways of living. We glimpsed ways of struggling against poverty and ecological devastation that are not based on a rush to imitate the Western ways of production and consumption. Rather, such communities draw on local resources in ways that both overcome poverty and restore peace and beauty to communities and their environment.

The International Buddhist-Christian Theological Encounter has now moved to a new phase of dialogue that is more intentionally focused on social justice issues. From dialogue on commonalities or differences of doctrine, we now have moved to solidarity in common social concerns, learning to use the rich resources of other traditions to address these social concerns.

The first session of the new stage of the dialogue focused on ecology. We asked how each tradition approaches the environment and how these approaches provided resources for responding to the ecological crisis. It is significant that for Buddhism the first item in the dialogue on social justice has been ecology, while Christianity has tended to get around to this issue only belatedly, if at all. This points to the wider vision of compassion in Buddhism for all sentient beings, while Christianity has been pervasively anthropocentric. Christians are suspicious of any concern for "nature." Nature is seen as unconnected with the "true God," defined as the God of history against the gods of nature. I will discuss this question of Christian problems with ecological spirituality more fully in my final chapter in this volume.

Our second topic for dialogue was war and peace. The two Christian papers focused on the just war tradition. They were particularly concerned to denounce what they saw as a tendency for just war to become "holy war" in Christianity. They suggested that, despite the theoretical commitment to love and peace in Christianity, there are key dynamics in this tradition that glorify violence and war. While I myself agreed with this critique and, indeed, wrote one of the papers for this dialogue, I became aware of the aggressive tone of Christians as they denounced their own tradition. Also noteworthy was the absence of any Christian from the peace churches, such as the Quaker church, whose presence I think would have brought a different perspective and style to the dialogue.

The Buddhists also critiqued their own tradition for not having been consistent in the ethic of peace. They pointed to periods in history when Buddhism had been associated with the state and condoned war. But their focus was on the cultivation of inner peace. For them, there could not be real peace in society without the nurturing of peacefulness within each person. The Christians tended to dismiss this connection of inner peace and social peace. This was based on the anthropology, shared by those Christians, of an Augustinian tradition that believed that humans are irreparably "fallen."

For these Christians of mainline Protestant and Catholic tradition, the self lacks the capacity for goodness, and so cultivating inner peace was not seen as really possible. Peace, like law and order, needs to be imposed from without, since humans are themselves incorrigibly violent. Clearly a deep difference in anthropological assumptions about the capacity of humans for goodness was uncovered in this discussion, although not adequately explored. Again I was struck by the aggression with which Christians insisted on the aggressive nature of the person, dismissing without question the alternative possibility that humans might be capable of peacefulness through spiritual development.

The dialogue in August of 2000 focused on poverty and economic justice. Both Christianity and Buddhism share a monastic tradition in which renunciation of wealth is the highest ethic. What does this mean for Christians and Buddhists today? How can it be connected fruitfully with questions of the global disparity between extreme wealth for a minority of humans and grinding poverty and destitution for the majority? Our dialogue has only begun to ask about the meaning of this move from discussing similarities and differences to expressing some solidarity in the face of a massive, common problem. We are just starting to ask how Buddhists and Christians can begin to work together for peace, economic justice and environmental harmony.

This discussion finds an important venue today in the meetings of the Parliament for the World's Religions. The first meeting of the Parliament, in 1893 in Chicago, brought Asian religions to a public platform in the United States for the first time. The second meeting in Chicago one hundred years later resulted in the development of a Global Ethic. This Global Ethic demonstrated a great deal of consensus on the basic social ethical concerns that face humans today. The third meeting, in 1999 in Cape Town, South Africa, sought to translate the Global Ethic into a body of concrete social projects. These projects draw on the principles of the Global Ethic to confront the major social institutions of society and call them to account.

As the Bangkok meeting on Alternatives to Consumerism demonstrated, those of us engaged in interreligious dialogue are now challenged to move to solidarity. We need to ask how we can create a more just and peaceful world, not only in some abstract future, but one in which we are able to begin to live today. I believe that Buddhist spirituality offers central insights on how we learn to do that. As Sulak Sivaraska would say, we need to start by "learning to breathe properly." Learning to breathe properly is fundamental. Only by basing ourselves in peacefulness and just relationality, here and now, can we become at all effective in doing something to create such relations around us.

RESPONSE BY RITA

I FIND IT intriguing that our chapters on what is most liberating about our own tradition and what we most admire about the other tradition are almost mirror images of each other. Rosemary wrote about Christianity's potential to be a voice promoting a prophetic, liberationist framework that subverts the patriarchal reading in her chapter on what is liberating in Christianity. In my chapter on what I most admire about Christianity, I discuss its "prophetic voice," explaining and defending my use of that term in my own work as a Buddhist feminist. In my chapter on what is most liberating for me about Buddhism, I wrote at length about the impact meditation has had on my life and thinking, especially its ability to tame aggression and develop the strength to be gentle in all situations. In her chapter "What I Have Learned from Buddhism," Rosemary describes her slow discovery of the virtues of Buddhist "mindfulness" practices and how much they can contribute to socially engaged spirituality. She writes,

> The Buddhist version of a social spirituality can supply what is often lacking in social Christianity—namely, the shaping of a calm, and peaceful interior self engaged in freeing itself from the egoistic impulses of greed, hatred, and delusion. So equipped, we are aided in seeking to free society from the collective ills generated by these ego-drives.

I am also intrigued by Rosemary's observations about the 1999 meetings of the International Buddhist-Christian Theological Encounter, which discussed war and peace. She observes that the Buddhists insisted on the need for each person to nurture individual peacefulness if there is to be general, social peace, and that the Christians dismissed the connection between inner peace and social peace. She writes, ". . . I was struck by the aggression with which Christians insisted on the aggressive nature of the person, dismissing without question the alternative possibility that humans might be capable of peacefulness through spiritual development."

She attributes this difference to different anthropologies in the two traditions. The Christians were speaking for an Augustinian reading of the human condition as irreparably "fallen," while the Buddhists were working out of the basic Buddhist perspective that all sentient beings possess "Buddha-nature" or "inherent enlightenment," which is more basic than self-centeredness and negative habitual patterns. I tend to

160

share that analysis of the source of these differences, which I discussed in my response to Rosemary's chapter on oppressive aspects of Christianity. I would suggest that direct dialogue on this issue might be important, though it is difficult for me to understand how the interpretation of Christianity that stresses fallen human nature, original sin, and vicarious atonement could be liberating or inspiring.

Is the way in which we mirror each other's concerns accidental? Would others come to similar conclusions? To me, it seems that an even-handed analysis of the two traditions made by someone not involved in either tradition would be likely to reach similar conclusions. And perhaps our mirroring of each other is proof of John Cobb's idea that dialogue promotes mutual transformation in which each tradition learns about itself and changes internally through dialogue. Or perhaps the fact that both of us share a similar feminist orientation predisposes us to notice the same things about our own and each other's traditions.

I would like to end with several comments about Rosemary's impressions of mindfulness. First, basic mindfulness practices are quite different from the contemplative (Christian) practices that she describes early in her chapter. Mindfulness practices, which usually use the breath as the reference point for the practice, are not attempts to understand an idea or a belief system or to "get in touch" with ultimate reality. Although anything could be the object of mindfulness practices, the breath is often chosen as the focus of meditation because of its neutrality and universality. Rather than instilling some idea in peoples' minds, mindfulness of breathing develops the mind's ability to hold its attention steadily on some object and to remain vividly in the present, moment by moment, whatever may be happening. Mindfulness practice is not even a deliberate attempt to be peaceful rather than agitated, though that is its effect. Given that it is a contentless technique, the question of whether it faces inward or outward doesn't really apply. It is hard for me to imagine mindfulness practices reinforcing the "spiritual narcissism" that Rosemary finds so problematic. In fact, one of the most important points to be made about mindfulness practices is that they are far from being a self-indulgent waste of time. As both of us have discovered, social action unnourished by mindfulness meditation is very likely to lead to burnout and aggression. That point cannot be made too often.

On the other hand, contemplative practices, which are found in Buddhism as well as in Christianity, involve ideas or content. One could contemplate the existence of God or the Four Noble Truths, for example.

Therefore, contemplative practices cannot be religiously neutral in the way that mindfulness of the breath is neutral. Depending on the content of the contemplations, they could pull one "inward" or "outward" and, given certain content, could promote "spiritual narcissism." In my view, what is significant about contemplation is the way in which it helps one internalize what one is learning, in contrast to more academic methods of gathering and grasping information, as I indicated in my chapter on what is liberating about Buddhism. However, I cannot imagine trying to practice contemplation without the foundation of mindfulness meditations. My guess is that it could be rather boring and unsatisfying to do so. At least that's what happened to me when I tried to incorporate the Jewish daily liturgy, which could be regarded as a contemplative exercise, into my life without any prior experience of mindfulness practices.

I have avoided the term Buddhist meditation for a reason. Mindfulness of the breath is widely practiced by Buddhists, but it is not ideologically Buddhist or non-Buddhist. Breath is breath; it is the same for both Christians and Buddhists. There is not a Christian way of practicing mindfulness of the breath as opposed to a Buddhist way. Because of this neutrality, mindfulness can easily be practiced by anyone of any religious persuasion. And because of its healing power, it would be beneficial if mindfulness practice became much more widespread, so that people did not have to stumble upon it by good luck or fortunate experiences, as happened to both Rosemary and myself.

Finally, mindfulness is a discipline. It is best practiced on a daily, or at least a regular basis. It is not something that one "gets" by understanding it theoretically. Reading books about mindfulness is not enough. One actually has to sit, following the breath, breath by breath, noting the thoughts that come and go. I would challenge and encourage all who are inspired by their idea of what mindfulness practice involves to actually develop a regular discipline of mindfulness practice in addition to the moments of mindfulness occasioned by circumstances.

8. What Buddhists Could Learn from Christians

RITA M. GROSS

OR ME, THE topic of what Buddhists might learn from Christians, or how Christianity may have influenced my own thinking is very convoluted, for obvious reasons. I have practiced three religious traditions seriously and have had some experience with several more traditions; beyond that, I have studied even more religious traditions. Who can say for sure which elements of my thinking came from where?

As religious traditions become more familiar with each other, I suspect my situation will become more common, without people necessarily being personally involved in more than one religious tradition. In a religiously plural world, people cannot help being at least minimally familiar with other religious traditions. In a religiously plural world, it is in everyone's best interests for the various religions to develop respect and sympathy for one another. As the religions' knowledge of each other grows through dialogue and comparative studies, various features of other religions are bound to rub off from time to time. It is difficult, if one has genuine and accurate knowledge of multiple religious traditions, to claim that any one tradition is complete and perfect or not to be impressed by certain aspects of other traditions. In such instances, learning something from another tradition and adopting one of its practices or ideas makes sense. This is in keeping with one of the major rules for interreligious exchange: the purpose of such exchange is to learn from the other tradition and possibly to expand or change one's own tradition, not to convert members of the other tradition, as was stressed in our introductory dialogue on dialogue. I see no reason to fear or resist this process.

For me, the process of identifying what might have carried over from monotheism into Buddhism is complex indeed. I did not consciously retain elements of monotheistic thinking because I thought Buddhism was incomplete. I was a feminist; I had become a Buddhist; therefore, I would be a feminist Buddhist—end of story, it seemed to me. Sometime in the mid-eighties, John Cobb suggested that I might want to think about whether I would be so outspokenly feminist as a Buddhist if I had not had any experience with Judaism or Christianity, if I had always been Buddhist and had been brought up in a traditional Buddhist environment. He had his doubts about that, he told me, suggesting that I should acknowledge my sources, or at least consider the possibility that my feminism stemmed more from the prophetic traditions of monotheistic religions than from anything Buddhist.

I took his suggestion seriously. What he said made sense. Western feminism clearly was in continuity with the prophetic stream found in the Hebrew Bible, and, to a lesser extent in my view, in the New Testament. There is no similar stream in Buddhist thought. It is not that Buddhism lacks a social ethic, as is sometimes claimed, but that its social ethic takes a form different from active confrontations with injustice and calls for reform of the social-political order. I found his suggestion that dialogue between religious traditions should be a process of mutual transformation quite appropriate and helpful. I began to present some of my own thinking as the result of an internal dialogue, an internal process of mutual transformation between the prophetic traditions of Judaism and Christianity on the one hand, and Buddhism on the other hand. I was especially interested in what might result from a serious conversation between the Buddhist emphasis on compassion and the Christian prophetic emphasis on justice and righteousness. Then and now, I would claim that these two ways of approaching social ethics are subtly but significantly different from each other, and have a good bit to say to each other. I also would claim that the discussion still has not been taken up in a serious manner between Buddhists and Christians.

This suggestion was presented as an important part of my book *Buddhism after Patriarchy: A Feminist History, Analysis, and Reconstruction of Buddhism* in a short but crucial chapter titled "Resources for a Buddhist Feminism." In that chapter, I claimed mutual transformation between Buddhism and feminism (not Christianity) as one of my resources for developing a Buddhist feminism and stated what that meant to me. I was ". . . taking permission, as a Buddhist, to use the prophetic voice."[1] I also stated that by "Biblical prophecy," I meant ". . . social criticism, protest against misuse of power, vision for a social order more nearly expressing justice and equity, and, most importantly, willingness actively to seek that more just and equitable order through whatever means are appropriate and necessary."[2] I explained further that, "in taking permission to use the prophetic voice as a Buddhist, I am seeking to empower compassion, as understood so well in Buddhist social ethics, by direct infusion of concern for righteousness, for the actual manifestation in Buddhist societies of Buddhism's compassionate vision."[3]

Buddhists' reactions to these passages caught me by surprise. I was not expecting this suggestion to be among the most controversial parts of my book. If I can summarize accurately, it seems that there were two main objections: first, I was subjecting Buddhism to evaluation and correction by monotheism and advocating a simple borrowing from Judaism and Christianity, which Buddhism didn't need because of its own self-sufficiency; and, second, distaste for the prophetic voice itself, claims that it is strident and oppressive, that it promotes intolerance, self-righteousness, and sometimes violence. Responding to these objections was one of the more significant elements of my paper to those who had participated in the conference on *Buddhism after Patriarchy* held in Toronto in 1995.

Revisiting those issues now, a number of years later, is interesting. I'm not sure what I would do if I were writing the book today, but I doubt I would retract anything and would only seek to express certain things more skillfully.

I will respond in several ways to the criticism that use of the prophetic voice involves inappropriate judgement by and borrowing from Judaism and Christianity. First, I don't think I could have made a stronger case that Buddhist feminism is necessitated by *Buddhist* views about the ultimate irrelevance and non-existence of gender. Buddhist feminism is *not* a direct borrowing from monotheistic feminism, nor does my work depend on imitating Rosemary, as one critic suggested in a comment that particularly galled me. Buddhist feminism does not need

---

1. Rita M. Gross, *Buddhism after Patriarchy: A Feminist History, Analysis, and Reconstruction of Buddhism* (Albany, NY: State University of New York Press, 1993), p. 134.
2. Ibid.
3. Ibid., pp. 234–35.

the prophetic voice, in the sense that it could not emerge or articulate itself except by incorporating aspects of Christianity into itself. I would want to maintain that one can make a case, purely on Buddhist terms, for Buddhist feminism, and I believe I amply demonstrated that case in my work. I would also maintain that if feminism were incompatible with Buddhism, all the "borrowing" in the world wouldn't help. So on the one hand, against some voices, I would maintain, as I did in my response paper, that if one removed from the book the few pages in which I suggested that Buddhists might want to take permission to use the prophetic voice as Buddhists, nothing would change regarding the arguments or the conclusions of the book. Perhaps it would be fair to say that, in my view, the prophetic voice is a very useful resource for Buddhist feminism, but is by no means the sole justification for a Buddhist feminism, or the foundation on which it stands or falls.

But second, I want to say to those same critics, "So what's the problem? Jews and Christians developed the prophetic voice and now Buddhists are taking permission to speak with it. What is the problem with that?" The source of a practice or an idea has nothing to do with its relevance. Some Buddhists who object to suggestions that the prophetic voice could be useful may be reacting to generations of negative evaluations of Buddhism by Christians. It is understandable that some Buddhists would find the prophetic voice unappealing for such reasons and not feel comfortable using it. But that does not logically invalidate altogether the cogency or relevance of the prophetic voice for Buddhism. Others probably object to what they call "borrowing." But the prophetic voice spoken by a Buddhist cannot be simply borrowed from Judaism or Christianity; it will have its own intonations and nuances because its speakers are speaking it with their own accent. *Inspiration* is probably a better word than *borrowing* for this process, given that mutual transformation is completely different from borrowing, the taking of something wholesale from one tradition and inserting it into another. Finally, I say to those critics that we no longer live in a world in which religious traditions are segregated from one other. In such a world it is futile to rail against influences from other traditions coming into one's own. It is more appropriate to be steeped enough in one's own tradition that these influences become inspirations, rather than insertions or borrowings.

Distaste for the prophetic voice may be a personal preference, of course, but I would argue that dismissing it altogether as always inappropriate, always strident and self-righteous, is simply inaccurate. Though I did not emphasize the point, I did suggest that the prophetic voice could also benefit from mutual transformation; training in meditation and the Buddhist emphasis on gentleness, I suggested, could modulate that sometimes strident voice.[4] Further conversations with the one person who most strongly expressed distaste for the prophetic voice revealed that our differing perspectives probably came from quite different personal experiences with that voice. My friend was a minister's daughter who recalled the prophetic voice mainly as admonishing and punishing, criticizing and demanding. Certainly it is quite possible to receive that kind of indoctrination as to what the prophetic voice means.

In my own case, when I used the phrase "prophetic voice," my main reference points were how I had experienced that voice in the Hebrew Bible and Judaism. For significant and formative years, some of my main mentors were rabbis. One of them used the prophetic voice as the basis for his passionate defense of the civil rights movement, which his congregation often resented. Others used the prophetic voice as the basis for their anti-war stance during the Vietnam era. One of them even used the prophetic voice as the basis for helping women obtain illegal abortions in the mid to late sixties, before Roe vs. Wade. In addition, I frequently studied the prophetic literature of the Hebrew Bible and experienced its use in Jewish liturgy. I'm still convinced by those examples. I have nothing to reject about those religious resources and experiences. By that time, I had largely forgotten about Jesus and, in any case, it would then never have occurred to me to include him in the prophetic voice. The Jesus I had learned about was obedient above all, and the only purpose of his life was to die a wretched death to make up for all the sins of humanity. If that's the prophetic voice, I, too, have extreme distaste for it. Only some years later, when I read Christian feminists' understandings of Jesus as a social reformer who took the side of the oppressed, did I see how Jesus could be part of the stream of the prophetic voice. I'm convinced by their arguments, even though it is now an abstract point in terms of my own religious understandings. But Jesus, understood as Christian feminists understand him, could easily be one note in that prophetic voice of which I speak.

Would I still use that phrase? As a Buddhist, I'm more interested in skillful means and getting the job done than in defending language and

---

4. Ibid., p. 235.

positions. If the phrase prophetic voice is an insurmountable obstacle to other Buddhists because of its Jewish and Christian associations, I'd rather give up the phrase than have other Buddhist reject what I think is behind the phrase.

At this point, I would like to turn to what is behind the phrase, to explore more closely whether there is something Buddhists could learn from Christians, or, if the word *learn* is too strong for some, to explore what about Christianity might be inspiring to Buddhists. To do this, I will need to summarize what I understand to be the Buddhist position on compassion, social ethics, and concern for others.

Buddhists may perhaps be unhappy with me because they think I am perpetuating the old stereotype that Buddhism is a religion of individual effort and salvation, with no concern for the world at large, but that is not my intention—nothing could be further from the truth. All Buddhists emphasize the importance of being kind to all beings; the first discipline on the path is to avoid harming beings. It is commonly said that we know this is the right thing to do simply because we know that we do not want to suffer and it takes no special insight to realize that all other beings feel the same way. The basic disciplines of Buddhism include "right livelihood," which means not engaging in livelihoods that cannot be executed without harming sentient beings. Furthermore, it is hard to image a more altruistic perspective than that of Mahayana Buddhism and the way of the Bodhisattva, who dedicates not only what could be accomplished in this lifetime, but also infinite future lives, toward promoting the well-being of all sentient beings. This path is based on understanding that liberation cannot be something individual; it makes no sense to proclaim one's own freedom in a world in which others are still enslaved. Such a vision is in accord with fundamental Buddhist teachings about universal and all-pervasive interdependence and the ultimate lack of difference between self and other, due to the emptiness of both. As pointed out in an earlier chapter, Buddhism teaches that when individuals begin to gain some ease from their own convoluted knottings, the natural tendency is to extend that ease and relaxation because our fundamental nature is *bodhicitta* ("awakened heart" in the sense of being awake to all suffering and wanting to do something about it), not the self-centeredness of private ego.

Thus, in terms of *view*, both Buddhism and Christianity talk about the importance of helping others, of being kind and generous, of acting so as to promote others' well-being above one's own. That is not the aspect of social vision that I have in mind when I discuss the prophetic voice. I am more concerned about *method* or *action*. (I am using traditional Buddhist categories here.) How would one be most able to help all sentient beings? The Buddhist answer is that if one were fully awake, a Buddha, or at least very advanced spiritually, one would have the skill and wisdom to know how truly to help beings and what to do. Short of that development, it is questionable how much one can help, whatever one's intentions may be, because one may still be acting on the basis of confused ego rather than *bodhicitta*. Therefore, the most useful thing one can do to help others is to engage in deep spiritual practice oneself, which often means withdrawing from worldly activities and practicing in solitude—social disengagement rather than social engagement. To understand Buddhists accurately, it must be understood that such social disengagement is not motivated by anti-social self-interest, but rather by deep-rooted intention to become of genuine service to all sentient beings. Nevertheless, social dis-engagement often seems to be preferred to social engagement. One is not encouraged to regard trying to improve society as a spiritually appropriate activity.

This attitude may well stem from a deeply rooted traditional Buddhist perspective; samsara (conventional cyclic existence) is unworkable and cannot be fixed. It must be left behind. This judgement seems to be applied especially to social, political, and economic systems. Buddhist ethical thought has thoroughly explored appropriate *individual* conduct. Right speech, right action, right livelihood, and non-harming have all been thoroughly discussed. However, for an outlook that is so thoroughly imbued with an understanding of all-pervasive interdependence, Buddhist thought seems strangely lacking in discussions of ethically appropriate *social, collective* systems and discussions of how an oppressive, unjust system undermines and sabotages individual ethical growth and maturity. For example, though Buddhists have recognized for a long time that male dominance makes women's lives difficult and often limits women from being able to practice, there is little traditional literature that finds male dominance ethically flawed. More problematic, I do not know of Buddhist literature that encourages me to criticize male dominance, to seek to undermine and change male dominant systems. (To be fair to Buddhists, it must be pointed out that analyses of systemic or structural violence and the discovery that human social institutions are due to human agency, not divine fiat or the cosmic order, are also relatively recent in Western and Christian thought. Only with these discoveries can it be understood that our social conventions can be changed, for better or for worse, by human agency.)

In traditional Buddhism, any justification for the role of the social critic and reformer is further limited by traditional ideas of karma—cause and effect—and rebirth, as already noted in my previous response to Rosemary's comments on what can be liberating about Christianity. An effect of traditional ideas of karma and rebirth can be to promote passivity and lack of a critical perspective vis á vis the status quo, to regard it as the inexorable workings of karma rather than unjust oppression. For example, regarding the way in which oppressive social systems limit individuals, it would undoubtedly be said that, just as evil deeds promote rebirth as a vicious animal who has little chance of accumulating merit, so evil deeds result in rebirth into a social situation that limits one's ability to accumulate merit. I have read innumerable texts urging one to regard misfortune, in the form of being the recipient of someone's enmity or cruelty, as good fortune in disguise because it allows one to ripen negative karma from the past, thus getting rid of it, as well as to practice the *paramita* (transcendent virtue) of patience. The word *oppression* does not occur in Buddhist contexts to my knowledge. Would one be encouraged also to regard oppression as good fortune in disguise which helps one purify negative karma? I do not know of Buddhist literature that guides one in saying, "No, this is unjust; this is oppression and I am not going to simply accept it because it is harmful to me and limits me from developing my potential as a human being and a bodhisattva." I know of no literature that encourages or guides one in applying the traditional Buddhist virtue of *prajna*—the discriminating awareness that enables us to properly differentiate *this* from *that*—to discriminating what is unjust and inappropriate in social systems from what is inevitable, though painful, in social living. I know of no traditional literature permitting one to regard social protest and social criticism as bodhisattva activity, or guiding one in how to engage in such activities specifically as a Buddhist and a bodhisattva. And I question whether it is appropriate to regard the social-political-economic orders as only and inevitably samsaric and, therefore, not worthy of Buddhist attention, impossible as a realm for bodhisattva activity.

I have always regarded my activities as a Buddhist feminist to be central in how I attempt to fulfill my bodhisattva vows. Furthermore, I do not see a fundamental contradiction between the more traditional Buddhist attitudes urging us to regard misfortune, even in the form of oppression, as a way of purifying negative karma and the prophetic voice of the social critic who attempts to change the system that leads to oppression in the first place. The former attitude would purify the stridency and self-righteousness that can damage the effectiveness of the prophetic voice while the latter attitude would purify the passivity that simply allows and leads to further oppression.

In summary, then, I have looked in traditional Buddhist ethical literature in vain for three things that I find important and for which I do find resources in the prophetic voice. First is the recognition that it is important to engage in ethical analyses of political, social, economic systems, not limiting ethical discourse to norms for individuals. Second, it is important to be able to discriminate what are unethical social systems and call their operations "oppression," even if on another level, they could also represent karmic ripening. Third, it is important to be able to regard active resistance to oppression and attempts to find an ethically more appropriate social order as part of spiritual discipline and bodhisattva activity.

This perceived lack of guidance in Buddhist teachings for activities that I experience as one of the most compelling dimensions of my bodhisattva activities, as well as active opposition I have frequently received from Buddhists, including those in my own community, encouraged me to take seriously John Cobb's suggestion that I look into the sources of my activities as a Buddhist feminist social critic more closely. It still makes sense to me that Buddhist social engagement in general may well owe something to Buddhist interactions with non-Buddhist thought, including Christianity. Some Buddhists have said that the rise of Engaged Buddhist movements, which are sometimes regarded as a Buddhist versions of liberation theology, proves that Buddhists don't need the prophetic voice because none of the leaders of these movements have appealed to it to develop their activist stances. But I would reply that such an observation is simplistic. These movements were developed by leaders who were well aware of global movements of social criticism and social protest, many of which, directly or indirectly, owed something to the prophetic voice, even though that was often unacknowledged. Nevertheless, my deeper question to such critics is "What's the problem? What's at stake in being so attached to the idea that Buddhism doesn't need and couldn't use any inspiration from anything non-Buddhist?"

The only valid counter-argument that I can accept is that possessing the prophetic literature and access to the prophetic voice does not, by itself, mean that these resources will be used to promote justice and equity. Given the colonialism, racism, and sexism that have so often been perpetrated by those whose heritage includes the prophetic voice, Buddhists could perhaps make the case that, given that actions speak louder than words, little is to be gained by listening to the prophetic voice. As Rosemary has shown in her chapter on what is oppressive in Christianity, at least regarding justice and equity for women, historically this prophetic voice has done almost nothing and has rarely been spoken. Just as traditional ideas of karma have been used to promote acceptance of the status quo, the prophetic voice has been used to promote obedience rather than social criticism. Even if we are aware of the prophetic literature and the prophetic voice, somehow, we still need the motivation and the *prajna* to activate it to speak for justice and equity, without stridency and self-righteousness.

If I were to employ a different tactic today, I would seek to develop a justification on purely Buddhist grounds for the same activities and attitudes that I then attributed, at least in part, of my knowledge of and respect for the prophetic voice. I believe it is possible to interpret traditional ideas of karma and rebirth in ways that could promote and justify social criticism and social activism, and my attempt to do so follows. My reasons for developing such interpretations of karma may well still have roots in my exposure to the prophetic voice. Who knows? But if other Buddhists find it difficult to acknowledge the power and validity of the prophetic voice, it would be good skillful means to develop other ways of talking about why bodhisattvas should engage in social criticism, social protest, and social reform.

To begin to inquire how karma and justice might be part of one framework for social ethics, or, to be more precise, to explore whether questions of justice and oppression can have any place in a Buddhist ethical system, let me begin with the fundamental principle of Buddhist ethics. All suffering is caused by self-cherishing, by attempts to protect and enhance a non-existent self that we take to be eternal and separate from the rest of reality. Therefore, all human suffering is caused by human beings; it is not random, inexplicable, or due to the will of God. We suffer because of our own desires, including an often strong desire to want things that are impossible to have.

This proposition seems indisputable to me. Nevertheless, two questions arise almost immediately. First, how do we know what is impossible? Is a just society impossible? Second, is this statement made of the collectivity of human beings, or of individual human beings? That human beings collectively cause human suffering is rather obvious. Wars, poverty, racism, sexism, and homophobia are all caused by human beings rather immutable nature. However, the statement that we cause our own suffering is often applied to the individual. Inexplicable misfortune in the present is attributed to misdeeds in a past lifetime, and even suffering as a civilian in the path of rampaging armies or suffering due to others' prejudices is explained as karma of one's own making. In the past I hunted animals, so now I am suffering the effects of war in the place where I live; or I was cruel to someone in a past life, so now people are prejudiced against me.

But Buddhism teaches all-pervasive interdependence with the same intensity that it teaches that the cause of all suffering is self-cherishing. In a worldview in which the individual has no ultimate reality, and in which everything is said to be connected with everything else, the notion that I, personally, cause all the suffering I now experience strikes me as much too individualistic. It would fit with a certain rhetoric, common in some political circles today, that emphasizes individual freedom and responsibility while discounting government and society, but it hardly seems to take account of the radical interdependence that Buddhism teaches. If I am interdependent with all other beings, then it would seem that their actions would have to have some impact on me and my well-being. To say otherwise, to claim that how well or poorly I manifest myself as a human being is completely independent of the matrix or container within which I find myself, is to come dangerously close to positing the independent self that Buddhism so carefully dismantles. The only level at which it could be claimed that others' actions are irrelevant to my suffering, that I alone am responsible for my suffering, is rather steep and advanced. Whether I respond to being a victim of war or prejudice with aggression or with compassion and equanimity is my own doing. However, that reality does not deal with or undo the initial pain of being on the receiving end of warfare or prejudice.

To help think about justice and karma, it would be helpful, first, to recall what karma is about. The word itself means "an action." As usually used, the term designates that fact that actions lead to inevitable reactions—the law of cause and effect. But in reflecting more carefully on karma and justice, I suggest that it is helpful to distinguish somewhat sharply between two aspects of karma, what I call "vertical" karma and what I call "horizontal" karma. By vertical karma, I mean the karma that comes from my infinite past as well as the past of this life, and which, dependent on my present actions, determines what kind of future I will have, both in this life and other lives extending into the infinite future. By horizontal karma, I mean the karma that extends out infinitely from this moment, this point, into all directions. This distinction is not new; Buddhists have always discussed cause and effect as both linear and simultaneous. Furthermore, the effect of recognizing the simultaneous dimension of karma is profound. A single cause for any event cannot be located because any single arising depends upon a multitude of causes and conditions; if any one of them is changed, the event itself would be slightly different. Making the topic of karma even more complex is the fact that it can be difficult to distinguish between cause and effect, since anything experienced in this moment is, first an effect from previous causes, but secondly, it can easily become the cause that produces effects both in the future and in the karmic matrix of the present constellation of events.

I want to suggest that the way in which we can meaningfully talk about both karma and justice, and the way in which we can discuss justice within a wholly Buddhist framework of explanation, is to distinguish between vertical and horizontal karma, and to explore and emphasize horizontal karma more than is typical. I make this suggestion because if only vertical karma is emphasized, there is little opportunity to talk of *present* injustice, or to justify, on Buddhist grounds, a critique and reformation of social institutions in their current forms. And vertical, linear karma is the type of karma that seems to predominate in explanations of present personal suffering. To be reborn as a woman in a male dominated religious and cultural setting certainly fills one's life with suffering. Unlike some Westerners, Buddhists have never disagreed that it is unfortunate to be a woman in a male dominated system. But the traditional reaction seems to be that it can't be helped.

There are two components to the reaction that present suffering, such as being a woman in a male dominated system, can't be helped. One component takes it for granted that the social system must be structured as it is currently. Buddhist traditions include two well-known descriptions of what makes female rebirth less desirable than male rebirth, known as the five woes and the three subserviences. Of the five woes, three are a male assessment of female biology—menstruation, pregnancy, and childbirth—as woeful, while the other two are social—having to leave one's own family to live with the husband's family upon marriage, and having to work hard all the time taking care of one's husband. The three subserviences are social rules; a woman must always be under the control of a man. In youth, it is her father, in midlife her husband, and in old age her son. Whether things *must* be this way is not asked. Instead, what is explained is how some people get to fill that unfortunate slot in society, which is the second component in the reaction that the way things are can't be helped. Being reborn as a woman is the result of misdeeds in some prior lifetime; it's too late now to improve one's lot for this life, though meritorious actions in this life will probably mean a male rebirth in the future. Similarly, a single woman pregnant by rape in a culture in which single women who bear children will be ostracized for life, irrespective of the circumstances leading to the pregnancy, attributes her misfortune to karma from a past life. If she resolves to rear the child herself, despite the almost insurmountable difficulty of that task, it is in order to earn merit for a more fortunate rebirth.

If one accepts both the reality of future lives and proposition that different social or economic arrangements are impossible, everything computes very well and the category of injustice dissolves. Furthermore, one has a perfect rationale to justify the status quo and to quell any thoughts of social criticism or rebellion, any assessments that one is being mistreated. If I deserve this treatment because of past misdeeds, what grounds can there be for seeking to change economic, social, or sexual systems even though they cause great suffering? The idea of karma, taken in this way, can function very much like the concept of "the will of God," as it is employed by social reactionaries.

I am hesitant to attribute suffering so clearly connected with actions taken by other humans in the present to vertical, linear karma. I would claim that vertical or linear karma should be confidently employed only to explain suffering that is truly inexplicable and mysterious, apart from the possibility of karma from past lives or the will of an inscrutable deity, such as disabilities with which one is born or finding oneself in the path of a powerful storm. Any suffering which can be traced to human agency—which could include some birth disabilities or deliberately settling somewhere that is known for its regular ferocious storms—might more cogently be explained by reference to horizontal or simultaneous karma. Certainly the suffering caused by war, poverty, sexism, and racism is due to human agency, not given in the nature of things in the same way as are the seasons or the elements in the periodic table. Suffering due to present human agency, to horizontal karma, is certainly not inevitable and unavoidable in the way that suffering due to vertical karma, or the inevitabilities of birth, aging, sickness, and death, is unavoidable.

Whether we are considering horizontal or vertical karma, one of the most crucial issues is to locate the arenas of freedom, the points at which one can make choices. If there were no such points, karma would be merely predestination and any talk of accruing merit and virtue would be nonsense. I would be predestined either to do virtuous acts, thus improving my chances for a better future, or I would be predestined to commit evil deeds, thus planting the seeds for an unpleasant and unfortunate future. But the teachings of karma not only state that I have created my present by my past, but also that I am creating my future by what I do in the present. Therefore, in each present moment, no matter how strong habitual patterns and familiar ways of reacting may be, Buddhist teachings about karma claim that I have some tiny opening of freedom. I cannot change my present lot, but I can deal with it in many different ways, and how I deal with that present situation will have some role to play in setting up my future situations. I can practice anger and aggression in reaction to my present situation, or I can practice equanimity. The first reaction automatically causes me immediate pain, whereas the second produces peace. In that sense it is accurate to say that we each personally create our own suffering.

Likewise, each person who is implicated in my present matrix has similar freedom. Here is where explaining oppression or misfortune (notice how much changes, depending on which term we use) as being due to vertical karma from the past breaks down. It breaks down because it takes away the freedom of those who share my current matrix, the freedom of my oppressors, of those at whose hands I experience misfortune. It would not do for any genuine understanding of karma to say that, because I "need" to suffer, due to misdeeds I have committed in the past, that there must be someone in the present compelled to cause me suffering, who *must* harm me, deal me misfortune, and oppress me. Rather, those present acts that cause me suffering, are the deliberate, freely chosen acts of someone with whom I share the present matrix. It would not do to say that because I have been reborn as a woman, for whatever reasons, therefore, men or some specific man must dominate or oppress me, or simply have privileges and comforts that I cannot have. To do so would deny their freedom to decide whether to participate eagerly and willingly in a male dominated system or to resist it. Even more serious, since harming others causes negative karma for oneself, these men are committing deeds that may result in unfortunate future births for themselves. No understanding of karma suggests that the deeds that lead to unfortunate future events are anything but freely chosen acts.

In this way, by focusing on horizontal karma, it is possible to say that I am experiencing injustice, which is the most direct cause of my present suffering, from within the framework of traditional ideas about karma. Given that no arising has a single cause and that karmic causes and conditions are very complex, this account does not deny that there could be contributing causes to my present sufferings in my karmic past. The point is not to deny vertical karma but to suggest that it alone is not sufficient to explain present suffering that involves human agency. Looking into horizontal karma more carefully allows us to takes into account what seems to be an obvious and direct cause of present suffering—the self-interest which keeps oppressive social systems going. Thereby, we discern a shorter and more empirical line of cause and effect than is provided by the explanation of vertical or linear karma by itself. And to explore horizontal karma more fully provides a Buddhist wedge for seeking to change present social systems—a wedge which vertical karma by itself cannot provide. We cannot change the past, but change and choices happen all the time in the present realm of horizontal karma. It is important to link the words *choice* and *change* with the words *oppression* and *justice* when discussing the topic of karma.

Looking more closely into present constellations of cause and effect also encourages us to see how systems, rather than individuals alone, cause suffering. I would argue that recognizing systemic oppression is one of the ingredients missing in traditional discussions of karma, which tend to be much more individualistic. This is important because usually, taking gender systems as an example, it is not really an individual man who wants to cause me suffering by oppressing me or limiting my options, but the male dominated system in which he participates, often without intention to harm. Because, according to Buddhism, intention plays such a large part in determining the extent and negativity of any karmic seed that is planted by our deeds, this distinction between individuals who do not intend harm and systems that cause harm is important. For Buddhism, with its intense concern for the practices of non-harming and compassion, it should be a grave concern that well-intentioned individuals nevertheless participate in systems that cause harm. Buddhist explanations for why I suffer can seem strangely individualistic in light of Buddhist teachings about interdependence, especially when one considers the causes of mass suffering, but ignores analyses of social, political, economic, and gender systems and how they perpetuate suffering with or without individual intention.

Systemic injustice and oppression can easily be connected with more traditional Buddhist concerns—non-harming and compassion. Injustice and oppression hurt people; therefore, Buddhists should be concerned with evaluating whether the economic, social, and political systems in which they participate are harming people, should attempt to withdraw from such systems as much as possible, and should work at changing them, using Buddhist principles of non-aggression to do so. It is not compassionate to perpetuate systems that cause harm simply because they are conventional and "that's what's always been done."

The motivations for non-harming and compassion would remain the same. Traditionally, one tried not to harm sentient beings because to do so would result in negative karma for oneself. It may be more difficult to think about non-harming as not participating in culturally sanctioned sexist, racist, or economically exploitative practices than to think of non-harming as not hurting one's neighbors or not killing animals—but the principle is the same. Committing harmful acts results in negative karma even if one is acting not as an individual, but as part of a collective within a system especially if one assents to the system. The motivation for compassion is less ego-based. In Mahayana Buddhism, compassion is said to arise spontaneously from the realization that one is not separate from other beings who want freedom from suffering as much as oneself. Therefore, one does what one can to help them. When one begins to contemplate all the suffering that results from conventional economic, social, political, and gender systems, it is hard to understand how Buddhists could not be concerned to do whatever can be done to change those systems.

Thinking about horizontal karma and systemic injustice can be taken one step further. Sometimes it is said that one should stop others from doing harmful acts out of compassion for them. Knowing how much they will suffer from the negative karma they will accumulate from such acts, one simply stops them, even at the cost of some negative karma to oneself. One of the most popular stories concerns the Buddha in a former life. Knowing that a certain passenger on a ship intended to kill all five hundred passengers and take possession of the ship's treasure for himself, the future Buddha killed him to save him from the terrible karma of killing so many people. I do not think the examples need to be nearly so dramatic. We can refuse to laugh at jokes that denigrate certain groups of people, thus discouraging their teller from repeating them. We can speak up against racism, sexism, homophobia, and excessive patriotism. We can refuse to be swept up into the orgy of consumerism. All of these acts undercut their perpetrators and discourage them from engaging further in these behaviors and accruing more negative karma.

We might want to consider even one more step. If we do not attempt to stop people from accruing the negative karma of practicing injustice and oppression, if we mindlessly participate in all these oppressive systems, regard them as perfectly normal and unavoidable, or justify them, we may well reap not only the karma due to our own participation in these systems, but the karma of not discouraging others from participating in oppressive, harmful systems.

I expect several objections from other Buddhists that I would like to try to defuse. I would expect many people to respond that the whole point of Buddhism is that samsara can't be fixed; it must be transcended or left behind, and politics, economics, and social systems are simply part of samsara. The Buddha, after all, left conventional society behind to create a monastic counterculture. The Buddhist tendency ever since has been to regard politics, economics, and social systems as not the realms most amenable to enlightened activity, which is focused more in universities, retreat centers, solitary hermitages, and in teacher-student relationships. I would reply that it is not so easy simply to divide human activities into worldly, samsaric activities like politics, economics, and social systems on the one hand, and samsara-transcending activities such as study and practice on the other hand, because these two realms are interdependent. Who gets to pursue samsara-transcending activities is often dependent on worldly systems of privilege and deprivation. For example, the Buddha did not observe conventional ancient Indian class and caste privileges when setting up his monastic counterculture, but he did observe male gender privileges. As a result, throughout Buddhist history, half the Buddhist population has found serious Buddhist study and practice more difficult to pursue than the other half of the Buddhist population. This is only one example of the way in which Buddhism's samsara-transcending activities are more available to certain socially elite groups. Regarding something as important as the opportunity to engage seriously in Buddhist practice and study, it would seem unwise and uncompassionate to rely solely on vertical karma to get everything right when the self-interest involved in horizontal karma is so obvious. To put the matter very succinctly, the practice of world transcendence requires a proper, just social matrix.

Furthermore, Buddhists have always recognized how crucial to our well-being is the context, the "container" (to use the jargon of one contemporary Buddhist sect), in which we experience our lives. This is one meaning of the practice of "going for refuge to the sangha," part of the Triple Refuge which is so basic to Buddhism. Given that the matrix in which one lives is central to one's well-being and important to one's spiritual practice, providing such a matrix should be a priority for Buddhists. And individual Buddhists should not be constrained from evaluating whether or not their right to a proper matrix has been met, as happens when vertical karma alone is used to explain why things happen the way they do. Relying on vertical karma alone does not permit one to evaluate what is happening to oneself and say, "This is not right! I am not being treated properly and certainly not in a way that is conducive to my being able to offer my best talents to the world. I don't deserve this."

At least in the contemporary Western Buddhist world, such a comment usually garners one scorn and the recommendation to practice more so that one will accept things as they happen and not complain. But I would argue that it is possible for such a statement to stem from *prajna*—the discriminating wisdom which can tell the difference between one thing and another—rather than complaint. A lot depends on the level of aggression or equanimity with which the statement is made. Therefore, the link between present suffering due to human agency and vertical karma should be used to do what it does best—encouraging people to accept what they cannot personally change in this moment *without resorting to the destructive emotions of vengeance and aggression.* Buddhists know how to accept what they cannot change, but that does not mean that what any individual cannot change about his or her life is, therefore, just and right. Much of what I would change about my life, but must accept because I cannot change it myself, could be due to the self-interest of others and the systems that foster and feed such self-interest. My life is harmed by those self-interested actions of others and my life would improve if those actions were changed. I may learn from these experiences, even turn them into fuel for insight, but my ability to work with negativity does not justify negativity nor prove that I "needed" such negativity in order to reach insight.

I see no reason why Buddhists should not engage in such analyses, should not name the reality of present oppression and take part in movements designed to change these systems, so long as the clarity of the analysis and the depth of practice short circuits the tendencies toward revenge and aggression that sometimes accompany the recognition that one is being treated unjustly.

However, from a Buddhist point of view, there is a major problem with many social action movements as they have manifested themselves to date in Western societies, and major psychological and spiritual benefits that come with the more traditionally Buddhist way of dealing with social and systemic evils. These issues must also be acknowledged and addressed in any attempt to meld social activism with Buddhism.

In their pursuit of their "rights," many activists and socially concerned commentators are at least as aggressive and confrontational as are their opponents. Shouting matches, yelling and screaming, pushing and shoving, and occasionally resorting to even more violent tactics to make one's point or stop one's opponents are quite common in movements that pursue social justice. Such tactics are often justified by the old argument that the end justifies the means or by claiming that only aggression and confrontation are noticed in a society that lives by the slogan "nice guys finish last." But having the "right" cause does not justify aggression, anger, and confrontation. If we are still fighting, but just fighting for the right things, instead of fighting to maintain our privilege, there is no "victory over warfare," the only goal worth pursuing in seeking social justice. Anger and aggression are regarded by Buddhism as the most poisonous and seductive of all the *klesha*-s, or conflicted emotions. They are unworkable and have no redeeming qualities, especially since they reproduce themselves so readily in those to whom one expresses them. Furthermore, they are at least as painful and counterproductive for the one who experiences and expresses them as they are to the recipient. And they are utterly unnecessary to maintaining one's passion for justice; in fact, they contribute significantly to the burnout and self-destructiveness that plagues some activists. The lack of alternatives to anger and aggression as the fuel to maintain one's activism or one's concern for justice is the greatest weakness of Western approaches to issues of oppression and equity.

By contrast, the traditional Buddhist approach, which is much less concerned with my rights and other peoples' obligations to treat me properly, promotes equanimity and cheerfulness, even in the face of considerable personal suffering, which is a major psychological and spiritual benefit. Such a person may well be happier than their counterpart who is evaluating whether their rights are being accorded them and is valiantly "fighting" for peace and justice. Buddhism stresses that all suffering ultimately comes from our own minds, our own attachments. Therefore, it is recommended that one look inward first and foremost when confronted with dissatisfaction, and cultivate inner peace, detachment, and equanimity. One's own mind is the only thing one has absolute power to change.

If the price for being concerned with rights, justice, oppression, and equity were the constant turmoils of anger, confrontation, and aggression, that price would be too high. Equanimity, detachment, and contentment that are not dependent on the external world are too hard won and too precious to discard for any reason. However, one does not have to make a choice between maintaining some level of equanimity and being concerned about justice and oppression. One can pursue peace and justice with equanimity and detachment. The attitude, the mindset of the person concerned with justice and oppression is not the issue from the Buddhist point of view. The issue is thinking about cause and effect in relationship to peace and justice. Why am I oppressed? What causes me to experiences the negativities of being a woman in a male-dominated world? What is the combination of my own karma from past lives and the present self-interested actions of others? I would argue that an answer which does not take horizontal karma into account is inadequate. I would also argue that, with Buddhist training in equanimity and detachment, it is possible accurately to assess and name horizontal karma without falling into either aggression or self-pity.

RESPONSE BY ROSEMARY

In her essay on "What Buddhists Could Learn from Christians," Rita struggles with a number of critical issues having to do with the use of the "prophetic voice" in Buddhism: karma, personal and collective responsibility, and gender. In her discussion of the use of the prophetic voice, Rita responds to critics who see this as a borrowing from Western Semitic religions and inappropriate in Buddhism. The objectionable suggestion is that Buddhism is somehow lacking in this regard and needs this borrowed element from Western religions. I would like to reply in terms of how I see questions of borrowing that may arise through becoming religiously multi-lingual and the integrity of each religion in such a religiously multi-lingual context.

Unlike Rita, who was first a Christian who then converted to Judaism before finding her primary identity in Buddhism, I have not journeyed through affiliation with several religions. But I have explored a number of religions, starting with the ancient Near Eastern and Greek religious worlds, and then Judaism, Buddhism, and Islam. I have not explored them as a world religionist, but more in the spirit of one learning other languages and seeking to experience the world through these religious lenses. Thus, I have sought to take them seriously in their own right, not in comparison with Christianity. My re-identification with and study of Biblical religion has much to do with my recognition in it, and its religious descendants, of the prophetic voice that seemed to be lacking in ancient Near Eastern and Greek religious world views.

In my explorations of religious world views, I have come to think of three major paradigms of religion: first, sacralization of nature, seen in seasonal and life cycles; second, prophetic, historical religions: and third, contemplative religions of inward transformation. There may be more paradigms than these, or other ways of naming them, but these are what I have identified. Complex religions that encompass a long development, from prehistoric roots through classical civilizations and into modernity, such as Judaism, Christianity, and Buddhism, are multi-dimensional. They contain all these paradigms, operative at different times and different contexts; some may be stressed at certain points in their history and become moribund in another time or context.

With new challenges, people may desire to renew one of the paradigms that has faded from the tradition of their own upbringing. Thus, many in the United States today who are faced with the ecological crisis desire a religion of seasonal and natural renewal, as well as a religion that includes a female personification of nature. Thus, they are engaged in what they believe is a revival of ancient Celtic or old Europe Stone Age religions. These new Goddess religions actually are modern creations, reflecting contemporary needs and appropriating and interpreting symbols from ancient cultures. Because there is little or no textual tradition and no institutional vehicle or continual practice of these ancient religions, their visual symbols provide vehicles for free creation which is not hindered by an inherited tradition. I regard such developments as perfectly appropriate, so long as people are clear about what they are doing and not doing. They are creating a new religion, not reviving an old one.

Encounters between living religions can also serve to renew elements in one's own religion that have become moribund, and to provide new insights and ways of understanding such insights. Thus, I believe that the prophetic voice in Christianity can be renewed through contact with prophetic, social justice Judaism. Judaism also can be renewed in its prophetic tradition through contact with Christian Liberation Theology, so that it can challenge its failures as a state religion in Israel. Jewish theological Marc Ellis has challenged Judaism in this way. Christianity can renew its contemplative tradition through contact with Buddhism. Buddhism may be challenged also by Liberation Theology to connect its social justice traditions with the prophetic voice. All these religions, which are the products of classical civilizations, can be challenged, through indigenous and neo-pagan religions, to renew their sensitivity to the sacrality of nature. These mutual enrichments are not borrowings of elements foreign to one's own religion so much as they are ways of renewing and redeveloping corresponding elements in one's own tradition.

The question of structural evil is a particularly important arena in which Rita feels the need for a more adequate development of Buddhist thought that would overcome the tradition of simply accounting for present evils in each person's life by invoking karma. Personally, I find this idea of karma to be deeply unacceptable. It seems to be based on an assumption of a substantial soul (an idea rejected by Buddhism) that can acquire merits or demerits in a previous life which are then passed on when the soul is reincarnated in a new life. Since I don't believe in substantive souls that are reincarnated, this makes no sense to me.

This is also a victim-blaming theory that makes women's situations a punishment for past sins, thus rendering impossible a critique of the miserable state of women as an injustice created by male domination. This seems to me to have a parallel in Hinduism, taken over by Buddhism, of the Christian idea that women's "natural" subjugation is to be reinforced as punishment for the past sins of disobedience of a mythical ancestor, Eve.

Rita has several times in these chapters described the Christian concept of Original Sin as one that makes no sense and is completely unacceptable to her. I would agree, if by "Original Sin" one means the theory that humans were created perfect in a mythical paradise, but lost their original immortality and capacity for goodness through a primal sin of disobedience, for which women were primarily responsible. In this understanding this sin and its resulting defective state have been transmitted through lust attendant upon a corrupted sexuality. The final element in this formulation of Original Sin is that humans are now incapable of contacting God and are in need of a redemptive intervention that transcends their own capacities. This is essentially the concept of Original Sin found in Augustinian and Classical Christianity; it should be rejected in all its major premises.

However, the idea that we have inherited a sinful state, but are also responsible for how we actualize it in our present historical context (Original and Actual Sin) has been reinterpreted in Christianity since the Social Gospel writings of the late nineteenth century. I find this reinterpretation very helpful for my own understandings of the collective, historical and personal dimensions of sin (as distinguished from tragedy or finitude). This reinterpretation is somewhat similar to what Rita is trying to do by distinguishing vertical and horizontal karma, although it avoids the victim-blaming of vertical karma by understanding the historical legacy of sin as collective rather than individual.

I have already discussed something of this modern interpretation in my chapter on "What I Find Liberating in Christianity," but will review some elements of it here. We are not born into an ethically neutral world. Rather we are born into a world that has been deeply shaped and distorted by our human ancestors who have created systems of injustice, such as sexism, racism, class inequality, militarism, and exploitation of the earth. These evils are not the work of some extra-human demonic powers. They are the work of humans acting in social groups. One can even, to some extent, trace its history; for example, the actual laws passed at particular times to establish the slave trade in America. These unjust and violent systems are transmitted to us socially. They come down to us as discriminatory laws, biased institutions, and social ideologies that justify these injustices and make them appear to be the "order of creation" and the "will of God."

Even though we are shaped by these structures of distortion and their ideological justification from birth, we have not lost our "good potential." It may be silenced and constrained, but it can be awakened through prophetic and transformative experiences to become the "seed" for liberating development. On the other hand, we may passively acquiesce to these evil systems, or, even worse, actively identify with them and seek to defend them and extend their sway. Thus, some whites born into South African apartheid were converted to oppose it, while others identified with apartheid and actively defended it, carrying out many crimes to keep it in place; the majority simply passively acquiesced in its benefits. It is the critical transformative minority who are the transformers of the world.

This way of looking at the combined ideas of historical and personal sin recognizes both that we inherit legacies of distortion and that we are personally responsible for our actions in response to them. While constrained by these evil systems and ideologies that have shaped us and our society, we are not lacking in potential for opposing them and transforming both ourselves and, to some extent, the society around us.

PART V

Religious Feminism
and the Future of the Planet

9. Christian Resources
for Ecological Sustainability

ROSEMARY RADFORD RUETHER

CHRISTIANITY HAS BEEN faulted by deep ecologists and ecofeminists as the chief source of the ecological crisis. In 1967, Lynn White, a historian of science published a widely quoted article, "The Historic Roots of Our Ecological Crisis," in which he pinned the blame for this crisis on the Biblical doctrine of dominion, found in Genesis 1:26, 28.[1] In this text, God gives humans dominating power and control of all living things: "Fill the earth and subdue it; and have dominion over the fish of the sea, and over the birds of the air and over every living thing that moves upon the earth." White saw this text as the major mandate in Western history for the notion that humans have absolute power over the rest of the earth.

Biblical scholars have sought to reinterpret this text as being about kindly, responsible stewardship. According to these scholars, humans are not given power over the earth to do whatever they will. Rather they have simply been given usufruct of the land, but God is still its ultimate owner to whom they are accountable. This view can be drawn from other texts of Hebrew Scripture, as we will see later in this essay. But it is important to note that the language used to bestow dominion over the earth upon humans in Genesis 1 connotes dominating power and sovereignty. The words translated "subdue" and "have dominion" are those used about a military leader who is trampling down and subduing a foe.

Deep ecologists and feminists have also pointed to the anthropocentrism and androcentrism of Christianity, to the notion that humans are

---

1. Lynn White, "The Historical Roots of our Ecologic Crisis," *Science*, March 10, 1967, pp. 1203–7.

189

the crown of creation and the only ones who are made in the image of God, a concept that links with the belief that humans were given dominion over the rest of nature. The sexist hierarchy that links maleness to the rational mind, which is seen as having sovereign power over the body represented by the female, heightens this anthropocentrism. A male ruling class elite is seen as having dominion over subjugated humans, such as women and slaves, as well as non-human things. Despising women and the body is integrally related to despising the earth. These ideas lend themselves to the belief that the earth is not our true home, just as the body is not our true self. Instead, redemption is seen as a flight from the body, the woman, and the world into an other-worldly disembodied immortality.

I fully concede that these themes are present in main lines of Christianity and have played a major role in making Christianity an auxiliary to the Western domination of the earth that is fueling the ecological crisis. Indeed, in my writings, I have been a major pioneer in the critique of these patterns in Christianity from the perspective of ecofeminism.[2] But I think the claim that these ideas in the Bible and Christianity translated immediately and directly into the abuse of nature is too simplistic. To a large extent, our present ecological crisis owes its major impetus to cultural, economic, and technological developments of the last five hundred years.

The scientific revolution of Bacon, Descartes, and Newton represented a shift away from belief in the earth and the cosmos as living and animate, and toward a belief that bodily things consist of dead matter in mechanical motion. It was claimed that this mechanical universe was ruled over by human knowledge lodged in transcendent, positionless intellects. It is this shift from belief in an animate cosmos to belief in dead, mechanistic matter that the historian of science Carolyn Merchant, calls the "death of nature."[3] Such a view of nature was not present in early and medieval Christianity, which followed a classical Greek view that saw the whole cosmos as alive. For the Greeks, the cosmos is ensouled. It is animated by the World Soul. Souls in humans are part of the World Soul. Thus there is a deep affinity between humans, animals, and the whole cosmos, since all partake in the same World Soul.

---

2. Rosemary Radford Ruether, *Gaia and God: An Ecofeminist Theology of Earth Healing* (HarperSanFrancisco, 1992).

3. Carolyn Merchant, *The Death of Nature: Women, Ecology, and the Scientific Revolution* (San Francisco: Harper and Row, 1980).

Christians drew on this same understanding that every human soul is an expression of the World Soul that animates the Cosmos when they interpreted Christ as the cosmological "ground of Being." The divine *Logos*, which is manifested in Christ, also dwells in each human soul and is the ground of being for the whole created world. Christ as redeemer is not over against this cosmological source of cosmic life, but is the re-manifestation of Word and Wisdom of God which is the source and ground of life for the whole creation.

In the New Testament letter to the Colossians, the Pauline author describes God as the one who has redeemed us from the "power of darkness and transferred us to the Kingdom of his Beloved Son." This "Son" is then defined as the one through whom the cosmos was created: "He is the image of the invisible God, the firstborn of all creation. For in him all things in heaven and on Earth were created, things visible and invisible, . . . all things have been created through him and in him. He himself is before all things, and in him all things hold together" (Col. 1:15–17).

For early Christians, God is not simply far away in a distant heaven, but is present in and through all life. As St. Paul says in the book of Acts, God "gives to all mortals and all things life and breath. . . . He is not far from each one of us," for "in him we live and move and have our being." (Acts 17:25, 27–8). This sense of the sacramentality of the whole Earth and cosmos was central to the sacramental spirituality of the early church, expressed in the anti-gnostic theologians of the second century, such as Irenaeus of Lyon. Irenaeus speaks of the Word and Spirit as the "two hands of God" used to create the cosmos. Humans have been made in the image of God and are mandated to grow into the likeness of God by which they, with the whole cosmos, will become the bodily manifestation of the indwelling Spirit of God.[4]

This sacramental view of the cosmos is continued in Medieval thought. In twelfth-century Victorine theology, the church's sacraments, as "outward signs of inward grace" or divine presence, are themselves expressions of the sacramentality of the cosmos.[5] Eastern Orthodox theology expressed this link between the sacraments and the cosmos in its theology of icons. Icons are the bodily manifestations of the holiness of

---

4. Irenaeus, *Ad Haer.* V.2.2.: See Ruether, *Gaia and God*, p. 235.

5. Hugh of St. Victor, *The Sacraments of the Christian Faith*, R. J. Defarrari, trans. (Washington, D.C.: Medieval Academy of America, 1951).

the cosmos.[6] The thirteenth-century Franciscan theologian Bonaventure, in his treatise "The Mind's Road to God," begins the human journey to God with the experience of the signs of God's presence in all created things.

Lynn White, a historian of medieval science, recognizes counter-trends to domination in Christian tradition. He particularly lifts up, as an exception to the Christian tradition of dominion over the earth, St. Francis, with his Canticle to the Sun, which hymns the sister- and brotherhood of humans with all created things. White suggests that Francis should be seen as the patron saint of an ecological Christianity. The notion of the earth as composed of dead matter in mechanical motion was a radical departure from these earlier views about the relationship between God, humans and nature, who all partake in a common soul that animates all living things and is rooted in seeing the presence of God as the creating and sustaining power of life.

It is important to see that Christian asceticism, which dominated Christian spirituality for fifteen hundred years, does not automatically translate into an abuse of the body and flight from the earth. Although negative views of the body and the earth are present in some forms of asceticism, the main lines of Western monasticism are suspicious of an asceticism that is carried to the extremes of body-abuse. The classic third-century hermit, St. Anthony, is seen as emerging from decades of fasting and struggle with demonic powers with a restored body. In the text, Anthony's body and mind are described as perfected, as "neither fat from lack of exercise nor emaciated from fasting....He maintained utter equilibrium, like one guided by reason and steadfast in that which accords with nature." In the ascetic, soul and body are no longer at odds, but are harmoniously integrated.[7]

Prayer and fasting by monks are seen restoring the original paradise from which humans departed in the flood. The monks return from the meat diet of fallen humanity to the vegetarianism of paradisiacal humanity before the flood. In Genesis, God gave humans only green plants to eat. But humans fell into violence, and God sought to purge creation through the flood. Those humans who survived God's retribution

---

6. See Vladimir Lossky and Leonid Oupensky, *The Meaning of Icons* (Crestwood, NY: St. Vladimir's Seminary Press, 1982).

7. Athanasius, *Life of Anthony* 14, Robert C. Gregg, trans. (New York: Paulist Press, l980), p. 42.

emerged into a harsher world. "The fear and dread of you shall rest on every animal of the earth, and on every bird of the air and on everything that creeps on the ground; into your hand they are delivered. Every moving thing shall be food for you, and just as I gave you green plants, now I give you everything" (Genesis 9:2–3).

Monastic vegetarianism and a simple, communal lifestyle restored the relationship that humans and animals had before the flood. Animals no longer feared humans as predators; friendship between humans and animals returned. Lions and wolves kneeled before desert monks, offering an injured paw for healing, and ravens dropped the monk his daily bread. Fanciful as such stories may seem to us, they express a vision of a lifestyle that was understood as restoring harmony between body and soul and between humans and nature, which had been lost through greed and violence.

For some Church Fathers, private property was also part of this fall into violence, creating the conflict between rich and poor. In monastic life, communal society without private property restores God's original intention of a shared creation. The Christian mandate to the rich to sell what they have and give to the poor is not beneficence, but simply restoring to the poor their just share in the goods of the earth unjustly stolen from them by the rich. In the words of the fourth-century bishop, Ambrose:

> Why do the injuries of nature delight you? The world has been created for all, while you rich are trying to keep it for yourself. Not merely the possessions of the earth, but the very sky, air and sea are claimed for the use of the rich few. . . . Not from your own do you bestow on the poor man, but you make return from what is his. For what has been given as common for the use of all, you appropriate for yourself alone. The earth belongs to all, not to the rich.[8]

These themes of harmony restored are continued in Western monasticism in the rule of Benedict. The Benedictine rule seeks to curb not only the wandering, greedy monk leading mob actions in Eastern Christianity, but also exaggerated forms of asceticism practiced in some Eastern sects that abused the body. Benedictine spirituality is rooted in an ideal of

---

8. Ambrose, *De Nabuthe Jezraelita* 11: see Charles Avila, *Ownership: Early Christian Teaching* (Maryknoll, NY: Orbis Books, 1983), pp. 66–67.

balance, neither too much nor too little. Monks should neither be gluttons nor emaciated zealots of self-punishment. Adequate nutrition, sufficient clothing according to the season, and a balanced regime of prayer, work, and study governs the Benedictine ideal. Monasteries were to be self-sustaining, the monks themselves tending the land.[9]

Such an ideal of the simple life lived in community is fundamentally anti-consumerist. It counters the ideology of consumerism, which is one of the major roots of modern ecological devastation. The Christian non-consumerist ethic of simple living in community is inspiring a new movement of ecologically oriented monastics, specifically women, in the Sisters of Earth movement in United States. Sisters of Earth, of which the Grail movement itself was an early example, joins monastic simple living with ecological spirituality. This movement recognizes that the private individual, or even the nuclear family, is too fragmented and isolated to be a base for ecological living. One must start with a community a little larger, living together with some roots in the land.[10]

The guru of the Catholic ecological movement has been the Passionist priest Thomas Berry. Berry was a professor of World Religions at Fordham University in the late sixties when he turned to a focus on ecology and cosmology. Berry founded the Riverdale Center for Religious Research in 1970, focusing on ways of creating a sustainable relationship between the human community to the Earth. His essays in *Dream of the Earth* (1988) have become classics of the ecological spirituality movement. Together with the physicist Brian Swimme, he authored the *Universe Story* (1991), which presented modern scientific cosmology as a new creation story to inspire wonder and reverence toward the unfolding cosmic process of which we humans are a small part.

Berry's most recent book, *The Great Work* (1999), defined the creation of an ecologically sustainable culture as the primary historical challenge of the present generation. Berry's seminars at the Riverdale Center and the distribution of his tapes and papers became musts for the

---

9. "The Rule of St. Benedict," in *Western Asceticism*, ed. Owen Chadwick (Philadelphia: Westminster, 1958), pp. 290–335, see particularly sections 38, 48, and 55 on food, clothes, and labor for monks.

10. See Miriam Therese McGinnis and Thomas Berry, *The Great Work of Our Time.* Sisters of Earth Conference, July 1996, Earth Communications, Laurel, Maryland. Videocassette and Audiocassette. The Sisters of Earth network can be contacted through Elm@woods.smwc.edu.

continuing education of American Catholic women religious. Other Catholic centers of ecological spirituality, such as the Sophia Center at Holy Names College in Oakland, California, have claimed Berry's work as the central pillar of their educational vision.

Berry is not the only influence on the Sisters of Earth Movement. Another important shaper of this movement on the practical level is Jesuit Al Fritsch, Director of the Appalachian Center, Science in the Public Interest. Fritsch's center has done ecological sustainability inventories for more than sixty women's religious orders in the United States. His resource audits include energy use, food use, land use, the physical plant, transportation, waste management, water, and wildlife. He recommends shifts to partial energy self-sufficiency by using solar, wind, biomass, and hydroelectric sources. He suggests solar food drying and cooking, the use of greenhouses, passive space, water heating, and photo-electric potential. He examines land use to promote self-reliance in food, edible landscaping, aquaculture, multiple land use, wildlife refugees, and the aesthetic and spiritual aspects of land.[11]

Why have women's religious orders become the primary agents for this kind of ecological community development? Men's monastic orders have similar Christian roots that might dispose them to similar concerns. The answer seems to lie in the greater prophetic consciousness of religious women as they have taken hold of the renewal of their communities in the last thirty-five years since the Second Vatican Council in 1962–65. An important factor in this prophetic consciousness has been the adoption of feminism as integral to the self-understanding of American women religious. American nuns have become aware of the injustice of the clerical establishment to women in general and to themselves in particular as churchwomen. This critical view of the male church establishment has fostered greater independence and initiative among these religious women to undertake their own work of justice, rather than depending on the leadership of the male clergy.

An ecofeminist approach that blends feminism, ecology, and justice seems to have particular appeal to Catholic women religious. Ecofeminism brings together spirituality: the poetic, artistic, and intuitive; scientific and technological reason; prayer and practical

---

11. Al Fritsch's program can be contacted at Resource Auditing Service, P.O. Box 298, Livingston, KY, 40445.

management; outreach to society and service to the poor; and cultivation of the inner self. Berry's vision and Fritsch's practicality make for a holistic reshaping of religious community life. They allow religious women to reclaim the best of past monastic life with the call for renewal. Ecofeminist religious leader, Sister Miriam Therese McGinnis, uses the metaphor of "re-inhabiting" for this process of conversion that both reclaims and transforms the places where one lives. Religious women are re-inhabiting their land and their religious traditions, redeveloping their call to religious community.[12]

Two decades ago, Catholic women's orders began to apply principles of ecological sustainability to their lands and buildings. In the early 1980s, the Grail, for example, transformed their property in Loveland, Ohio, to create a permaculture garden and a solar heated greenhouse. They added how-to courses on permaculture to their regular course offerings, using their own work as demonstration training sites. Many other women's orders underwent similar conversions: conversion to the ecological issue itself, conversion of their lands and properties, and the creation of training centers to help others learn from their experience. Sisters of Earth, founded in 1994, brought together these many centers into an organized network for communication and mutual support.

Although the transformation of motherhouses into centers for practicing and teaching ecological sustainability suggests a rural focus, much of the work of members of Sisters of Earth ranges across urban institutions as well. Most notable is the application of energy and food conservation and waste recycling to hospitals, one of the major ministries of Catholic women religious. Parishes and schools have also been sites for ecological practice and teaching. Many members of Sisters of Earth are trained in science, and ecology has given them a new way to bring together their scientific knowledge with their spirituality and concerns for justice.

The most important site that Catholic women religious have developed for ecological spirituality and learning is the Genesis Farm, located in Blairstown, New Jersey. Genesis Farm was founded by Miriam Therese McGinnis in the 1980s. McGinnis has written extensively on the new universe story and ecological spirituality, and is a frequent lecturer on

----

12. For a detailed study on Sisters of Earth and Genesis Farm, see Sarah McFarland Taylor, "Sisters of Earth: Catholic Nuns Reinhabiting Religion at Genesis Farm," Ph.D. Dissertation, University of California at Santa Barbara, 1999.

these topics around the United States and the world. Genesis Farm offers major training courses in such areas as "The Universe Story and Bioregionalism," six and twelve week courses in earth literacy, and focused short seminars on topics such as "simplifying our lifestyle" and "revisioning the vowed life."

Ecological spirituality and practice are also reshaping prayer and liturgy for these religious women. Several have developed ecologically-focused labyrinth walks. Genesis Farm has created a sacred space on their land as an earth meditation walk. The stations of this walk bring together the stages of the universe story with the stages of each person's life story. Other Catholic women's ecojustice centers feature meditation walks modeled on the stations of the cross. The theme of the meditation is the crucified earth. Each station focuses prayer and meditation on a particular form of the sufferings of the earth and its creatures, such as pollution of water, fouling of air, poisoning of the soil, extinction of species, social violence, and poverty.

The prayers of the church year also allow for a recovery of the relation of liturgy to the seasonal cycle, the winter and summer solstices, the fall and spring equinoxes. Prayer is integrated into the daily rhythms of life, rising and sleeping, food preparation, eating and cleaning up in community, fasting and feasting. Sisters of Earth is a significant example of how a very old form of Christian life, the monastic community, is being re-inhabited today to make it a vehicle of ecological living and learning. Christian monasticism, which itself arose as a survival spirituality and way of life when the great cycle of empire building of the ancient Mediterranean was collapsing in the fifth century, returns in an ecofeminist form as we face global collapse due to the capitalist exploitation of the earth at the end of the twentieth century.

These expressions of ecological practice and spirituality are being deepened today by increasing reflection on the theological resources in the Christian tradition for ecological theology. In my book *Gaia and God: Ecofeminism and Earthhealing,* I explored two complementary forms of ecological theology from the Biblical and Christian traditions: covenantal ethics and sacramental cosmology. Covenantal ethics, which is found particularly in the sabbatical legislation in Hebrew Scripture, gives us a vision of the local land and household, with its rooted community of humans, animals and soil living in one covenantal relation with a caretaking God. Although the patriarchal assumptions of this vision need to be rejected, what is significant is that humans do not own this land and cannot do with it what they will. Humans are caretakers of a land that ultimately comes from and belongs to God. They are accountable for the well-being of all those who live together—fellow humans, animals, and the soil itself. It is this tradition, not Genesis 1:26, that is the basis for the stewardship ethic lauded by Biblical proponents of ecological sustainability.

In the sabbatical legislation, God demands limited use of human and animal labor and of the soil itself, and also mandates periodic rest and restoration. Every seven days, all creatures must rest and be restored. There is no mandate here for a workaholic ethic. To work all the time to maximize production and consumption is a sin, not a virtue. Not only must there be a weekly rest, restoration and celebration that balances the six days of work, but on a periodic basis, every seven years, there is a larger rest and restoration in which the land lies fallow for a year.

Finally, every seven times seven years there is the Jubilee, the great restoration. During the Jubilee, systems of unjust accumulation of land and enslaved labor that have occurred over the previous cycle of years must be dismantled. Debts must be cancelled and slaves freed. Land that has been alienated from peasant farmers through debt and enslavement and appropriated by great landlords must be restored. There must be a land reform that recreates a society of small farmers in which each household has sufficient land for its own maintenance. Unjust centralization of power and possessions is dismantled, animals and land are given rest, and the society as a whole is restored to a just and sustainable balance of humans with each other, with animals and with the land. (Leviticus 25). In short, the Biblical sabbatical legislation enshrines a call for a continuing revolution, a revolution of restoring right relations between humans, God, and creation.

This vision is not simply an ancient dream without relevance for today. The symbol of the Jubilee is inspiring a global movement to cancel unjust accumulations of global debt by the poor countries to the rich countries and their banks whose policies toward the developing world are a vivid expression of exploitative economic practices in the world today. Under the United Nations, the world's peoples are coming together to negotiate environmental agreements to limit the toxic waste dumped into the seas or blown into the air. One international group has been working to develop an "Earth Charter" that would parallel the Declaration of Human Rights as a charter for regulating humans and the environment in sustainable relations.[13] These movements are restoring the sense that humans are a part of a community of life on earth, a community that must live together in a covenantal relationship.

The preamble to the Earth Charter reads:

> In our diverse yet increasingly interdependent world, it is imperative that we, the people of Earth, declare our responsibility to one another, to the greater community of life and to future generations. We have entered a critical stage in history when we must unite to bring forth a new global order founded on respect for life, environmental protection, freedom and justice, sustainable human development and a culture of peace. We are one human family, and one Earth community with one common destiny.

The preamble concludes with the statement:

> there is an urgent need for a shared vision of basic values that will provide an ethical foundation for the emerging world community. Therefore, together in hope we affirm the following interdependent principles for sustainable development, as a common standard of achievement by which the conduct of all persons, groups, businesses and nations is to be guided and judged.

The common principles which the Earth Charter details include: respect for the Earth and life in all its diversity; care for the community of life with understanding, love, and compassion; building societies that are free, just, participatory, sustainable, and peaceful; and securing Earth's bounty and beauty for present and future generations.

These principles continue with specific commitments around what it would take to secure ecological integrity, a just and sustainable socio-economic order, democracy, and peace. Most notable in the Charter is a clear recognition that justice and peace between groups of humans and between humans and the earth are interconnected. There can be no flourishing for humans if the Earth is impoverished and devastated. The Charter ends with a call to action that must include all the cultures of the earth: "Let ours be a time that is remembered for an awakening to a new reverence for life, a firm resolve to preserve Earth's evolutionary potential,

---

13. For copies of the Earth Charter and information on its process of formation, see Steven C. Rockefeller, Chair, Earth Charter Drafting Committee, P.O. Box 648, Middlebury, VT, 05753. The website is www.Earthcharter.org.

a quickening of the struggle for justice and peace, and joyful celebration of the mystery and wonder of being."

Covenantal ethics is complemented in the Biblical heritage with the sacramental cosmology found in the Jewish Wisdom tradition and New Testament sacramental Christology built on the Wisdom tradition. Here we have a sense of the whole cosmic community of nature as alive, as grounded in and bodying forth the divine spirit which is its source of life and renewal of life. As I mentioned earlier in this chapter, this sacramental sense of the earth and cosmos governed Christian thought, both in Eastern Christianity and in the West, until the scientific revolution, colonialism, and the industrial revolution.

This theme has been renewed by ecofeminist theologians, such as Sally McFague, who calls us to renew a sense of the whole cosmos as God's body.[14] For Christians this is represented in renewed form in the understanding of the redemptive community as the Body of Christ, the community where the alienation and separation of individuals from God's sacramental presence in creation is overcome. We are called to commune with God, not by turning away from bodies, but in and through the mystery of bodies that are the sacramental presence of the divine to and for one another.

Thus, Christianity has rich resources for an ecological theology, but it needs to renew and develop these not in an exclusivist way, but in solidarity with other world religions that are also seeking to question the patterns in their traditions that furthered the abuse and neglect of nature and to identify and redevelop the themes in their traditions that can inspire ecological living. Many forums around the world are bringing scholars of world religions together to engage in this critique and development of their traditions from an ecological perspective.

One of the major efforts in this direction was a series of ten conferences sponsored by the Harvard Center for the Study of World Religions. These ten conferences gathered scholars of ten different world religions, each working to reclaim the resources in their respective traditions for an ecological theology and spirituality. With impressive dedication, Buddhists, Hindus, Sihks, Jains, Confucianists, Taoists, Jews, Christians, and Muslims, and representatives of indigenous spiritualities gathered in

---

14. Sallie McFague, *The Body of God: An Ecological Theology* (Minneapolis, MN: Fortress Press, 1993).

separate conferences to examine the resources of each of their traditions for ecological spirituality and practice.

The papers from each conference are being published as a book series by Harvard University Press. The volume *Christianity and Ecology*, edited by Dieter Hessel and me, appeared in 2000. An additional two conferences brought together representatives of the world religions with scientists and economists to discuss both the interface between the religions and areas in which they might dialogue with secular specialists. This major commitment indicates both the urgency felt by the world's religions and their interest in finding their own resources for ecological living. It also makes clear that this process of recovery must be integrated into dialogues between not only world religions, but also with scientists and economists.

One of the results of the 1994 Parliament of the World's Religions I have already discussed was the passage of the Global Ethic. While members of the different world religions may not easily find it possible (or necessary) to knit together their religious symbols into a unified theology, they find that they have a very large area of common ethical principles on which they can all agree. The call to justice, peace and ecological sustainability found broad acceptance among all of the world's faiths.

Five years later, in 1999, representatives of the world's religions met in Cape Town, South Africa, for the third Parliament of the World's Religions. In this meeting, the Global Ethic was taken for granted as a common basis for dialogue on social commitments. In this gathering, the assembly of the parliament, drawn from representatives of each religion, worked together on concrete projects by which the Global Ethics might be applied to specific countries, contexts, and social concerns.

This work was structured around the "call to our guiding institutions." In this document, developed in consultations before the Parliament, the major institutions of human society— government, economics, the media, education, NGOs, and the religions themselves were examined to ascertain what the key ethical service was to humanity to which each of these institutions is called. The assembly sought to concretize these calls to the guiding institutions by developing a great range of actual projects directed at each of these institutions to help realize their proper service to humanity in light of the Global Ethic.[15]

---

15. The website of the World Parliament is www.CPWR.org.

It has become apparent to thousands of people who have been involved in these many forums for dialogue on religion, ecology, and social justice that the threatened earth can no longer afford rivalries between the religions. Neither can we afford the continuing rivalry between religion and science. Only a dynamic interrelationship of the world's cultures can help save the earth that is our common home. The world's religions, operating out of a new sense of mutual respect and solidarity with one another, have a key role to play in this process of Earth's "redemption."

THOUGH WE BOTH wrote about environmental issues and sustainability in our chapters on religious feminism and the future, that was not the result of collusion or prior agreement. When initially asked to frame my last talk for the Grailville workshop (that led to this book) around the question of what my tradition had to offer for the future, I immediately thought about things I had emphasized in previous writings I had done on Buddhism and ecology—Buddhism's lack of a pro-natalist ideology, its emphases on interdependence, the unworkability of attachment, and the freedom detachment brings. I assume Rosemary had a similar reaction that the only possible issue for the final chapter would be ecological sustainability. It would be hard to argue that there is a more pressing issue than developing lifestyles of ecological sustainability. Where will peace and justice be accomplished if the earth has become uninhabitable due to human-induced environmental devastation?

I am again intrigued by some crossover in our thinking. In her chapter on what she had learned from Buddhism, Rosemary talked about how much the Buddhist concept of pervasive interdependence resonated with her basic outlook. The main theme of my chapter on ecology is interdependence and how much difference it makes when we really understand that we are included in the interdependent matrix of life. Many of the examples of Christian resources for ecological sustainability about which Rosemary wrote strike me as manifesting an understanding of interdependence without using the word. Buddhist concepts of interdependence would not allow for a creator of the interdependent world, something that most Christians would probably want to affirm. But I would suggest that being able to work together on the basis of shared views that all life is interdependent with all other life is more important than solving theological issues about where deity does or does not fit into interdependence.

Rosemary's earlier discussions of sacramental thinking as a resource for ecological spirituality resonated with me in the past, and they resonate again in this book. I, too, have slowly recovered, at least somewhat, from being taught to view the world of nature as dead and mechanical and am attracted to seeing all of nature as alive and interconnected. Actually, my studies of Native American traditions have helped me the most in this regard, but I suspect that growing up alone in the country made the process easier. Is the view that the world consists of dead matter operating by mechanical laws the end result of a theology that posits an external creator? I don't know. But I have been happy to learn from Rosemary that Christianity has such a deep underground tradition of sacramental thinking and practice, and I agree that the European enlightenment, more than the Biblical worldview, is responsible for the "death of nature." And I concur deeply that the "death of nature" makes it much easier for humans to view the world as theirs for the taking, as something to be exploited.

The terminology used in Buddhism is different, but I would suggest that elements of Buddhism are quite similar to Christian sacramental thinking. Tibetan, Chinese, and Japanese forms of Buddhism are especially well-known for their celebration of the natural world and their delight in mountains, waterfalls, flowers, and wild animals. The forest, far from the noisy, crowded conditions that prevail in towns or cities, has always been regarded as the ideal environment in which to pursue serious spiritual discipline. Even today here in North America, my Buddhist community maintains several centers where individuals can rent primitive, isolated cabins in which to do the solitary retreats that are required of all of us. The Buddhist concept that may be closest to a sacramental theology is the esoteric Vajrayana concept of "sacred outlook." In this outlook and the practices that develop it, the distinction between sacred and mundane is completely collapsed, so that everything one encounters and does is seen as sacred. Indeed, recognizing pervasive interdependence may well promote a sacramental outlook. If all beings are "mother sentient beings," as discussed in my chapter on ecology, reverence and respect is the only proper attitude to have toward all beings.

I was also intrigued by Rosemary's discussions of asceticism and monasticism in the context of ecological living. As I read about the communities she described, the key Buddhist phrase "the Middle Way" continued to reverberate in my consciousness. The ideal Buddhist lifestyle, whether monastic or lay, has long been described as a middle way between self-deprivation and self-indulgence, though, as with Christian asceticism, extremes have sometimes occurred. The lifestyles of the Christian and the Buddhist monastic are actually quite similar in many ways, turning on communal living, few personal possessions, and a vegetarian diet. In Buddhism, this lifestyle is seen not as a way of returning to ideal conditions that had prevailed before some catastrophe, such as the flood, but as an ideal way to cultivate equanimity and gentleness. It is also important to note that, though I did not emphasize it in this set of writings, renunciation is an important theme and virtue in Buddhism, so basic that it is called the "foot" or foundation of meditation in one Buddhist liturgy. In Buddhism, renunciation focuses not only on material possessions, but on negative emotions and on the desire for "honor and gain."

The sentence that most caught my attention concerned the Sisters of the Earth movement, and its recognition that the individual or even the nuclear family is too fragmented and isolated to be a base for ecological living. One of my greatest concerns is developing meaningful community life in our society of lonely individuals. I believe that there is an important cause and effect relationship between a lack of meaningful community life and consumerism. People try to make themselves feel better and less lonely by buying things. Happy people do not need to run to the mall every evening, and I do not believe most people are happy when they are lonely and have no meaningful community. I would argue that finding ways to live communally is essential for solving ecological problems, not only because it is redundant for every tiny household to have its own private lawnmower, but also because friendship and meaningful conversation give people the happiness that we often try to find in material objects and consumerism. I would also suggest that a shared spiritual perspective is a strong basis for building a community that can stay together and work. Communities that are based merely on personal affinity are much more precarious. For a community to be viable, we must share something more basic than personal affinity, so that we will be able to live among people some of whom we may not like very much personally.

Though communal living in a Buddhist community is not an option for me most of the time, some of the happiest periods of my life have occurred while living at one particular Buddhist meditation center that I frequently visit. The center is a large tract of land isolated in the frontrange in northern Colorado. Once one turns off County Road 68 C and passes through the gates, we are a community in a world totally of our own making. Despite my consistent advocacy of diversity, living in this world gives me some insight into the virtues of a community that is homogeneous in one regard. An oddball and a minority of one in many other social settings, here I can feel at home, among people like me, even though few of them are academics or feminists, and even though I am still alone. Food preparation, cooking, and cleaning are all done communally. Living in a tent, sharing a bathhouse with about fifty other women, and eating all my meals communally are just fine—I am content with very little in the way of material conveniences. One of the things that has most struck me about living communally at this center is how healthy it can be for the children, and how much having enough children in a safe enough environment for them to form a children's culture helps the parents. This issue of community-building, of lifestyles beyond the nuclear family, has only been discussed tangentially in our book. But it is one of the many critical tasks that Buddhists and Christians might well work on co-operatively.

Finally, though Rosemary devotes only a few sentences to discussing how the practice of the sabbath undercuts workaholism, I could not agree with her more that workaholism is a major problem in our society today. Buddhists don't observe a day of rest every seven days. But we have the equivalent, I believe—that practice that our ridiculers deride as time-wasting navel-gazing—the practice of meditation. They say that we're just doing nothing when we meditate, instead of accomplishing something. I once heard a Zen teacher say that there is all the difference in the world between doing NOTHING and DOING nothing. I have finally learned how essential it is to take the time to be with friends, to work in the garden, to pet the cats. Doing nothing that produces something or consumes something is very good practice.

10. Sustainability and Spiritual Discipline

RITA M. GROSS

A STRONG CASE can be made for the fact that environmental degradation is the greatest threat and challenge we face as we look into the future. Global warming, depletion of vital resources, loss of arable land to urban sprawl or desertification, loss of wilderness areas and the extinction of many species, declining reserves of fresh water, endless amounts of toxic and non-toxic wastes that must be dealt with, severe air, water, and land pollution, overcrowding, noise and light pollution, unregulated urban and industrial growth—the list goes on and on. And yet, in Buddhist analysis, there is but one source for environmental degradation and the widespread misery it is already causing in many parts of the world and will eventually cause everywhere if present tendencies remain unchecked—human greed, an insatiable desire for more, more things, more children (or at least one male child), more wealth, more luxury, more ease and comfort. The second noble truth of Buddhism states that compulsive desire and addictive clinging are the causes of suffering. And compulsive desire or addictive clinging are states of mind that human beings enter voluntarily, though the habitual patterns of consumerist culture make those states of mind attractive to many.

But Buddhism also teaches that we can be happy and content when we learn to live within the limits of our existence. Since desire is insatiable, we will never be able to satisfy all of them, thereby constantly thwarting ourselves. We need to learn, instead, to enjoy the simple, tenuous life we have. In fact, only if we learn that getting the next thing—whatever that next thing might be—will *not* make us happy, can we ever be *truly* happy, paradoxical as that may sound. Many people have a mistaken impression of Buddhism, thinking that it is a depressing, dark religion because it talks so much about how much suffering there is in a conventionally lived life. Some people even think that Buddhism teaches,

207

not that people *do* suffer, but that people *should* suffer. But Buddhism does not glorify suffering. In fact, Buddhism's attitude is quite the opposite; all beings treasure their lives and want to enjoy them. The problem is that people go about living in ways that produce the exact opposite of what they want. People want contentment and happiness, but because so many lives are so riddled with desires, compulsions, and clinging of all sorts, the exact opposite happens. And Buddhism is keen to point out how much of what masquerades as pleasure is really pain.

The basic teachings and practices of Buddhism are so opposite to the values promoted by advocates of consumerism, endless economic expansion, and unlimited population growth, that it is hard to imagine their co-existence. Buddhism has many resources with which to respond to the ecological and social crisis in which we find ourselves, though Buddhists previously did not have to use their values and practices to deal with consumerism and disastrous rates of growth in both goods produced or consumed and in population. For this reason, there is little explicitly ecological literature in traditional Buddhist sources, which leads some commentators to claim that current Buddhist ecological writings and movements are not "genuinely Buddhist," but a fashionable response to current Western concerns. I would reply in two ways. First, the current ecological crisis is not the product of the Buddhist worldview and Buddhist values, but of the Western worldview and values, so why would traditional Buddhist sources address the intellectual and spiritual sources of this crises? It is true that Asian countries have enthusiastically mimicked these Western inventions, but, nevertheless, the Buddhist worldview and values did not produce the current situation. Second, as with my comments about the prophetic voice in my last chapter, I would claim that in the modern world, with its interconnected communication networks and problems that affect all parts of the globe, Buddhists naturally will take up issues that have not been central in earlier times and will think about them in Buddhist ways.

I would suggest that the most important aspect of Buddhist resources for an ecological ethic is that, if internalized, these views and values would help people adopt more ecologically appropriate lifestyles without feeling personally deprived. In my view, much of what drives the consumerist, expansionist lifestyle is the fact that so many people, when faced with the choice between what is ecologically appropriate for them to do and what they want to do, will chose to do what they want to do, whatever its costs to the future of the planet and sentient beings. Therefore, an ecologically appropriate lifestyle needs to be a satisfying choice rather than an obnoxious duty. Otherwise, the prospects for developing ecologically sustainable lifestyles are not great. I do not believe that the consumerist, expansionist ideology can provide the tools that would enable people to make that transition, because its very survival depends on creating more and more desires in people, desires that most people would not even know they had were it not for advertising and the examples of other consumers. I believe that Buddhism has highly relevant and workable resources, both in terms of view and in terms of action or practice, that can foster that transition. It does not have the only resources, or all the resources needed at this point in time, of course, but working in concert with other traditions, religious or secular, Buddhism has something important and perhaps unique to offer to the effort to craft ecologically sustainable lifestyles.

In this chapter, I will discuss views and practices that are deeply transformative when personally internalized. This is my focus because I would argue that in the long run, basic shifts in the values and behaviors of large groups of people require each individual, individual by individual, to understand and accept, without feeling deprived, the limits imposed by sustainable ecology. Once one understands what ecological sustainability requires, it is totally unreasonable to feel deprived by submitting to those requirements. But I do not believe that laws, coercion, "oughts," and holding the right ideas, by themselves, are powerful enough to effect the transformations required to reverse the forces let loose by global industrialization, global capitalism, and massive population growth. Those forces are based on notions of a right to individual choices regarding consumption and reproduction without regard to the impact those choices have on the matrix of life. Once one understands certain basic realities, such as pervasive interdependence, claims about the right of the individual to do whatever he or she wants to do regarding consumption and reproduction vanishes. There is no truly existing *individual*, given interdependence. Thus, somewhat paradoxically, I am advocating that each individual—in the common-sense meaning of *individual* as a discreet personality who makes choices—assimilate and internalize a more accurate understanding of the place of individuals in the context of the interdependent matrix of life. I am seeking a solution to problems caused by excessive individualism, individual by individual, which can be the basis for a powerful tectonic shift in basic values and orientations, from valuing growth and consumption above all to valuing sustainability and acceding to a more modest lifestyle.

The Buddhist view most relevant to thinking about the environment and ecology is pervasive interdependence, which is very closely linked with karma, as was discussed in my last chapter. In fact, in many ways, I will be elaborating even further on horizontal karma. Interdependence happens to be one of the most basic of all Buddhist views about reality. It is said that the Buddha attained enlightenment when he understood interdependence, that the discovery of interdependence was the final and liberating insight of that momentous night of the May full moon some five hundred or so years before Jesus lived and taught. Teachings about interdependence have not been given an ecological twist traditionally in Buddhism; there has been little need to do so until recently. And the ecological twist to teachings about interdependence, admittedly, does have more to do with horizontal than with vertical karma. But these teachings readily lend themselves to an ecological interpretation. Basically put, things exist only in relationship with everything else; there is no independent existence of anything apart from its matrix, which is what Buddhists mean when we say that no individual *truly* exists. If the matrix in which I live and move have my being were different, I would be different. So I do not *truly* exist as an independent and eternal entity, but as part of a web or matrix of life. But, because I am part of that web and matrix, actions that I decide to undertake, such as buying a large car vs. a small car or having a(nother) baby vs. having no children at all, affects everything in the matrix of life. These are not private choices that implicate myself alone. Once we realize that, the chimera that this (whatever *this* may be) is my private matter, irrelevant to you, dissipates.

One aspect of Buddhist teachings on interdependence concerns how the human species fits into the matrix of life. On this point, Buddhists are unequivocal; human rebirth is considered to be very fortunate because it the most conducive state in the web of life from which to pursue enlightenment and freedom. (However, the preciousness of human rebirth is dependent on whether or not one is reborn into circumstances in which one can actually cultivate one's innate wakefulness, a point about which more will be said later in this chapter.) A clear implication of this view is the fact that rebirth into other realms is possible, that human beings are not essentially different from animals or other sentient beings that are believed to exist within the Buddhist "six realms," but are invisible to normal human eyesight. (The other realm most often glimpsed by humans beings is that of ghosts and other unhappy wandering spirits.)[1] The scope for non-harming and compassion is always "all sentient beings," not just all human beings. A phrase commonly used in Tibetan Buddhism is "mother sentient beings." This phrase is used to reinforce the view that since "beginningless time" we have all been in every possible relationship with every other sentient being. We are so interdependent with all other sentient beings that at some time they have been our parents and we theirs.

Therefore, cruelty toward animals or regarding animals as existing primarily to be used by humans has never been condoned by Buddhists. In climates where a vegetarian diet is possible, it has always been the preferred diet. In my travels in Buddhist countries, I have sometimes encountered an equation between being Buddhist and being vegetarian. Hunting and butchering have never been considered right livelihood and very few Buddhists engage in them. Buying and releasing animals headed for the slaughter house is a widespread "merit making" practice.[2] Clearly, such beliefs would discourage unnecessary experimentation on animals, such as those that merely reduplicate, for teaching purposes, results that are already clearly known, or to test useless, unnecessary products, such as cosmetics. (Imagine all the frogs that have uselessly lost their lives to high school dissection exercises.) And, as a Buddhist, I have grown used to something that would probably strike most people in our society as strange—funerals for animals. If a funeral is performed for an animal, it is the same as the ceremony performed for human beings, the one that will someday be performed for me. It is a simple ceremony

---

1. In Buddhist thought, there are six realms into which sentient beings can be reborn. All of them are in samsara, or cyclic existence, and rebirth into them is thus impermanent. They are, in terms of ascending order from greatest amounts of suffering to greatest amounts of pleasure, the hell realm, the hungry ghost realm, the animal realm, the human realm, the realm of the jealous divine beings, and the realm of the gods. They are interpreted as both physical realms of rebirth and as psychological experiences. Thus someone with a human body could experience any and all the six realms. These realms are often commented on, especially by Tibetan Buddhists. For one popular discussion of them, see Chogyam Trungpa, *Cutting Through Spiritual Materialism* (Berkeley: Shambhala, 1973), pp. 138–48.

2. Buddhism talks of the "two accumulations," the accumulation of merit and the accumulation of wisdom. The accumulation of merit, which is gained by generosity and virtue in general, brings one into fortunate situations, which means a situation in which one is able to study and practice the dharma. By studying and practicing, one accumulates wisdom, which is necessary for freedom and enlightenment.

encouraging the deceased to cease clinging to the past life and offering assistance for finding a fortunate rebirth. Recently, close friends of mine lost all three of their aged pets within a short period of time and they matter-of-factly told me how they took their animals' bodies into their shrine room for a day and then performed the funeral service. When my beloved fifteen-year-old cats have to move on, I certainly will do the same for them. Once, I participated in this service performed on behalf of mice who had invaded a large Buddhist sanctuary in Boulder, Colorado, and, unfortunately, had to be exterminated because no way could be found to get them out of the building again. "All sentient beings" means all sentient beings.

More directly linked with ecological concerns is the need to limit human production and reproduction to preserve habitat for animals, which also preserves wilderness for human beings. I cannot imagine wanting to live on an earth which has been so completely overtaken by and overrun with human beings that many animal species and most or all wilderness areas have disappeared. Nor can I imagine anything so important about what humans are doing that we could consider it our "right" to push other sentient beings out of our way so that we can take over the whole earth. Thus, the phrase "all sentient beings," so basic to Buddhism, so universal in Buddhist language, has profound implications for the proper conduct of human beings in the interdependent web of life.

The term *interdependence* is often used in a celebratory way by both Buddhists and non-Buddhists who use it in environmental contexts. It is a great relief to realize our kinship with all that lives, especially in our cultural context, which has favored views of individualism and human supremacy. In such a context, it has become difficult to experience our profound interconnectedness with other human beings, to say nothing of our connectedness with other species. But the reality of interdependence also has more sobering implications. Not only kinship, but harmful acts also reverberate through the entire planet. We are now used to hearing about depletion of the Antarctic ozone layer due to human activities, which is coupled with rising rates of skin cancer and an increased need to protect oneself from the sun's rays. We are used to hearing about northern lakes where loons no longer live, probably due to acid rain, and we are used to hearing about dying forests far from the source of the pollutants in the rain which is causing their death. We are used to hearing about dire predictions of the consequences on global weather patterns of clearing the Amazon rain forest so that more beef can be raised for export. People are becoming more aware of the negative consequences of global capitalism—which benefits only a few rich people—on the majority of the earth's peoples, to say nothing of unique cultures, other species, and the habitats in which they live.

The pain of realizing this dimension of interdependence is intensified when we realize that we too are locked into the system. What we do may seem small and inconsequential, but it becomes part of the global matrix. It is very painful that we are locked into patterns and systems not of our making or liking, but in which we cannot avoid participating. There is no more obvious example of such a pattern than the need for a personal automobile, which is very convenient, but more wasteful and degrading to the environment than anything else common to our lifestyle. Think of the endless acres paved over with concrete to make superhighways and parking lots, the endless emissions into the atmosphere, habitat for wildlife destroyed by oil fields, pipe lines and refineries, endless photographs of sea birds covered with crude oil from yet another oil spill. It is extremely frustrating and painful to realize that a personal automobile could be fundamentally unnecessary if more attention were paid to the interdependent web of life and less to profits, and yet to be helpless to do without an automobile in the absence of alternate modes of transportation. Or to realize that the personal automobile could probably be much less damaging to the environment if there were serious attention to fossil fuel alternatives. Or to see large cargo that should be moved by trains cruising inefficiently down the highway. Or to realize that other countries, now less automobile dependent than the United States, are moving as fast as possible into the same insanity of making it very difficult to rely on public transportation for one's transportation needs. Because I must have a car to shop or to visit friends, a reindeer calving ground in Alaska may be destroyed; it sits on top of oil reserves that could supply the United States' oil needs for a maximum of six years. No, interdependence is not just about celebrating kinship with all life; it is about recognizing how implicated we are in the web of environmental destruction and doing whatever we can to lessen our negative impact on that web.

The reality of interdependence is also my motivation for talking, not only of the havoc wrought by excessive consumption—most, but not all of which occurs in the affluent nations—but also of the havoc brought about by excessive population growth, something about which both rich and poor nations need to be concerned, though for different reasons. It troubles me that so many people who are quick to point out the evils of excessive consumption on the part of the affluent lack the courage to discuss the environmental costs of overpopulation. This timidity seems to stem from at least two sources. One is peoples' intense emotionality about sex and reproduction. People who can be quite calm and rational when discussing other issues demonstrate adamant and unquestioning attachment to their pro-natalist views about reproduction. I experience this in part because, though I never discuss the issue of population without also addressing the issue of consumption, people often react negatively to my discussions of the warped reasons people have for uncritically reproducing. Second, many people from affluent nations feel that they should not discuss the evils of overpopulation because so many wealthy people talk as if population control is an issue only for poor people. This obviously is not the case, given that the children of the rich will cause much greater environmental devastation than the children of poor—at least until more equitable methods of distribution are in place. Furthermore, there is more than enough to discuss concerning excessive reproduction among the wealthy and in wealthy nations. This is not an issue that pertains to the poor but not to the rich. My discussion of population is in no way pointing a finger at "them." I am not exempt from the limits on my reproduction required for the health of the web of life. I grow very weary of my affluent acquaintances who regard limiting the number of births as relevant only to other people. They think that their desires regarding children are more important than the well-being of the matrix of life, and that their children will be so wonderful that it doesn't matter what their ecological impact will be.

Once we really understand interdependence, it is easy to understand that, even if excessive consumption were curbed and equitable methods of distribution were devised, there could easily be more people on earth than can be supported at a reasonable standard of living by sustainable methods of production. Simply looking the other way and pretending that this issue does not exist is willful ignoring—the taproot of all trouble and suffering according to Buddhism. I can think of no reason to prefer huge, crowded populations living at low standards of living to populations of a stable and sustainable size living with a good standard of living. I have argued before that if there is a "right" that most Buddhists could agree upon despite the fact that this word does not occur in traditional Buddhist contexts, it is the right to be born into a situation in which one's parents and one's community have enough time and resources for one to be well cared for physically, emotionally, and spiritually. Human birth, by itself, is not enough. A precious human birth, a birth that is free and well-favored, requires being born into a situation in which one can awaken one's inherent Buddhahood, for which adequate physical, emotional, and spiritual resources are needed, in most cases. Producing children under other conditions do not constitute the practices of non-harming and compassion that are so central in Buddhism.

I will not repeat all the arguments I have made on this topic in other publications.[3] I will only point out a few things that pertain to our own society and to the rich in general. I never cease to be amazed at the subtly pro-natalist policies of the United States and never cease to wonder why we should be encouraging people to have more children when we, as a society, don't do very well at taking care of so many that are already here. For example, why should health insurance policies not pay for contraception, given that they do pay for the costs incurred in pregnancy, childbirth, and early childhood? Reproductive choices made by women and families are supported only if they are pro-natalist. Is this another reason why Viagra for men is often covered by health insurance while contraception for women is not? Then there are the tax benefits that go with reproduction, especially the fact that there is no limit on the number of exemptions that can be taken for children. Likewise, the family rate for insurance coverage is the same whether health care is being provided for two people or twenty. This, of course, results in higher insurance costs for people who have no or few children. (I regard this as another reason to support universal health care rather than private insurance.) Many peoples' reactions when I bring up such facts demonstrates that, though they have never thought about whether pro-natalist policies make any sense, they are deeply attached to the view that more births are better than fewer births.

An especially important dimension of the population question concerns the effects of crowding on people. To look into this question, we do not need to look somewhere else; there is ample evidence of the negative effects of crowding even in my own community, which is less densely populated than many places, but is much more crowded now than it was thirty years ago. A great deal of that was once open and wooded or being farmed has

---

3. Rita M. Gross, *Soaring and Settling: Buddhist Perspectives on Contemporary Social and Religious Issues* (New York: Continuum, 1998), pp. 75–93, 108–24.

been paved over and built upon. I find it difficult to evaluate this as a positive development. Traffic has become intolerable at some times and in some places, and the relatively new phenomenon of road rage has increased dramatically, attributed by most analysts to more crowding on the highways. Many people would probably react by saying that more and wider highways should be built, but I ask why we need an increasing population that needs more and wider highways. What do we gain? Furthermore, road rage is probably only the beginning of increasing aggression, as people live in more and more crowded conditions. This is especially the case for a society like the United States in which aggression not only is tolerated but is encouraged by many institutions and by much of popular culture.

I am mystified by the easy assumption made by most people that population growth is both inevitable and good. I routinely read columnists in the local paper railing against the fact that, in some countries, the fertility rate is less than that required to replace the current population. They talk as if this is an unmitigated tragedy. I shake my head, asking "What's the problem with a stabile or a declining population, especially in crowded places? Is it not possible that the *quality* of life within the interdependent matrix of life and the well-being of all sentient beings would be *improved* by such a development?

I am passionate about the issue of excessive population, not only because so few people are willing to take it up, but also because of all the environmental problems facing us, I would argue that this is one of the easiest to solve. All it takes is contraception. I wish it were so easy to defuse the nuclear wastes that will last far longer than their containers or the land mines that render parts of the earth useless for any sentient being. I wish it were so easy to undo global warming or the decrease in the ozone layer, which will take many generations to correct, even if their causes were stopped immediately. By contrast, population problems could be solved in a generation or two, but only if people were willing to do so. I am not optimistic, however. There are too many forces pushing too many people to have too many children. Instead, warfare, starvation, and disease are likely to be relied upon. Many populations are kept in balance with their environment by predators; we humans have no predators left, so we become each others' predators in the form of aggression and warfare. Microbes, which spread more easily in crowded conditions, are also efficient predators on human beings. And people starve to death every day, though much starvation is due to economic imbalances or military actions, to greed and aggression, rather than to an absolute lack of food.

Strong pro-natalist pressures are an extremely important issue for women, given that under traditional child-rearing patterns, women bear most of the burden of fulfilling these demands. Throughout history, many women have suffered greatly from enduring too many pregnancies for their health. Their heavy child-rearing responsibilities have also forced them to be culturally illiterate and irrelevant in many societies, an extremely high price to pay. Furthermore, many religions tell women that they need not involve themselves in time-consuming serious religious and spiritual study and practice, on grounds that their child-rearing responsibilities prevent such involvement. As if all these woes were not enough, women are often then subjected to a vicious circle in evaluating their worth; many religious traditions, including Buddhism, have said women are less worthy and important than men, precisely because they spend all their time and energy fulfilling pro-natalist agendas rather than studying and practicing spiritual disciplines!

Excessive population growth is also a religious issue, because so many religions bear heavy responsibility for promoting pro-natalist attitudes and practices. This is one of the reasons that I discuss population issues so much: religious condemnations of greed and excessive consumption are well in place, but religions have often been on the wrong side regarding excessive population growth. In many religious contexts, having large families is regarded as a virtue, not an ecological problem. Reproduction is a religious duty in several religions, including some in which simple reproduction is not sufficient; there must be a son. Asian women have talked with me about "that scourge of Asian women, the need to bear a son." Other religions may not require reproduction as a religious duty, but forbid birth control or the most effective means of contraception, with the same results as when reproduction was a religious duty. In addition, sexual activity itself is often regarded negatively by religions.

How does Buddhism rate on these issues? I have argued extensively in another context that one of things Buddhism could offer to the future of the matrix of life is the example of a religion that is not especially pro-natalist or negative about sexuality.[4] In part, this is because so much of traditional Buddhism was focused on monastic life and very little attention was paid to developing detailed codes and norms concerning the behavior of laypeople. Laypeople could take the precept to avoid sexual

4. Ibid., pp. 108–24.

misconduct, one of the five basic precepts of Buddhism. But the very broad phrase "sexual misconduct" can be and has been subjected to a number of interpretations. For the most part, sexual norms for lay Buddhists simply follow indigenous cultural customs. The monastic prohibition of sex is not because sexual activity is degraded or negative but because family life is so distracting and demanding, both financially and emotionally. Sexuality itself is an important positive symbol in Vajrayana Buddhism, which could hardly have happened in a religions that regarded sexual activity as degraded. Buddhists have never been told to "be fruitful and multiply" or regarded reproducing as a religious requirement. In fact, especially in China, Buddhism was heavily criticized because, unlike the indigenous traditions, especially Confucianism, it permitted the options of celibacy and not reproducing. This earned Buddhists the label "unfilial," about as serious a flaw as one could have in Confucian evaluations. Finally, though abortion is highly problematic for Buddhists, birth control is not. I have heard traditional teachers saying that they could see no problems with a couple using contraception even in situations in which Western students were arguing the opposite.

The reality of interdependence gives me the big perspective on my habits and choices, my consumption and reproduction. I would argue that the Buddhist recognition of interdependence offers compelling reasons to limit both. But someone might say, I don't care about the bigger picture as much as I want a big car or another child. I have a right to have my desires fulfilled. This, in fact, seems to be the logic by which many people in our society make many of their decisions, which fuels global capitalism and consumerism very well. But if I cannot be convinced to modify my behavior due to the big picture of interdependence, Buddhism encourages me to look into the link between desire and happiness more personally. Buddhist logic on this point, if taken seriously and internalized, would break the back of consumerism by defusing the belief that we will be happier if we have more, the belief that happiness is the result of something outside our own being and state of mind.

These contemplations are found especially within the Four Noble Truths that come from the Buddha's first sermon, rather than his enlightenment experience, which culminated in the discovery of interdependence. In some ways, we could say that the Four Noble Truths bring insight into interdependence down to a more personal level. Why am I suffering? How can I stop suffering so much? Two words, if fully understood, would answer those questions—*attachment* and *detachment*.

The Four Noble Truths suggest that we should look into our own desires when we experience dissatisfaction and misery. What does this have to do with ecology? As already stated at the beginning of this chapter, ecological devastation doesn't just happen. At rock bottom, it is caused by human desires. When that is understood, we have a basis for developing an ethic of adopting limits for the sake of the matrix of life. The First and Second Noble Truths foster especially fruitful contemplations relevant to ecological ethics. The First Noble Truth states that conventional lifestyles inevitably result in suffering; the Second Noble Truth states that suffering stems from desire rooted in ignorance. Translated into more ecological language, a conventional lifestyle of indulging in desired levels of consumption and reproduction results in the misery of an environmentally degraded and overpopulated planet.

The Second Noble Truth, with its emphasis on desire as the cause of suffering, is especially important. The first step in understanding what the Second Noble Truth has to do with sustainability is clarifying the meaning of the term *desire*. That term is widely misunderstood, with the result that Buddhism is often caricatured as a gloomy, pessimistic, world-denying religion. The usually-chosen English word *desire* translates the Pali *tanha* and the Sanskrit *trishna*, but the connotations of the term *desire* are not strong enough to carry the meaning of Second Noble Truth. Most English-speaking people regard desire as inevitable and only a problem if it gets out of hand. But, in Buddhist psychology, *trishna* is always out of hand, inevitably out of control. Therefore, I believe more accurate connotative translations of *trishna* would be "addiction" or "compulsion" which more adequately convey its insatiable demands and counterproductivity. "Grasping," "attachment," "clinging," "craving," and "fixation" are also possibly more accurate translations, and the way the term *greed* is now used when discussing some multinational corporations also could translate *trishna*. All of these terms suggest that the object of desire is actually more powerful, more in control, than the desiring subject, which is precisely why *trishna* causes *duhkha*—misery.

Trishna is not about having lightly-held plans or about preferring an adequate diet to malnourishment, as many people think when they try to refute Buddhism by saying that life without attachment is impossible. *Trishna* is about the extra weight we bring to our plans and preferences when they so control us that any change throws us into uncontrollable, heedless emotional turmoil. That is how *trishna* causes *duhkha*. *Trishna* is also about the mistaken view that getting something—wealth or a male child, for example—will bring happiness and satisfaction. Because of this view, such goals are pursued compulsively and, therefore, suffering is the result. Thus, it is clear that from a Buddhist point of view, *trishna* is at the root of both excessive consumption and overpopulation. Neither would occur if people did not think that more wealth or more children would satisfy an existential itch that is only cooled by equanimity. "I want . . ." are the two words that fuel the suffering of excessive consumption and overpopulation.

Because it is so counter-intuitive in our culture to suggest that attachment is the cause of human miseries, let us perform a mental exercise I often use with my students. Buddhists, contrary to popular Western stereotypes about them, regard happiness as favorably as any other people. The First Noble Truth is not about preferring misery to happiness but about noting that conventional ways of pursuing happiness produce sorrow instead. Most people think that happiness results from getting what we crave, whereas Buddhists would say that happiness happens when *trishna* is renounced. Thus, craving and happiness are incompatible. Some reflection on one's last experience of unrelieved, intense longing will quickly confirm that it was not a pleasant experience. One endures the longing because of the pleasure that comes when cravings are satisfied. But the satisfaction is short-lived, quickly replaced by yet another longing. The satisfaction of our cravings is virtually impossible because of the insatiable, addictive nature of *trishna*, which always wants more. Since craving and happiness are incompatible, which one should be renounced?

The good news of Buddhism is that the mental attitude of grasping and fixation is not the only alternative. "I want . . ." can be replaced with simply noting what is. The enlightened alternative to *trishna* is detachment—equanimity and even-mindedness beyond the opposites of hope and fear, pleasure and pain. It is the unconditional joy that cannot be produced by the satisfaction of cravings, but which arises spontaneously when we truly experience unfabricated mind. Equanimity has nothing to do with getting what we want and everything to do with developing contentment with things as they are. It is the hard-won ability to be at least somewhat even-minded, whether one gets one's heart-desire or is denied it. It is the ability to put space around every experience, to realize that nothing lasts forever without feeling cheated, and to be at least somewhat cheerful no matter what is happening. Therefore, fundamentally, *trishna* and equanimity are states of mind; they have little to do with what we have or do not have. According to Buddhism, external factors, whether other people or material objects, are not really the source of our joy or suffering; rather our *attitudes* toward people and things determine which we experience. With such understanding in place, one will experience limits to consumption and reproduction, not as personal loss but as normal, natural, and pleasant in an interdependent matrix. They are not a problem.

On the other hand, greed is normal in conventional people because of a pervasive and deep-seeded erroneous view of the self. Craving for more is rooted in ignorance. Ignorance of what? Classically, craving is rooted in ignorance and denial of our fundamental nature, which is the lack of a permanent individual self—*anatman*. But *anatman* is simply another name for interdependence. Because we are interdependent with everything else in the matrix of existence, we do not exist in the way we conventionally believe that we do—as self-existing, self-contained bundles of wants and needs that end with our skin, or, if we feel generous, with our immediate families. That imagined independent self which greedily consumes and reproduces itself is a fiction. It has never really existed and so giving up on it is not a loss but a homecoming. This is the aspect of Buddhism that has been so inspiring to deep ecologists, who have claimed that Asian world views are more conducive to ecological vision than Western emphases on the unique, independently existing, eternal individual.

Fortunately, these Buddhist views are not merely theory but attempts to express what happens experientially when spiritual disciplines are taken seriously. This means that these insights about interdependence and the counterproductivity of attachment can be realized by anyone who makes some effort to contemplate these teachings and engage the practices. The behaviors are appropriate for someone who realizes these insights are not really "shoulds" or commands—they become self-existing, the only way one can behave. In my view, the most valuable Buddhist contribution to the discussion of sustainable patterns of consumption and reproduction is this potential for fundamental transformation. On the other hand, practicing a spiritual discipline is a "should," and one whose relevance can escape people for long time.

RITA'S WORK ON a Buddhist ethic to respond to the problems of consumerism and expanding population is an important contribution. I particularly appreciate her focus on the touchy issue of population typically avoided in circles of interreligious dialogue. I also believe that it is crucial to deal with consumerism and population expansion in interconnection with each other. Reduction of consumption will do little good if population is not also curbed. The often used equation for the ecological impact of populations is: Technology × Consumption × Population = Impact. That is to say, the amount of resources used to produce, transport, and deliver a product, and to dispose of the waste products at each of these stages, times the level of consumption of the average person in a society, times the amount of people in that society equals their ecological impact.

People in high consumption societies, such as the United States, are often said to have about a hundred times the ecological impact of people in simple societies in which they walk or bicycle and consume local products. Thus the populations of rich societies are clearly the problem, not simply in terms of their high rate of consumption, but also in terms of how many of them there are! The combination of the three factors are a multiplier factor, not simply an "add on." This means that in order to lessen the ecological impact, one has to reduce each of the three factors in their interconnection with each other.

Thus, for example, if one seeks to reduce smog in Los Angeles by passing laws that require a 30 percent reduction in fuel emissions per vehicle, but meanwhile the population expands by 15 percent and there is a 15 percent increase in the number of households driving two cars, the net effect is that there will be more fuel emissions than before. All efforts to reduce consumption are nullified by expanding population, although, of course, the impact of this increasing population would have been even worse without the reduction in consumption. Nevertheless population is a key leg in the tripod that has to be included equally in the equation.

Rita emphasizes the need for one-by-one conversion to the low consumption, low reproduction ethic to make a sustainable society. She is critical of any coercive means as counter-productive. I personally believe that while a small number of people can be converted to such a life style by personal appeal of its goodness for the total community, this will be completely inadequate for mass change, particularly in the context of the urgency of this change within the next few decades. This is not simply because people are irredeemably selfish and won't respond to the appeal for the common good, even though it will also be for their own good and that of their (fewer) children. Rather, what keeps the present expanding consumption and high (though falling) reproduction pattern in place is structural and ideological, and not simply personal greed. One doesn't choose to drive a private car out of greed, but primarily because there is no other adequate means of transportation to get between home, work, shopping, and other aspects of one's life. To choose a large gas guzzling car for this purpose, on the other hand, is unnecessary and greedy!

The changing of these patterns needs to be addressed both on the level of curbing this excess greed, but also in changing the parameters of what people find necessary—having to have a private car at all because there is no accessible public transport. Private choice and the development of personal convictions on these issues of consumption and procreation are crucial. Many media of communication can be used to help spark such personal decisions. But these too are institutional efforts, even if aimed at shaping individual choice. Individual choice needs to be addressed by a complex package of incentives provided by laws and public policies that include disincentives.

Tax laws, for example, can be a crucial means to shape personal decisions. Presently, our tax laws promote high consumption. Tax breaks for using alternative energy and retrofitting one's houses for energy efficiency should be combined with high taxes on environmentally destructive practices, including the use of private cars. But disincentives need to be combined with the creation of attractive alternatives. Good accessible public transportation is needed to give people an alternative to the private car. (This also means electing public officials who are tied to environmental concerns and not oil companies!) A few people will reduce consumption because they recognize it is right for the good of all, even if it is personally difficult. Many more will do so if it is relatively convenient to do so, and almost everyone will do so if it is also considerably more expensive not to do so. Public policy is about creating this environment of choice. Religious and cultural institutions need to reinforce this disposition to right choice by educational campaigns that explain its compelling reasons.

People do things in a better spirit if they feel they have some choice and are not simply the puppets of coercive government. But the idea that we have a totally free choice about consumption is an illusion. There is a bottom line of basic needs for nutrition, clothing, and housing. But the elaboration of consumption far beyond basic needs is an enormous superstructure, most of which is enforced by what is possible, available, and acceptable in particular cultural contexts. An environmentally friendly society will involve reshaping this entire superstructure and its cultural incentives.

Take, for example, the cultural incentives to reproduce. While Americans may not feel they have to have a male child to take care of their funeral, there is still lot of pressure to produce grandchildren to carry on one's family. One child is still considered too few and growing up as an only child a recipe for pathology. Women are still told in many subtle and not so subtle ways that they are unfulfilled without children. There is also the distinct sense that a single person will be lonely in old age and part of the need for children is to provide a community of support as one ages. Shaping a different public culture requires more than simply insisting that it is okay to be single and/or childless. One also need to shape other ways to fulfill some of these same longings for community, intimate relations to others, and parenting the next generation.

What if religious and cultural institutions promoted practices that connected childless adults with a child and his/her parents in Godparent or co-madre/co-padre relations, as is already an integral part of Hispanic society? This larger circle of adults that have a committed relation to a child could not only lessen the stress of parenting on the biological parents by providing substitutes for the available aunts and uncles of earlier extended families, but also give those who choose not to parent biologically a partial social participation in parenting.

One needs more ways of creating familial community than biologically producing children. One single female professional friend, who lives with another woman, decided at a certain point that she needed a family, but she wasn't going to have children. She then, with her partner, created a "chosen family" by affiliating with several young people as her chosen "children." These young people themselves were rootless and much in need of parenting. These relations have continued now for twenty years. She had helped them through marriage, divorce, childbearing. They gather for Christmas and holidays and can count on each other in personal and group crises. When one moves to a new house, the others can be counted on to show up to help. Their pictures adorn her piano. She has the joys (and the troubles) of an extended family of children and grandchildren without herself reproducing.

While her example is somewhat unique, cultural institutions could encourage many ways of bonding between people that reproduce the needs for familial community without demanding that every adult produce two or more children to have "families." These cultural alternatives can mediate population reduction without leaving people feeling that they are thereby deprived of primary committed relationships. Creating a new future for planet Earth demands as much one-on-one conversion to a new ethic and culture of sustainability as possible, but these personal changes will only happen on a large scale if they are embedded in massive changes of culture and legal, social, economic, and technological structures.

Suggestions for Further Reading

BUDDHISM

Allione, Tsultrim. *Women of Wisdom.* London: Routledge and Kegan Paul, 1984.

Blackstone, Kathryn R. *Women in the Footsteps of the Buddha: Struggle for Liberation in the Therigatha.* Surrey, England: Curzon Press, 1998.

Boucher, Sandy. *Turning the Wheel: American Women Creating the New Buddhism.* Boston: Beacon Press, 1993.

Campbell, June. *Traveller in Space: In Search of Female Identity in Tibetan Buddhism.* New York: George Braziller, 1996.

Dowman, Keith, trans. *Sky Dancer: The Secret Life and Songs of the Lady Yeshe Tsogyel.* London: Routledge and Kegan Paul, 1984.

Dresser, Marianne, ed. *Buddhist Women on the Edge: Contemporary Perspectives from the Western Frontier.* Berkeley, California, North Atlantic Books, 1996.

Edou, Jerome. *Machig Labdron and the Foundations of Chod.* Ithaca, New York: Snow Lion Publications, 1996.

Friedman, Lenore, and Susan Moon, eds. *Being Bodies: Buddhist Women on the Paradox of Embodiment.* Boston and London: Shambhala, 1997.

Gross, Rita M. *Buddhism after Patriarchy: A Feminist History, Analysis, and Reconstruction of Buddhism.* Albany, New York: State University of New York Press, 1993.

———. *Soaring and Settling: Buddhist Perspectives on Contemporary Social and Religious Issues.* New York: Continuum, 1998.

Horner, I. B. *Women under Primitive Buddhism: Laywomen and Almswomen.* Delhi, India: Motilal Banarsidass, reprint, 1989. (Original edition, 1930).

Klein, Carolyn Ann. *Meeting the Great Bliss Queen: Buddhism and the Art of the Self.* Boston: Beacon Press, 1995.

Lama Chonam and Sangye Khandro, trans. *The Lives and Liberation of Princess Mandarava: The Indian Consort of Padmasambhava.* Boston: Wisdom, 1998.

Paul, Diana W. *Women in Buddhism: Images of the Feminine in Mahayana Tradition.* Berkeley, California: Asian Humanities Press, 1979.

Rhys-Davids, C. A. F., and K. R. Norman, trans. *Poems of the Early Buddhist Nuns: (Therigatha).* Oxford: The Pali Text Society, 1989 (joint revised reprint).

Shaw, Miranda. *Passionate Enlightenment: Women in Tantric Buddhism.* Princeton, N.J.: Princeton University Press, 1994.

Simmer-Brown, Judith. *Dakini's Warm Breath.* Boston: Shambhala, 2001.

Tsai, Kathryn Ann, trans. *Lives of the Nuns: Biographies of Chinese Buddhist Nuns from The Fourth to Sixth Centuries.* Honolulu: University of Hawaii Press, 1994.

Tsomo, Karma Lekshe. *Sakyadhita: Daughters of the Buddha.* Ithaca, New York: Snow Lion Publications, 1988.

———. *Buddhist Women Across Cultures: Realizations.* Albany, New York: State University of New York Press, 1999.

Willis, Janice Dean, ed. *Feminine Ground: Essays on Women and Tibet.* Ithaca, New York: Snow Lion Publications, 1989.

Wilson, Liz. *Charming Cadavers: Horrific Figurations of the Feminine in Indian Buddhist Hagiographic Literature.* Chicago: University of Chicago Press, 1996.

CHRISTIANITY

Aquino, Maria Pilar. *Our Cry for Life: Latin American Theology from the Perspective of Women.* Maryknoll: Orbis Books, 1993.

Boerresen, Kari. *Subordination and Equivalence: The Nature and Role of Women in Augustine and Thomas Aquinas.* Kampen: Pharos Publishing House, 1995.

———. *The Image of God: Gender Models in the Judaeo-Christian Tradition.* Minneapolis: Fortress Press, 1995.

Chung, Hyun Khung. *The Struggle to Be the Sun Again: Introducing Asian Women's Theology.* Maryknoll: Orbis Books, 1989.

Fabella, Virginia, and Mercy Oduyoye, eds. *With Passion and Compassion: Third World Women Doing Theology.* Maryknoll: Orbis Books, 1988.

Gebara, Ivone. *Longing for Running Water: Ecofeminist Theology: Ecofeminism and Liberation.* Minneapolis: Fortress Press, 1999.

Graff, Ann O'Hare. *In the Embrace of God: Feminist Approaches to Theological Anthropology.* Maryknoll: Orbis Books, 1995.

Grey, Mary. *Redeeming the Dream: Feminism, Redemption, and Christian Tradition.* London: SPCK, 1989.

Heyward, Carter. *Touching Our Strength: The Erotic as Power and the Love of God.* San Francisco: Harper and Row, 1989.

Isasi-Diaz, Ada-Maria. *Mujerista Theology.* Maryknoll: Orbis Books, 1996.

Johnson, Elizabeth A. *She Who Is: The Mystery of God in Feminist Theological Discourse.* New York: Crossroad, 1993.

Jones, Serene. *Feminist Theory and Christian Theology: Cartographies of Grace.* Minneapolis: Fortress Press, 2000.

LaCugna, Catherine, ed. *Freeing Theology: The Essentials of Theology from a Feminist Perspective.* HarperSanFrancisco, 1993.

McFague, Sallie. *Metaphorical Theology: Models of God for an Ecological Nuclear Age.* Minneapolis: Fortress Press, 1987.

Oduyoye, Mercy. *Daughters of Anowa: African Women and Patriarchy.* Maryknoll: Orbis Books, 1995.

———, et al. *Women Resisting Violence: Spirituality for Life.* Maryknoll: Orbis Books, 1996.

Ruether, Rosemary. *New Women, New Earth: Sexist Ideologies and Human Liberation.* New York: Seabury, 1975. Reprint, Boston: Beacon Press, 1995.

———.*Sexism and Godtalk: Toward a Feminist Theology.* Boston: Beacon Press, 1983. Reprint, 1993.

———.*Womenguides: Texts for Feminist Theology.* Boston: Beacon Press, 1985. Reprint, 1995.

———.*Women-Church: Theology and Practice in Feminist Liturgical Communities.* New York: Harper and Row, 1986

———.*Gaia and God: An Ecofeminist Theology of Earth-Healing.* HarperSanFrancisco, 1992.

———. *Women and Redemption: A Theological History.* Minneapolis: Fortress Press, 1998.

————, with Rosemary Keller, eds. *In Our Own Voices: Four Centuries of Women's Religious Writings.* HarperSanFrancisco, 1992. Reprint, Westminister Press, 2000

————, eds. *Women Healing Earth: Third World Women on Feminism, Religion, and Ecology.* Maryknoll: Orbis Books, 1996. Spanish edition, Santiago, Chile: Sello Azus, 1999.

Also of interest from Continuum International

Buddhists Talk about Jesus, Christians Talk about the Buddha

Edited by Rita M. Gross and Terry C. Muck

"Thought-provoking enough for specialists, these articulate views from informed followers of the 'other' faith are also accessible to general readers. This book is an excellent follow-up to Thich Nhat Hahn's *Living Buddha, Living Christ* and the Dalai Lama's *The Good Heart: A Buddhist Perspective on the Teachings of Jesus."* —*Library Journal*

"Originally a dedicated issue of a small, professional journal, this set of essays has little of the musty academic's study about it. The scholarly contributors, six Buddhists and six Christians, speak personally to clearly convey the exceptions they take with either Jesus or the Buddha. . . . Each side has plenty of intelligent appreciation for the other, making the whole book a model of nonpussyfooting civility." —*Booklist*

Soaring and Settling
Buddhist Perspectives on Contemporary Social and Religious Issues

By Rita M. Gross

"This thoughtful, thought-provoking, personal encounter with serious contemporary religious issues belongs on all undergraduate and graduate libraries. Also recommended for general readers and practitioners."
—*Choice*

"Gross discusses social issues ranging from environmental ethics to children's rights and religious issues from immanence and transcendence to the feminine principle in Tibetan Vajrayana Buddhism. Her courageous willingness to reveal how these issues affect her personally makes for powerful reading. A treat and a challenge, this book is highly recommended . . . as a very special contribution to the field." —*Library Journal*